BODY OF TRUTH

ALSO BY PHILIP CALLOW

BODY OF TRUTH

D. H. Lawrence:
The Nomadic Years, 1919–1930

PHILIP CALLOW

Ivan R. Dee

CHICAGO 2003

To John Lucas

Library of Congress Cataloging-in-Publication Data:
Callow, Philip.
    Body of truth : D. H. Lawrence, the nomadic years, 1919–1930 / Philip Callow.
      p. cm.
    Includes bibliographical references and index.
    ISBN 1-56663-494-6 (alk. paper)
    1. Lawrence, D. H. (David Herbert), 1885–1930—Journeys. 2. Lawrence, D. H. (David Herbert), 1885–1930—Last years. 3. Lawrence, D. H. (David Herbert), 1885–1930. Lady Chatterley's lover. 4. British—Foreign countries—History—20th century. 5. Authors, English—20th century—Biography. I. Title.

PR6023.A93 Z587 2003
823'.912—dc21   2002035102

Lawrence's entire output, made of fiction, drama, verse, philosophy, psychology, and books on travel, to say nothing of thousands of letters, adds up to a unity to be read rather as one reads the Bible (there is even a work called *Apocalypse*). It records the adventures of a personality . . . but it has, as one of its purposes, the redemption of a race. He wanted to bring his own people, the British, to a kind of promised land. Like all Britain's prophets, he preached to a wilderness.

—Anthony Burgess, *Flame into Being*

Dazzling and tremendous how quick the sunrise
   would kill me,
If I could not now and always send sunrise out of
   me.

—Walt Whitman, *Song of Myself*

Contents

Preface

WHEN I CAME to try my hand at biography for the first time, D. H. Lawrence was a natural choice. I can remember even now my first contact with his unique voice, picking up a paperback copy of *The White Peacock* on New Street Station in Birmingham, England. He was evidently a poet, he was of my time, and I could identify with him at once. Emotionally, he spoke my language. Like me he was a Midlander. We had class in common. He began his working life in a factory, as I did. My first marriage into a Nottingham family meant that Nottinghamshire became almost as familiar to me as my own county. I once met a disabled Eastwood miner, short of breath, pushing his bike up a country lane near the colliery where Lawrence's father had worked.

What kind of writer was this, whose prose shone like newly mined coal? "If the unconscious plays so large a part in Lawrence's work," writes Anthony Burgess, "it may be because, in his youth, it had a physical counterpart in the coal mines." At the end of his life he spoke of the importance of staying faithful to one's roots, with an emphasis I could readily appreciate. At the same time I am as deracinated as he was. The moment I began to really immerse myself in his work, this figure whose life in no way resembled mine cast a spell on me. His writings made immediate sense, and they disturbed. In the beginning I accepted him totally, no matter how *ex cathedra* or extreme his views, for he seemed extraordinary in having the clue to the course of the twentieth century, against which he never ceased to rage. He could see into things; he sounded right. The trust he inspired seemed, like his charm, to be part of his Englishness.

For all his vacillations and contradictions, he was nothing if not consistent. Annable, the gamekeeper in *The White Peacock*, was "a man of one idea—that all civilization was the painted fungus of rottenness. When he thought, he reflected on the decay of mankind— the decline of the human race into folly and weakness and rottenness," urging Cyril the young narrator to "Be a good animal, true to your animal instinct." In the second version of *Lady Chatterley's Lover* Lawrence says categorically, "It is useless to talk of the future of our society. Our society is insane." With Lawrence, like it or not, we have to start from here, from a position that never changed.

Yet in spite of this despairing worldview, here was a writer who radiated hope. How could this be? In his early twenties he worked as a teacher, and he remained one in every book he wrote, more and more convinced—like Blake before him—of his prophetic mission. Needing to earn a living he was forced to seek a wider audience, but in one sense he was always a populist.

One is tempted to say that what animated all the older Lawrence's writings—as it did the man himself—was sheer rage. This is the burden of John Middleton Murry's argument, that behind Lawrence's brave and wise words lurked a secret discontent with himself, amounting at times to crucifixion. In other words, his rage against the modern world masked a bitter knowledge of his own insecurity. Murry's book was the first on Lawrence to appear after his death. Much maligned in 1931, it was called a slug's-eye view by Aldous Huxley. Frieda Lawrence burned her copy and presented Murry with the ashes in a cardboard box. Treacherous though the onslaught is, simultaneously hailing his friend as "the future" and interpreting all his work in terms of an inability to love women, it would nevertheless be foolish to dismiss out of hand the insights of this keen critical intelligence. Murry's readings of the novels, stories, and poems, interspersed with insinuations about the Lawrence marriage, had for their justification his personal experience of an intimate friendship. What, he might have said, were friends for? He had witnessed the savage fights in Cornwall, he was Frieda's lover briefly in the mid-twenties when her marriage nearly foundered, he had denounced *Women in Love* publicly as degenerate and been told in letters and to his face that he was a Judas and a worm. This was a time to settle scores. All the same, his charges have never, to my mind, been properly confronted.

No one was more ruthless with Lawrence's doubts and weaknesses than Lawrence himself, as we shall see in the books and correspondence of his last decade. Murry readily acknowledged this, but then added that the apparent candor of Lawrence's confession was yet another hiding behind words, at best a self-deception, at worst a cunning evasion of the truth. And the truth for Murry was that by the time Lawrence was twenty-six his fate was decided: his mother's death had left his soul in bondage, doomed him to a life of sexual failure.

In the middle of his diatribe, Murry suddenly delivers an extraordinary "tribute." "Lawrence was abnormal; his experience was abnormal. . . . Vital issues were tried out to a conclusion in him: the stress of suffering their resolution devoured and destroyed him." In two exalted pages he raises Lawrence to a different order of being, a genius—that word Lawrence always detested like a curse. A symbolic and prophetic man cannot make mistakes, cannot be judged, says Murry in his exalted state: "all that he is and does is his destiny." If the language of judgment is used, "it is used only as a means of discourse." Murry's facing-both-ways performance has reached its climax.

In one respect, however, Murry understood perfectly the nature of his friend's artistic shortcomings, realizing that at bottom he was not concerned with art at all. Lawrence makes this clear himself, even as a young man, with his "Study of Thomas Hardy." Nowhere in this long essay is he in the least interested in the virtues of Hardy as a novelist, and by the third section is announcing with obvious impatience that "This is supposed to be a book about the people in Thomas Hardy's novels." What it rapidly becomes is the outline of a philosophy of law and love, with Hardy the excuse. Nor is Lawrence interested in being a great novelist himself. He has no time for the modernist movement. Joyce is puerile, Proust feeble. Conrad scarcely receives a mention.

Murry puts it this way. Lawrence "gave up, deliberately, the pretence of being an artist. The novel became for him simply a means by which he could make explicit his own 'thought-adventures.' His aim was to discover authority, not to create art. The artist today finds no spiritual authority which he instinctively acknowledges. To charge him with a lack of form is to be guilty of irrelevance." He goes on: "In actual fact Lawrence was neither a great novelist nor a great poet. More than any other single thing he was the great life-adventurer of modern times." Burgess makes the same point when he says that in all the novels the characters wear clothes, smoke cigarettes, take tea, but sooner or later "their impulses overcome reason," they are naked, they speak from the unconscious.

Harold Bloom comes to a similar conclusion in an introduction in 1985 to a symposium on Lawrence. Lawrence is for him the odd man out among major British writers of the twentieth century, despite the strenuous efforts of F. R. Leavis to include him in the "great tradition." Both Blake and Lawrence, notes Bloom, believed that touch, "the sexual sense proper, is the least fallen of the senses," and remarks, "To say that Lawrence was more a Puritan than Milton is only to state what is now finely obvious." More important, he recognizes that Lawrence is first and foremost a religious writer, an apocalyptic one. "Beneath their narrative procedures, Lawrence's two great novels, *The Rainbow* and *Women in Love*, essentially are visionary prose poems, inhabited by giant forms acting out the civil wars of the psyche."

Visionaries among writers of fiction were virtually extinct after the terrible slaughter of the war to end wars. Mary Butts, a twenties novelist on the margins of modernism, overlooked in her lifetime and now being rediscovered, felt an exultation in the presence of the natural world that was Lawrentian. So was her sense of the devastation inflicted on her generation by the war, and her refusal to get on that postwar merry-go-round painted by Mark Gertler, which Lawrence applauded as a symbol of modern brokenness. Her great grandfather was Thomas Butts, the patron of Blake. Like Lawrence she saw the threat of the "democratic enemy," aware like him that "the worst is coming to the worst with our civilization," but also that "something . . . is trying to get born. . . ." Her urban, mechanical, "fabricated man" at the close of one novel reminds us of Loerke at the end of *Women in Love*, detached from everything with his "insect-like" comprehension.

Lawrence's temperament had in some respects a startling similarity to that of Dickens. Both men saw life as essentially "a battle": both were instinctive, fluent writers who worked themselves up into a passion in order to write. The "mercurial changeability" noted by biographers of Lawrence was remarkably like that of the "cheerfullest man of his age," as Peter Ackroyd quotes one description of Dickens, a man who "also brooded apart, who was filled with a sense of emptiness and of that one thing missing in his life which he could never find. The man of farcically high spirits and endless imitations of his friends was also the man who was perpetually susceptible to slights and who in some deep sense felt himself to be unwanted and vulnerable. . . . By all accounts Dickens was also a very restless and 'driven' man, always attempting to do the impossible and, as it were, continually beating violently against the gates of the world."

Son and Lover, my account of the young Lawrence first published in 1973, concludes with him leaving England in 1919 more or less for good. Poor, he lands in Italy alone, nine pounds in his pocket and about twelve in a London bank. Let us start here. He is thirty-four, with ten years left to live. The older Lawrence will never really be old.

Here he is in November 1919 on a "dark, wet, wintry evening." We have the exact moment recorded in his introduction to *Memoirs of the Foreign Legion* by Maurice Magnus. Lawrence has written to Norman Douglas in Florence for help in finding a cheap room. Always frugal, he is quite prepared to live on bread and cheese until his wife Frieda arrives. Passing the end of the Ponte Vecchio he sees the portly Douglas approaching with another man, a stranger. This man, short and strutting, is smart, all in gray, but "there was a touch of down-on-his-luck about him. His voice was rather fastidious, his manner a little patronizing. I realized at once that I ought, in this little grey-sparrow man's eyes—he stuck out his front tubbily, like a bird, his legs seemed to perch behind him, as a bird's do—I ought to be in a cab. But I wasn't."

Lawrence wrote nothing better than this long introduction. Brilliant, witty, poignant, it was remarked on by Norman Douglas himself, never a bosom friend of the Nottinghamshire rising star. Lawrence's portrait of Maurice Magnus dressed like a little pontiff in his blue silk dressing gown was, he thought, "a perfect etching—not a stroke too much or too little. . . ."

So here is Lawrence at the top of his form, a big name already with a banned book behind him, scraping by on very little but with a zest for life undiminished by shaky health. Travel always perked him up. Bright-eyed as a bird himself, his beard raggy because he had a thing about entering a strange barbershop, he was immediately curious about this fellow who looked so clean and natty and alert, "like a sparrow painted to resemble a tom-tit."

He had had a bleak war, his disgust with literature turning him into a farm laborer at Zennor, hounded out of Cornwall with his German wife, humiliated in three successive army medicals by supercilious doctors with absolute power over him, and was now overjoyed to be free and on the move, a twentieth-century English exile who would remain passionately English to the end of his days. And soon in a mounting rage against his time, his fate, even his own body which so cruelly betrayed him. "The time is out of joint," Hamlet ranted, and cursed the fate that compelled him to rail against it. His was an isolation Lawrence would come to know for himself, as his hatred for the Western world grew more intense. Wanting to break out of Europe, unable to persuade friends to join him in a small boat sailing round the world, he traveled from Sicily to Ceylon to Australia in a dream of escape that carried him eastward to America and then Mexico.

His rage ebbed and flowed erratically, extending, some would say, his precarious life span. And between rages he knew rapture. He was a poet and he praised creation and the gods he saw at work in the natural world, relishing his workingman's aptitude for turning his hand to anything, from the baking of bread to the mending of a roof. What kept him going, as well as literally sustaining him, though he was poorly paid for it, was writing. "Without it," he said once, "I would have been dead long ago." When he became sick at last of words, with death staring him in the face, he turned to the painting of visceral canvases, and then to squibs and doggerel aimed at the London literati and the hypocritical bourgeoisie, calling these ejaculations *Pansies* and *Nettles*. In Mexico the natives saw him as a fox, because of his russet coloring and his watchfulness. Not pleased, he would rather have been a mountain lion.

Finally his anger found an outlet that earned him money: he broke the taboo against using in literature the Old English "obscene" words for sex and bodily functions, and wrote *Lady Chatterley's Lover*. Critics of the novel have observed that the impotent Sir Clifford, wounded and paralyzed in World War I, has some of the author's more attractive traits, whereas the gamekeeper (in the angrier final version) is now and then a coarse bully. It is no surprise to find Lawrence, who had been close to death so often, writing poignantly of his wheelchair-bound aristocrat that "He had so very nearly lost life that what remained was wonderfully precious to him." His own unhealing psychic wound had been inflicted in a different war.

He went on to resurrect a blasphemous sexual Christ in a tender novella called *The Man Who Died*, without mentioning Jesus by name, and celebrated the obliterated culture of the Etruscans with instant sympathy in one of his finest travel books. The black fury of his letters subsided, replaced now by a renunciation of his old self's "battle battle" as he lost his passion for changing the world. He sang the song of the cosmos in a final work, *Apocalypse*, and to the bitter end clung to his wife, the fundamentally married man he had always been.

BODY OF TRUTH

1

A Strange, Quaking Star

(1919–1920)

Middleton Murry saw Lawrence's life and work as falling into four distinct periods. Of course nothing in life is as clear-cut as that, but this schematic outline does make a kind of sense. We are concerned with the third period, when Lawrence leaves England in 1919. According to Murry, this ends in 1923 with the abortive visit to England. Then we go on to his death on March 3, 1930.

Heading for Italy alone, with Frieda visiting her mother and about to plunge into the postwar confusion of travel in order to get from Baden-Baden to Florence, Lawrence was in a curious state, telling himself he was from now on a desperado, prepared to live on his wits and damn everyone, but in reality in need of his wife at his side, as he would always be. But for the moment he was euphoric. After the bitter years of penury and alienation in Cornwall there was the prospect of money at last. Martin Secker promised to bring out *Women in Love* and reissue *The Rainbow*, and there was the possibility of American editions. The American poet Amy Lowell sent him fifty pounds. His novella *The Fox* brought him a welcome thirty pounds.

He had escaped the influenza epidemic that swept the postwar world in 1919, but was so ill in Derbyshire that the doctor feared he would succumb. His sister Ada had found them a cottage, and despite Frieda's opposition she had nursed him through this crisis. The two women never got on. As for the sick man, he wrote bitterly to his friend Samuel Koteliansky in London that "I am not going to be left to Frieda's tender mercies until I am well again. She really is a devil—and I feel as if I would part with her for ever—let her go alone to Germany, while I take another road. I have been bullied by her long enough. The time comes to make an end, one way or another." This was bluster, and he had done his own fair share of bullying. But the marital strife in Cornwall had been bloody; he had cruelly turned his back on her at Zennor, and he knew these words would be music to Koteliansky's ears. The Russian Jew detested Frieda and saw the marriage as a disaster.

Certainly the honeymoon after the wedding in 1913 bore little relation now to reality. But to leave Frieda without a pang was beyond him. He traveled alone happily in the knowledge that they would soon be reunited. Reaching Turin and staying a couple of nights as the guest of some wealthy English with whom he was barely acquainted, he felt like a freebooter, marveling at the luxury and only too glad to sing for his supper. "Rather nice people" they may have been, but his hosts were given satirical treatment when he came to write *Aaron's Rod* in the improvised, cocky style that was the nearest he ever came to modernism, and that he would use to great effect in *Sea and Sardinia* and *Kangaroo*, though not in *Mr. Noon*, where the tone veers about disastrously. By presenting himself nakedly in the present in *Aaron's Rod* he creates a narrative of freshness and veracity, and his own exhilaration with the freedom he has granted himself is very clear. In fact it is the war and his treatment by the authorities that has made him feel like a renegade, out of patience with traditional literature. How ridiculous were the masks everyone wore: Aaron—Lawrence in the novel—standing by himself in his sumptuous bedroom of blue silk, decided there and then to be nakedly himself, true to his nature come what may. It was as if "he had dropped his mask on the floor, and broken it. His authentic self-describing passport, his complete and satisfactory idea of himself suddenly become a rag of paper, ridiculous. What on earth did it matter if he was nice or not?"

There is nothing "nice" about *Aaron's Rod*. Feminists have loathed it more than any other of his books. Brenda Maddox in her biography manages to have fun with this novel which is misogynistic from start to finish. The time to desert one's wife, it seems to Aaron, a colliery worker who plays the flute alone in his front room, is Christmas Eve, with his two little girls decorating the Christmas tree and mince pies baking in the oven. He walks off into the night with his flute, wanting to be by himself, and just keeps walking. In London he meets Rawdon Lilly and his wife Tanny. This couple seems to have solved the problem of marriage ("stuck together like two jujube lozenges") by living much of the time apart.

In the autumn of 1917 Lady Cynthia Asquith took Lawrence to the opera in London. Sitting in a box listening to the gossip becomes a comic episode for Aaron. Lawrence's personality is divided between Aaron and Lilly, and Frieda's complaints ring out clearly when Tanny says of her husband, "He can't give himself; he always kept himself back," and again when she says scornfully, "Because I hold you safe enough all the time you like to pretend you're doing it all yourself." Lilly and Aaron talk over their discontents, agreeing that women will sacrifice eleven men for one baby. Tackling their relationship dilemmas they are in complete accord: "Men have got to stand up to the fact that manhood is more than children—and then force women to admit it."

When it came to forcing, of course, Lawrence was in difficulties with Frieda, who did what she pleased and was a big woman. Arthur Lawrence, when he met his son's wife, wondered why he had put himself at such a disadvantage. She was, said Lawrence approvingly to his friends at the outset, "a gushing woman." His father was far from keen on women who talked so much. "When 'er oppens 'er mahth," he said dubiously, "aif room's dark."

The novel is permeated by Aaron's resistance to love. Sharing a bed warily with a *marchesa* in Florence, he reflects that "The years of marriage had made a married man of him, and any other woman than his wife was a strange woman to him, a violation. . . . When a man is married, he is not in love. A husband is not a lover. Well, I am a husband if I am anything. And I shall never be a lover again, not while I live."

When the chronically ill Katherine Mansfield read *Aaron's Rod* she felt "as if the book was feeding me." One can see why. Aaron's insistence on a separate, creative life was like her own need to be less dependent on Murry's letters and visits.

The novel's real attraction is its spontaneity, for Lawrence saw no difference between a novel and a poem when their composition was concerned. Murry insisted quaintly on claiming this as the greatest of his novels, probably because it suited the purposes of his argument to do so, and because he was imitating the contrariness of its author. It is in fact the rapidly expressed description of a mood, the satirical portraits of people met in chance encounters hit off with great verve to enliven it. Norman Douglas, for instance, appears in it as James Argyle. Brenda Maddox truly calls it one of his lesser works and brackets it with *Kangaroo* and *The Plumed Serpent* as a "flight-from-Woman novel."

He had started the novel in 1918 when relations with Frieda were dire and when he could see little future for himself as a writer. When he took it up and swung through the rewriting early in 1921 he was still as defiant, but Italy was working its magic, and markets in England and America were opening up to him. From the autumn of 1920 he was engaged in *Aaron's Rod*, writing enough new poems to fill two books, and completing *Studies in Classic American Literature*, begun in the dark days of Cornwall. As well as all this he was writing essays on *Education of the People*—the genesis of *Fantasia of the Unconscious*—a short story, "The Blind Man," and revising his manuscript of *The Lost Girl*, a novel in the Arnold Bennett mode that he hoped would be a money-spinner.

ARRIVING FROM TURIN in the rain of Florence, amused with himself for taking so readily to the luxury of his host's accommodation, he was reminded everywhere of those blissful prewar days in 1912 at Gargnano on Lake Garda, when he and Frieda had been so happy and carefree. There he had lived "in sunshine and happiness, in exile and poverty." It was a world of flowers, and even in winter they came, the wild cyclamens "very cold and fragrant . . . as if blossoming in the landscape of Phaedra and Helen," the Christmas roses, "large pure cold buds, like magnolias in the winter sunlight that was so still and pure, like iced wine." A landlady in Riva had sent them to the lakeside village that was accessible only by steamer, where they found a villa for two pounds sixteen a month with bedrooms "clean as a flower." Now he was carefree once more, rejoicing in the beauty of Italy after drab Derbyshire towns, and wanted Frieda with him so that he could share his delight. The Arno ran greenly under the bridges and the markets were in full swing, white oxen pulling the farm carts over the cobbles, the horses "in great brilliant scarlet cloths. . . ."

But where the devil was Frieda, what was keeping her? He was on the threshold of so much new work he could feel it pressing up through him urgently, but he needed his wife to anchor him, to buttress him with her belief, otherwise his energy would have no focus. He roamed around in Florence, he sat in his cheap pension overlooking the Arno, lonely at times but stimulated by the company of that old whimsical hedonist Norman Douglas, who made him forget his puritanism and his natural frugality. And it was comical to sit with him and this curious little American adventurer Maurice Magnus, who was strangely fey, yet appealing in some way to the feminine in Lawrence. Douglas was a natural opposite, cynical but charming, "handsome in his day, with his natural dignity and his clean-shaven strong square face." As for the entertaining Magnus, he had, it seemed, knocked about in all the capitals of the world and somehow survived. Lawrence was fascinated by him above all as a survivor, feeling cosmopolitan himself as he sat listening to the other's chatter in a *trattoria* and shared their Chianti. Back in his room he scribbled postcards to everyone, all with the same refrain. "Here I am on my lonely-o, waiting for Frieda." "Here I sit in my room over the river Arno, and wait for Mrs. Lawrence." "Am waiting for Frieda—had a wire from her."

When she came at last it was four in the morning, and her elated husband refused to let her rest until she had seen Florence by moonlight. He was enamored of the town, he told her, because of its natural culture, its aura as a town of men, and because the statues in the piazza were naked males.

Shortage of ready money took them south, via Rome which he found "vile," to a farm in the Abruzzi which they had been told they could "borrow"—probably by a London friend, Rosalind Baynes, whose father, Sir Hamo Thornycroft, was a sculptor. Orazio Cervi had been a model for the sculptor, and he lived in remote Picinisco (called Califano when Lawrence came to subject Alvina, heroine of *The Lost Girl*, to its icy fastness. In Gargnano he had read Bennett's *Anna of the Five Towns*, which had suggested his own novel with its Dickensian troupe of actors, until in the rewriting in 1920 it changed direction and in its final chapters became totally Lawrentian). Once at Picinisco they were dazzled by the mountains, snowy and beautiful, "glittering like hell," and everything was marvelous but too much, just too "staggeringly primitive." To reach it from the nearest village meant crossing a stony river bed, followed by an icy river over which you crossed on a plank, an ass bringing up the rear with the luggage. Then the farm! It was unbelievable, icy cold, as cold as the outside, the kitchen a huge barrel-vaulted hole, chickens wandering in and out, the ass tethered to the doorpost depositing its droppings on the threshold, braying like mad. Cooking was done "gipsy-fashion" over a wood fire in an enormous dark open hearth, and the only way to eat was on your knees. For utensils they had two cups, a plate, two glasses, a teaspoon, and that was the whole supply of crockery. It was December 16, beginning with an unearthly commotion under the window made by bagpipes, together with "a wild howling kind of ballad, utterly unintelligible." This was the Christmas serenade, a daily occurrence until Christmas.

Their contact, Orazio, was a nice but slow, vague creature. Upstairs they had a room with a little fireplace and tried to decide whether or not to settle in. The nearest railway station was fifteen miles away, and to reach a shop or get letters meant scrambling by the river "pale and fizzy with ice" and up a goat's track for about an hour and twenty minutes to the "godlost" village of Picinisco. They both fell in love with the local costume, the men in "white swathed strapped legs," the women in white skirts with full sleeves, but the prospect of a winter which was only just beginning, no matter how wonderful to look at, was too much. There was no bath, only a big copper boiling pan where they cooked the pigs' food, and at night they froze.

Escaping, they got up at 5:30 to find it had snowed all night. They tramped five miles with their luggage to catch the post omnibus at Atina, then on to the station at Cassino. The afternoon boat from Naples to Capri found them caught in a storm, unable to land in the shallow port as the seas were running so high. Boats that were to take them off couldn't come out. All night they lay rolling on board, in the semi-shelter of Sorrento, surrounded by sick Italians. Next day the boats did come out, and this time they were assisted by Compton Mackenzie, who steered them to a barely furnished flat with two rooms and a kitchen perched at the top of an old house, miraculously comfortable after Picinisco. Happily settling into the Palazzo Ferraro, Lawrence wrote to their friend Cecily Lambert at Grimsbury Farm in England, "I really think we shall stay here for a while."

Frieda was not so sure. The island was small, if incredibly beautiful, and the little town with its maze of streets cooped her in. Also it was spilling with gossip, and there was an incestuous English colony. All the same she liked the idea of swimming in the sea.

Elaine Feinstein, whose biography of Lawrence is in the main admirably fair, suggests that he and Frieda were now permanently at odds and that Frieda was winning. As she puts it, "Lawrence feared Frieda's triumph over him so intensely that he saw evidence of it in her every act." This is close to Murry's hostile portrait. Nevertheless it does help shed light on his puzzling friendship with Douglas and his fascination for the equally camp Magnus.

As Compton Mackenzie was in effect financing their stay in Capri, his tone seemed offensively patronizing to the touchy Midlander who was finding the island swarming with "cosmopolitans." He resented Mackenzie's wealth, thought his silk pajamas an affectation and didn't hesitate to tell him so. Mackenzie in his autobiography makes clear that he thought the wandering pair amusing, commenting on Frieda's calico underwear, which she supposedly showed him to demonstrate her husband's *pudeur* regarding finery.

Lawrence, who soon agreed with Frieda's impression of Capri as a stewpot of scandal, was ambivalent about Mackenzie from the beginning, though if one allowed for the "generation of actors" behind him, he thought he was basically nice. As for his friends, some rich drunken Americans, "Monty," as Lawrence now called him, though not to his face, made a fool of himself entertaining them with champagne, in his pale blue suit to match his eyes, and a large woman's brown velour hat "to match his hair." But at least he was a genuine writer and got down to work. "Well," Lawrence reported to Catherine Carswell with that touch of honesty that often redeems him, "I find I am nearly as spiteful as the rest of Capri." And we shall meet very often in the years to come that streak of waspish malice he had.

What compensated for a great deal in Capri were their two rooms on top of the old palace, and the Italians with their insouciance which was nearly but not quite gone, and anyway he liked them deeply, instinctively, "and the sun shines, the rocks glimmer, the sea is unfolded like fresh petals." How lucky he was not to be in England. Living was not too expensive, even here among the flesh-pots, and the air itself was somehow freer. One was reminded always of the Greeks—"Ulysses' ship left the last track in the waves." And the unchangeable "morning-delicate sea" was a joy as always.

HIS SURPRISING business flair came to the fore in his letter on January 16, 1920, to Martin Secker from Capri. He had been getting useful advice from Mackenzie and was eager to use it to good effect. Referring to a letter from Secker, he said he would never agree to sell *The Rainbow* outright for two hundred pounds. He had lived long enough with next to nothing and knew he could survive, so he had no intention of jumping at a paltry sum. There seems to have been some talk of a triumvirate, with he and Mackenzie and Francis Brett Young in a joint publishing venture. Apparently it was a scheme proposed by Mackenzie, though nothing came of it. Meanwhile he would retain the copyrights to all his books, and he asked Secker for two hundred pounds for *The Rainbow*, three hundred for *Women in Love*, and five hundred for a book that was in the post for him to complete, called provisionally "A Mixed Marriage." This was *The Lost Girl*. He wanted plain speaking between Secker and himself in future dealings, and announced at the same time that he was breaking with his agent Pinker. *The Lost Girl* manuscript, which was two-thirds done, had been in Bavaria since 1914. All in all he was about to become immensely productive on several fronts.

While in Capri he spoke intimately with Mackenzie about his problems with sex. The urbane Mackenzie found these discussions comic, and the more innocent Lawrence evidently did not. He was living too with a sexually experienced woman, imbued with Freudian ideas and experimentation with Otto Gross, a previous lover. Whatever the truth was, she was clearly not going to be told by her insecure husband how to behave in bed. We have to take into account Mackenzie's prejudice when we read his memoirs, published in 1933, since by then he had been annoyed by a satirical portrait of himself in Lawrence's story "The Man Who Loved Islands." Especially laughable for Mackenzie apparently was Lawrence's distress at Mackenzie's opinion that the sexual act was basically comic.

John Middleton Murry received the first of many blasts of abuse when Lawrence was still on Capri. In January 1919 Murry had been made editor of *The Athenaeum*, and in his new position of power in the London literary world he rejected an innocuous essay about a pet rabbit, "Adolphe," and followed up this "betrayal" of his old friend by returning several other pieces. "I have no doubt," wrote Lawrence on January 30, 1919, "you 'didn't like them,' just as you didn't like the things you had from Derbyshire. But as a matter of fact, what it amounts to is that you are a dirty little worm, and you take the ways of a dirty little worm. . . ." Contact was resumed later, though warily, Murry being notoriously difficult to insult. And Lawrence was still fond of Murry's wife, Katherine Mansfield, in spite of this rupture.

The question arises: what impelled him to write to Maurice Magnus as soon as he reached Capri? He hardly knew the fellow, though he did know he was a little adventurer who wouldn't hesitate to touch anyone for cash, since he was always out of funds and rather desperate. But then Lawrence's first instinct after meeting someone new was to reestablish contact by writing to them, that is if they interested him. And there is no doubt that he was intrigued by his short acquaintance with Magnus. Let us look at his first impressions in that introduction to Magnus's book. This person who eyed him shrewdly, a little impertinently in the way of actor-managers, cosmopolitan, knocking shabbily around the world, "was just the kind of man I had never met. . . . He was a new bird to me." Yet he would surely have met the type in London, the voice precise and a little mincing, with now and then a funny high squeak. This fey, finicky individual, dancing attendance on the old reprobate Norman Douglas, running his errands fussily, "queer and sensitive as a woman with Douglas," didn't in the least repel Lawrence in the way he had been revolted by Keynes and his homosexual colleagues at Cambridge. But the intrigued novelist with an eye for interesting characters was in an uncaring mood. He had got away from postwar England and its miseries, and the adventure of being in Italy again made him indifferent. Besides, he found he admired Magnus for his pluck, surviving on next to nothing for many years, and he was stung to think that Magnus despised him for his thrift. When he tried to explain that he had difficulty in spending for himself when he had little anyway, with a wife to support, Magnus simply laughed at him. "Why, that's the very time to spend money," he said, "when you've got none. . . . That's been my philosophy all my life: when you've got no money, you may just as well spend it." He laughed his squeaky laugh, and Douglas joined in with a hearty, "Precisely. Spend when you've got nothing to spend, my boy. Spend *hard* then."

It was time for Lawrence to declare himself. "No," he said flatly. "If I can help it I will never let myself be penniless while I live. I mistrust the world too much."

The spruce little outsider who lived on his wits and yet knew how to live well had somehow made him feel inferior and cowardly. To cap it all, Lawrence thought his accent was common, with a hint of American. All he could discover about him was that Magnus was a Roman Catholic convert. There by his bedside in his room next to Douglas was a life of St. Benedict. The Benedictines appealed to him, he said, because they knew how to live better than any of the others. When Lawrence asked Douglas about him he was told, "Oh, you never know what he's at. He was manager for Isadora Duncan for a long time—knows all the capitals of Europe—knows them as you and I know Florence." His line was mainly theatrical, Douglas went on. He edited the *Roman Review* till the war put an end to it. "Oh, a many-sided sort of fellow."

Douglas, it turned out, had met Magnus in Capri sixteen years earlier. It seems he was a frequent guest at the famous old monastery south of Rome and was thinking of becoming a monk himself. Would his new friend Lawrence like to visit the monastery at Monte Cassino? It was unbelievably beautiful. Yes, Lawrence thought he might. Just say the word, cried Magnus, and I'll arrange it. Off he went on the train to Rome, first class of course. "Why not," he said. "It's beastly enough to travel at all."

No sooner had Lawrence written to Magnus from Capri that he got a reply by return. There was no direct appeal for money, though Douglas had made it clear that when he had first been approached by Magnus, a total stranger, the man had been begging. Lawrence guessed by the rueful tone of the letter that Magnus "was in trouble, in monetary difficulty." Strangely, the letter came from an expensive hotel in Anzio.

About to leave Capri, that "stewpot of semi-literary cats," and concerned to husband his resources, having only just shaken free from an existence of precarious borrowing himself, Lawrence sent off five pounds. He felt in debt to Magnus for a dinner in Florence and loathed the idea of owing him anything. He disliked even more the thought of Magnus regarding him as miserly. Also he felt sorry for him. Amy Lowell had just presented him with a hundred dollars, and it made him guiltily rich.

The letter of thanks he received was no longer wistful but buoyant, and Lawrence detected in it "a curious little tenderness." It said: "Your cheque has saved my life. Since I last saw you I have fallen down an abyss. But I will tell you when I see you. I shall be at the monastery in three days. Do come—and come alone." Lawrence had forgotten, he comments in his introduction, that the man was a woman-hater.

It was a surprise to find himself expected when he had only expressed a vague interest. Another letter came, warmer still. He suspected he would be touched for more money if he went, and Frieda vehemently objected. They had slender enough resources, and what right did he have to give away part of their money? She had a point, he agreed, but something made him want to go. It would be only for a stay of two days. He set off in the black dark of a January morning, "the thin line of the lights of Naples twinkling far, far off."

AFTER A HAZARDOUS JOURNEY by steamer and train he was deposited at twilight by a cab at the huge old gateway of the monastery, looking like a massive fortress palace of the sixteenth century, and there was Magnus coming to meet him, quite at home, walking with his perky little step. "I'm so *pleased* you've come," he said. "And he looked into my eyes with that wistful, watchful tenderness, rather like a woman who isn't quite sure of her lover."

Lawrence was led by the arm under the tunnel-like entrance into a grassy courtyard like a cloister. Black monks chatted, an old peasant was driving sheep along and an old monk was entering a little post office. Peasants were working, one carrying a two-handed saw. Then came Magnus's friend Don Bernado, a tall, good-looking gentle monk about Lawrence's age. "One felt one was at college. . . ."

Don Bernado produced the key to his room: an elegant little bedroom with an ante chamber, on the wall an engraving of an English landscape, with a balcony looking down on the garden, beyond that the farm and oak woods and arable fields of the hill summit. Down below lay the "world's valley," with mountains that stood in Italy on the plains "as if God had just put them down ready-made." It was sunset, the snow on the mountains glowed rosily, shadows gathered in the valleys. "One heard, far below, the trains shunting, the world clinking in the cold air."

Magnus at his side was exclaiming, "Isn't it wonderful! Ah, the most wonderful place on earth! The peace, the beauty, the eternity of it." He put his hand wistfully on Don Bernado's arm and began to prattle about becoming a monk, going to college in Rome for two years to prepare, "when I have got the money for the fees."

The charming Don Bernado, who spoke English like a native, suggested a cup of tea and they went to Magnus's room for it. It was cold as a tomb everywhere. Lawrence's clothes worn in hot Capri were thin, so Magnus made him wear a big sealskin coat of his own, buttoning it up solicitously at the throat for him, until he felt warm and as pampered as a millionaire. This splendid coat had been made specially in New York fifteen years ago, Magnus told him. "We don't want to die of cold in the monastery, do we? That's one of the mortifications we will do our best to avoid." He liked to give the impression he dealt with the best shops and stayed in the best hotels, whereas Lawrence stood and "grinned inside the coat, detesting best hotels, best shops and best overcoats."

They went down for dinner to the guests' refectory, Lawrence still in his "sealskin millionaire monster" coat, Magnus in his gray overcoat. They had a decanter of good red wine but the food was cold—it had come so far from the kitchen. The next morning Lawrence woke to a nice old lay brother bringing his water, and to a motionless, sunny day in the grip of the Middle Ages. "And the poignant grip of the past, when blood was strong and life flamboyant with splendors and horrible miseries, took hold of me till I could hardly bear it. It was really agony to me to see the old farm and the bullocks slowly working in the fields below . . . and to see an old, old man driving an ass slowly to the monastery gate, with all that lingering nonchalance and wildness of the Middle Ages, and yet to know that I was myself, child of the present." Down there far below he could see the white road he had traveled along, and trains steaming at the station "and tiny people swarming like flies." To see all this from the monastery, from the last vestiges of the Middle Ages, "made almost a wound."

That evening Magnus showed him his manuscript about life in the Foreign Legion, "rather raggedly" typed out. Lawrence read it when he went to bed and when he woke in the morning. He thought it not well written, "And yet there was something in it that made me want it done properly." Magnus promised, not too willingly, to tackle it again.

In the afternoon they walked through the woods and over the bit of moorland covering most of the summit. It was sunny and warm as they came to the ruined convent which lay on the other brow of the hill. A barefoot little boy

> was tending a cow and three goats and a pony, a barefoot little girl had five geese in charge. We came to the convent and looked in. The further part of the courtyard was still entire, the place was a sort of farm, two rooms occupied by a peasant-farmer. . . . Some creature was crying—crying, crying, crying with a strange, inhuman persistence. Almost it might have been a sharp-voiced baby. We scrambled about, looking. And at last . . . found a blind black puppy crawling miserably on the floor, unable to walk and crying incessantly.

On the road outside they met a man, a peasant, thin and black and dirty. He said the bitch-mother had gone off with his son and the sheep. They would be back at sunset.

> They were the old-world peasants still about the monastery, with the hard, small bony heads and deep-lined faces and utterly blank minds, crying their speech as crows cry, and living their lives as lizards among the rocks, blindly going on with the little job in hand, the present moment, cut off from all past and future, and having no idea and no sustained emotion, only that eternal will-to-live which makes a tortoise wake up once more in spring, and makes a grasshopper whistle on in the moonlight nights even of November. Only these peasants don't whistle much. The whistlers go to America. It is the hard, static, unhoping souls that persist in the old life. And still they stand back, as one passes them in the corridors of the great monastery, they press themselves back against the whitewashed walls of the still place, and drop their heads, as if some mystery were passing by, some God-mystery, the higher beings, which they must not look closely upon. So also this old peasant—he was not old, but deep-lined like a gnarled bough. He stood with his hat down in his hands as we spoke to him and answered the short, insentient answers, as a tree might speak.

Then came a scrap of dialogue in his introduction that would be exemplified and repeated again and again in his novels.

"The monks keep their peasants humble," he said to Magnus.

"Of course!" Magnus said. "Don't you think they should be humble?"

"Well," Lawrence said, "if there's any occasion for humility, I do."

"Don't you think there is occasion?" Magnus cried. "If there's one thing worse than another, it's this *equality* that has come into the world. Do you believe in it yourself?"

"No," Lawrence said. "I don't believe in equality. But the problem is, wherein does superiority lie?"

"Oh," chirped Magnus complacently, "it lies in many things. It lies in birth and upbringing and so on, but it is chiefly in *mind*. Don't you think?"

And what Lawrence thought was that it was terrible to be agreed with by a man like Magnus. "All that one says, and means, turns to nothing. . . . But if I had had to choose, I would have chosen the peasant." And being Lawrence, he had to make absolutely clear what he meant. "No, if I chose the peasant it would be for what he *lacked* rather than what he had. He lacked the complacent mentality that Magnus was so proud of, he lacked all the trivial trash of glib talk and more glib thought, all the conceit of our shallow consciousness." Here is the fierce clarity that one values so much in Lawrence, together with the dilemma that always faced him. The past, poignant and nearly dead, was no longer an option for anyone. "One can't go back," he said to Magnus. The way to the future lay through the modern world down there, and that was agony, and would always be so. Sinking to the elemental beneath the civilized characters in his novels would be his unique achievement. "There on the steamer I sat in a bit of sunshine, and felt that again the world had come to an end for me, and again my heart was broken. The steamer seemed to be making its way away from the old world, that had come to another end in me." He had looked down on the future from his mountaintop foothold with its illusory peace, and saw democracy, aggressive industrialism, communists, fascists, and the sterile, barren world that had been engendered. Somehow it had to be got through, to somewhere beyond it, to a reality where the demands of its society no longer applied.

He had half expected to be asked for money, and to forestall this had left his checkbook behind. In the event Magnus's hand did not come out. Going down to the station they had stopped at a cavelike café. Magnus paid a franc for the wine, refusing Lawrence's shamefaced offer of twenty lire, the only spare cash he had, apart from his journey money. His host shook his head and turned back uphill.

IF LAWRENCE HOPED he had seen the last of Maurice Magnus he was mistaken. The ingratiating little man was not so easily shaken off. The Lawrences had been told about Taormina on Sicily, and by the time the Italian spring arrived they already felt themselves to be "old inhabitants," installed on the top two floors of Fontana Vecchia, just outside the village. Mount Etna was out of sight, obscured by other peaks, but from their veranda they looked out on splendid views across the straits of Messina to the Calabrian coast. To their right beckoned the Ionian Sea. At the end of March 1920 Lawrence wrote to John Ellingham Brooks of his joy in the dawns: "The world's morning—that and the wild cyclamen thrill me with this sense. Then there are the pink gladioli, and pink snapdragons, and orchids." Sicily had, he thought, a fascinating interior: "If I can only get some money and finish this novel I shall walk into the middle of it." The fifty thousand words of a novel that amused him but "perhaps won't amuse anybody else" was no doubt the contentious *Aaron's Rod*.

Pacing the decks high on the top of Fontana Vecchia he counted his blessings, and the work was flowing. In swift succession he completed *The Lost Girl*, prepared new versions of the groundbreaking essays in *Studies in Classic American Literature*, and added to poems in a volume that would become *Birds, Beasts and Flowers*. (From childhood onward, Lawrence loved charades. "He could act, mimic, turn himself into a frog or fish," writes Anthony Burgess. "Some of his animal poems are a kind of charade, in which he boasts an inner understanding of what no human soul can ever hope to understand.") Before long he would finish *Aaron's Rod* and dash off *Sea and Sardinia* and *Fantasia of the Unconscious* in an extraordinary burst of work, prodigious even for him.

This was for Lawrence his first real postwar spring, and to celebrate it the poems streamed forth, struck off hit-or-miss with perverse delight, all of them reveling in a new freedom, teeming with ideas, argumentative, and all intrinsically religious. Impossible without the example of Whitman, they were in a manner uniquely his own.

> What rot, to see the cabbage and hibiscus-tree
> As equals!
> What rot, to say the louts along the Corso
> In Sunday suits and yellow shoes
> Are my equals!
> I am their superior, saluting the hibiscus flower, not them.
> The same I say to the profiteers from the hotels, the money-fat
> ones,
> The same I say to the pale and elegant persons,
> Pale-face authorities loitering tepidly:
> *That I salute the red hibiscus flower*
> *And send mankind to its inferior blazes.*

Of course no paradise is complete without a devil, and soon a serpent arrived in the form of Magnus. On the run from his creditors, he had left Monte Cassino in a hurry and fled to Rome, then making for Lawrence—who had hoped to keep him at arm's length with letters—in Taormina. It was April. As it happened, the Lawrences were away, visiting Syracuse with their friends the Jutas for a few blissful days. Magnus waited, running up bills at one of Taormina's expensive hotels while he did so.

Lawrence must have realized why he had been invited to Monte Cassino, yet he had still gone. He was always willing to help aspiring writers, giving generously of his time if there was talent there to encourage, and Douglas had no doubt told him of what he knew of the memoir. Now Magnus hoped to enlist Lawrence's help in either selling the manuscript or obtaining magazine serialization.

The memoir, called *Dregs: Experiences of an American in the Foreign Legion*, had been unearthed for Lawrence to look at in the monastery, and he had read it quickly. Back in Sicily, he wrote to Magnus suggesting that he revise the last five chapters and then Lawrence would approach Stanley Unwin. On April 2 he was true to his word, asking Unwin to look at the book, an inside story of life in the Legion which pulled no punches. One censored passage indicted the Legionnaires for "their evil mindedness which attributed every action to the lowest motives, their physical filth, and finally their drunkenness and sodomistic habits. . . ."

Returning from Syracuse with the young South African painter Jan Juta, the Lawrences found Magnus waiting with a tale of woe. Frieda took an instant dislike to him, turning on her husband for aiding and abetting him. Lawrence had no choice but to show Magnus the door, relenting to the extent of settling his Taormina hotel bill. Meanwhile Frieda went on Magnus's list of women he hated: he wrote to Douglas saying that Lawrence was sympathetic but not "She, the bitch." At the monastery he had been acid about women, telling Lawrence, "Why, it's all a fraud. The woman is just taking all and giving nothing, and feeling sanctified about it. All she tries to do is to thwart a man in whatever he is doing." Lawrence had noticed a photograph of a beautiful woman on the wall of Magnus's room, who turned out to be his mother.

He continued to do his best for the memoir, posting half the manuscript to Unwin with a recommendation, saying that in his opinion its amateurishness was redeemed by a courageous honesty.

The tragicomic story of Maurice Magnus, American gentleman, is nearly, but not quite done. The "impossible little pigeon" with his conceit as a gentleman and his insistence on keeping up appearances no matter how desperate, now came up with another request. He was eternally grateful to Lawrence for settling his hotel bill, but would he mind going back to Monte Cassino to gather up the baggage he had left, containing valuable manuscripts, when he had fled from the police? Plausible though the fellow always was, Lawrence managed to refuse: facing that arduous journey again was too much. Instead he gave the man, who had decided to head for Alexandria or Malta, a hundred lire to assist him on his way. Magnus wrote indignantly to Douglas that Lawrence wanted him to move to a miserable *pensione* in Taormina. What's more, "he never asked me for a meal or offered a room in his most commodious house."

Finally he departed for Malta and Lawrence breathed again. Alas, not for long. Lawrence, who responded by letter to everyone, even the Magnuses of this world, heard that the "prime hypocrite" had reached Syracuse, still on his way to Malta. He had been written into *The Lost Girl* as Mr. May, the shady but likable stage manager. On May 7, for all his relief at getting rid of the pest his American acquaintance had become, Lawrence thought he would like to see Malta himself. Their friend Mary Cannan had expressed a desire to go there and would pay his and Frieda's expenses: it would be only for a few days.

Reaching Syracuse they were confronted by a steamer strike. In the hotel where they had to stay the night, a note arrived for Lawrence. It was from Magnus, staying at another hotel where of course he had run up a bill. Could Lawrence lend him—only till he reached Malta where he had friends and resources—ninety lire?

Lawrence paid up again. What Frieda said is not recorded. On the steamer at last they gazed on a remarkable sight: Frieda and Mary Cannan were both furious at the sight of Magnus resplendent in gray, boarding the steamer with a porter behind him. Later he smiled down with "condescending nods from the first-class deck to the Lawrences and Mary Cannan in second class. The farce—which would soon be black farce—was capped by the appearance of Magnus chatting with a royal naval officer.

It was impossible on an island as small as Malta for Lawrence to avoid Magnus, and according to Brenda Maddox's account he did not even try. Magnus now had two charming young Maltese friends in tow, and the four went for a drive around the island together. After they parted and the Lawrences returned to Sicily, Magnus continued to woo his English friend, who wrote Martin Secker on July 20 after Unwin had rejected "Dregs," telling him he thought the Legion manuscript was "awfully good."

Postcards arrived from Magnus, and letters, urging Lawrence to come back to Malta and spend a month with him, but he had had enough. Magnus's friends Mazzaiba and Salonia were very pleasant young men, but he found the island "stark as a corpse, no trees, no bushes even: a fearful landscape . . . weary with ages of weariness, old weary houses here and there . . . and a sordid, scrap-iron front." He had no intention of ever visiting the beastly island again, though he was relieved to think of Magnus established there in a tiny house costing five pounds a year, with his two kind friends for company. Letters kept coming, which he refused to answer, telling Jan Juta, "No, I don't like him—shall not bother with him any more." But if he ever did think about him it was with a "fatal sinking feeling."

Mackenzie was tempting him with descriptions of his newly acquired boat *Lavengro*, named after George Borrow's book—perfect, he said, for sailing the South Seas. If Lawrence ever had sufficient funds he would "go whacks" in running her. It was one dream he would never achieve. How wonderful it would be to sail away from everything. England sounded as sickening as ever. "I hate Labour and Capitalism and all that frowsty duality in nothingness."

In August 1920 Frieda went to see her mother in Germany, worried by her struggles to cope with postwar shortages. Lawrence accompanied her as far as Milan, then they parted and he visited friends at Argeno on Lake Como and after that had a reunion with

Rosalind Baynes, whose sculptor father Lawrence had known the previous year in Berkshire. In the throes of a divorce, she chose Florence after hearing Lawrence's praise of it. She found a villa in a small village, San Gervasio, a tram journey from Florence, and when Lawrence called to see her he brought presents for her small daughters. Some of the poems in *Birds, Beasts and Flowers* have the designation San Gervasio.

Rejoining Frieda in October and returning with her to Taormina, he was relieved to find no word from Magnus. Had the infernal nuisance really gone out of his life? A short letter from Don Bernado with the grim news of Magnus's suicide was followed by a Maltese newspaper that Salonia had posted, with the marked notice: "The suicide of an American gentleman at Rabato. Yesterday the American Maurice Magnus was found dead in his bed. . . . By his bedside was a bottle containing poison." Two detectives intent on charging him with fraud had accosted him in the street. Magnus, always punctilious about his dress, asked if he could go into his house to change. He was found with a bottle of prussic acid at his side. He was nearly forty-four.

Lawrence, his feelings in turmoil, realized too late, he says in his introduction, what it must have meant to be that hunted, desperate man. The world stood still for him when he thought that he could, by giving half his money, have saved his life. "I had chosen not to save his life."

He goes on: "The worst thing I have against him is that he abused the confidence, the kindness and the generosity of unsuspecting people like Mazzaiba and Salonia. For after all, he was never mean. Absurdly generous in fact when he had the means. The *human* traitor he was. But he was not traitor to the spirit. In the great spirit of human consciousness he was a hero, little, quaking and heroic: a strange, quaking star."

2

An Absolute Necessity to Move

(1920–1921)

The blazing summer at Fontana Vecchia had come and gone, when he had lived for weeks in a pair of pajamas and nothing else, gone barefoot, and seen the snake of his famous poem. Then, after Frieda returned from Germany, the late autumn of October had suddenly drenched everything, turning Sicily "like a land inside an aquarium—all water—and people like crabs and black-grey shrimps creeping on the bottom." He passed the time in the endless wet days copying a classic Italian picture—making careful copies of paintings was something he had always done (Birkin in *Women in Love*, asked why he copied rather than doing something original, answered, "I want to know it")—and "swotting Italian history" for an additional chapter to his Oxford *Movements in European History*.

Looking out at the rain he wrote of "Wet almond trees in the rain / Like iron sticking grimly out of the earth," and when the sun broke free and his perch over Taormina and the sea seemed "so pleasant, magical," he tried to subdue his dream of leasing a sailing boat—like Robert Louis Stevenson before him—and cruising the world in absolute freedom from houses and possessions. Then the blow fell of Magnus's tragic end, and perhaps to throw off the pall of that news he conceived the idea of an excursion to Sardinia. Frieda was game, as in those days she invariably was. And Sicily, especially Taormina, seemed to "go dead without their foreigners, torpid, as if they were waiting to be wound up." He was in a mood that will soon be very familiar to us: waiting to go somewhere, anywhere, yet with a commonsense voice in his ear telling him to stay. Fontana Vecchia cost only ten dollars a year. But once he found fault, imaginary or otherwise, with somewhere, he swiftly had the confirmation he needed. Sicilians, living in such close proximity to Etna, were "intelligent daimons," intelligent but soulless. Living near Etna drove men mad.

He recognized that something drove him to move, without knowing what. "Why can't one sit still? "Leaving Etna aside, he had to admit that Sicily was agreeable, and so was the sunny Ionian Sea, Calabria like "a changing jewel." So where could he go? Africa was near, and a book by a German historian— it could have been Spengler, whose *Decline of the West* was being read widely—had stirred him with evocations of its dark heart. But for the moment Africa was too drastic a step. Spain, then, or Sardinia. All at once Sardinia attracted him as a place where he might like to live. In those days it was little known or visited. Its attraction for Lawrence was that it lay untamed, still primitive, even with its Italian railways and buses. Somehow it existed "outside the circuit of civilization." Working himself up to an animus with those "maddening, exasperating, impossible Sicilians . . . sulphurous demons" under the sway of that witch, Etna, he set out for a boat sailing once a fortnight from Palermo. They had a mere three days to wait—no time to change his mind.

He and Frieda spent no more than nine days in Sardinia, and thus he came to write one of his most magical books, a travel log that is so many things: enchanting, zestful, comical, boiling with rage, and giving us an invaluable blow-by-blow account of his life with Frieda. It is perhaps his most popular, certainly his most accessible book, and is immensely successful, with its off-the-cuff, highly personal style, in capturing the place and the people as never before. Angry about so much, it could be called indulgent were it not for the fact that Lawrence freely ridicules himself and his towering, absurd rages, parodies himself even, and can see perfectly well how laughable he and Frieda are at times. He writes of Frieda, furious about an evening meal, "working up to the rage I had at last calmed down from." He came back to Sicily, probably without a single note, full of this brief, packed experience, sat down and wrote his book *Sea and Sardinia* in six weeks. It was quickly serialized and then published by Seltzer in America the following year.

IT WAS TIME to go, one cold morning early in January 1921. As always he was full of misgivings at the last moment, feeling pangs at leaving, "slinking out" in the dark under the great carob tree after swallowing a cup of tea and a bit of toast. Then the working-class touch: "Hastily wash up, so that we can find the house decent when we come back." On their travels they always carried a little bag called the kitchenino, with methylated spirit, a little saucepan, two spoons, two forks, a knife, two aluminum plates, salt, sugar, tea. Oh yes, and the thermos flask, sandwiches, a few apples, and a pat of butter. At the outset it amused him to refer to Frieda as the queen bee: "Then my knapsack, and the q-b's handbag."

So off he went, ambivalent as ever at leaving "the dawn-place," Sicily, Europe's dawn, "with Odysseus pushing his ship out of the shadows into the blue," propelled by his desire to escape, to move. It was only an excursion, a matter of a few weeks, but in his heart he knew it was a foretaste of a more drastic leavetaking. For Murry the book confirmed all his charges: Lawrence's false turning toward the pagan, his delight in the survival of "the hardy, indomitable male" that he was unable to be himself, his fear of woman as the Devouring Mother. All this in a lovely book that for Murry seethed with weak and childish contradictions.

Contradictions there certainly are, and ambivalence galore. The book's appeal has to do with the constant striving to be honest to life as he sees it, and a willingness to show himself at his worst, his most irrascible, his most vulnerable.

Above all there is enchantment, along with mad irritation and vituperative disgust. But first the shiver of awfulness at the naked beauty of the world, the sky and sea "parting like an oyster shell, with a low red gape." Cocks crowing as they went down to the highway and the civilization he dreamt of shaking off, to an island that had perhaps slipped through the net. On their way to the station they passed a factory for making citrate, then houses flush to the road, whose occupants threw out dirty slops and coffee dregs, over which they walked.

At the station Lawrence marveled at his fellow passengers, who might be an early morning crowd waiting for a train on a North London suburban station. As far as features go they might be, but there the resemblance ended. These lower-middle-class young fellows were not socially self-conscious as their English counterparts would have been. Not at all: they were lively, they threw their arms round one another's necks, "they all but kiss. One poor chap has had earache, so a black kerchief is tied round his face, and his black hat is perched above, and a comic sight he looks." Yet more comic than this, Lawrence was looked at askance because of his knapsack instead of a new suitcase, "as if I had arrived riding on a pig." They grabbed the one with the earache by the arm and could not be sympathetic enough. "Do you suffer?" they asked.

Lawrence must have seen much of this physicality already during his time in Italy, but the Sicilians were more so, he claims, than anywhere else. "They pour themselves one over the other like so much melted butter over parsnips. . . . Never in the world have I seen such melting gay tenderness as between casual Sicilians on railway platforms. . . ." He adds that this was more true of the middle classes than the lower. His English antennae for class differences are forever quiveringly alert. The working men he observes were thinner and less exuberant. "But they hang together in clusters, and can never be physically near enough."

The journey to Messina was only thirty miles, but they shuffled along tediously for two hours. They stopped and started, hurrying and crawling

> beside the lavender grey morning sea. A flock of goats trail over the beach near the lapping waves' edge, dismally. Great wide deserts of stony river-beds run down to the sea, and men on asses are picking their way across, and women are kneeling by the small stream-channel washing clothes. The lemons hang pale and innumerable in the thick lemon groves. Lemon trees, like Italians, seem to be happiest when they are touching one another all round. . . . Women, vague in the orchard under-shadow, are picking the lemons, lurking as if in the undersea. There are heaps of pale yellow lemons under the trees. They look like pale, primrose-smoldering fires. . . . When there comes a cluster of orange trees, the oranges are red like coals among the darker leaves. But lemons, lemons, innumerable, speckled like innumerable tiny stars in the green firmament of leaves. So many lemons! Think of all the lemonade crystals they will be reduced to! Think of America drinking them up next summer.

From Messina they went on to their port, Palermo, where they had to find a hotel for the night. At last next morning they were in a boat making for their steamer. "Climb up, climb up, this is our ship." Frieda had already, with her substantial body, confronted three·giggling young hussies in the streets of Palermo after insisting on going shopping. Now Lawrence, the miner's son, was about to feel insulted by the casual proletarian manner of a bunch of men in black canvas jackets, "a loutish crew with nothing to do, and we the first passengers served up to be jeered at."

"Who is going?"

"We two."

"Tickets!"

The crew stood there, "exactly like a gang of louts at a street corner. And they've got the street to themselves—this ship. We climb to the upper deck."

How he loved the sea! One is reminded of Stevenson's joy on board ship in the vast Pacific. "Sweet, sweet wide morning on the sea," rhapsodizes Lawrence, with the sun coming, swimming up to greet them. "The lovely dawn, the lovely pure, wide morning in the mid-sea, so golden-aired and delighted. . . ." Then comes the dream in all its glory which pursued him all his days, and should be quoted in full:

> How glad to be on a ship! What a golden hour for the heart of man! Ah, if one could sail for ever, on a small, quiet, lonely ship, from land to land and isle to isle, and saunter through the spaces of this lovely world. Sweet it would be sometimes to come to the opaque earth, to block oneself against the inertia of our *terra firma*! But life itself would be in the flight, the tremble of space. Ah the trembling of never-ended space, as one moves in flight! Space, and the frail vibration of space, the glad lonely wringing of the heart. Not to be clogged to the land any more. Not to be any more like a donkey with a log on its leg, fastened to weary earth that had no answer now. But to be off. . . . To find three masculine, world-lost souls, and saunter along with them across the dithering space, as long as life lasts! Why come to anchor? There is nothing to anchor for. Land has no answer to the soul any more. It has gone inert. Give me a little ship, kind gods, and three world-lost comrades. Hear me!

And it goes without saying, no women and no work. One can see Murry throwing up his hands at this "bewildering inconsequence." But Lawrence was writing as he felt, and tomorrow would feel something else. All through this book he is in violent reaction against the status quo, in a restless search for something else. To penetrate a place like Sardinia, he will say, "is like a most fascinating act of self-discovery—back, back, back down the old ways of time. Strange and wonderful chords awake in us. . . ."

Yet we are immured in the present in this book, which is why it is so entrancing, so vivid and so transient. The kaleidoscope is always shaking, the rainbow forever hanging. This for Lawrence is the truth. Not for him the dreamy Utopian, struggling to believe in something that can never be. Pipe dreams are as anathema as the democratic uniformity he sees engulfing the world. Utopian visions may come and go, but they exist only to express a longing or to make a point. *Sea and Sardinia* is filled with these adjustments in the face of realism, enchantments that disappoint, noble savages who on close contact turn out to be sordid and repulsive. He dreams dreams, and jettisons them just as quickly, in swift spasms of reaction.

He seems to sense these shifts in attitude even before they disembark, when land appears ahead that is "more transparent than thin pearl." Sardinia! The eagerness of his anticipation is poignant because one knows the place will not live up to his vision. He is aware of this himself. "Magic are high lands seen from the sea, when they are far, far off, and ghostly translucent like icebergs." Even sailing ships, "as if cut out of frailest pearl translucency," sailing away toward Naples, seem to us like images of his frail hope for something different, better, a greater reality existing somewhere.

Soon, not quite yet, he will come down to earth with a bang. Ahead is Cagliari, nothing like Italy, with no trees, looking remote, like a town in an illuminated missal. "One wonders how it ever got there." The air cold, the sky bleak, with clouds all curdled, yet the piled-up town for some reason makes him think of Jerusalem. And of course he wants it to be Jerusalem, golden, holy.

THE SHIP is hauled to the quayside. He shoulders his knapsack, and a man like a bluebottle jumps forward.

"You pay nine francs fifty."

He pays, and they get off that ship.

And at first he approves of the starkness, the lack of glamour, "none of the suave Greek-Italian charms," no airs and graces. Nothing like Sicily. No, it is rather stark, bony, yellow, and cold, somehow like Malta: he has forgotten how he loathed Malta a few months before. A north wind is blowing, and they are hungry. It is January after all.

They find a hotel, which is at least clean, the people warm-seeming, "like human beings." He has no time now for the suave "completely callous" Sicilians of his experience, with their ancient souls.

He approves too of the men standing about in groups in the stony streets, who don't have the Italian watchfulness that never leaves you alone. And he clings to his sense of a place "lost between Europe and Africa and belonging to nowhere . . . never having belonged to anywhere . . . as if it had never really had a fate. Left outside of time and history." Here is his famous spirit of place in operation, always illuminating and instinctive, sometimes unerringly right, sometimes wildly wrong. Not content with registering the strangeness, he cannot resist a swipe at "our mechanical age" which tries to override the spirit of place and inevitably fails.

Down to earth he comes in the dark humid streets, thin as crevices, threading up to the cathedral. Suddenly a huge pail of slops hurtles down from above. It misses him narrowly, as it does a small boy who looks up in impersonal wonder like a child staring up at a star.

They are at a table at the Café Roma, which has coffee and milk but no butter. Lawrence sees his first peasant costume and at once his heart responds, he has a "heart yearning" for something he has once known and wants back again. It's not a dream, he says vehemently, not an illusion, for there the man is. He admits the nostalgia. Why should he be so nostalgic?

The peasant is elderly, upright, a handsome proud man in his black-and-white costume. Can a man be called beautiful? He describes the costume of this beautiful apparition in detail. "How handsome he is, and so beautifully male!" Frieda would have no doubt agreed, but this is between men. "How beautiful maleness is, if it finds its right expression. And how perfectly ridiculous it is made in modern clothes." Now he expounds on an obsessive theme, in a great generalizing sweep. "One realizes with horror that the race of men is almost extinct in Europe. Only Christ-like heroes and woman-worshipping Don Juans, and rabid equality-mongrels." The lovely thing for Lawrence about this man is his unapproach-ableness, indomitable. So there we have it. "The old, hardy, in-domitable male is gone. His fierce singleness is quenched." Here are the last sparks. "Nothing left but the herd-proletariat, and the herd-equality mongrelism, and the self-sacrificial cultured soul." All detestable.

But what is it about this black-and-white peasant costume that so enthralls him, flashing before his eyes? "I seem to have known it before: to have worn it even: to have dreamed it. . . . It belongs in some way to something in me." The yearning he expresses is in-tense. He bursts out, "Here they don't make those great leering eyes, the inevitable yours-to-command look of Italian males. . . . Give me the old salty way of love!"

In the sunless streets, as in most Southern towns, the streets are cold as wells. He and Frieda dodge in and out of the sunny scraps. She would like to explore the shops, such as they are. He is still tak-ing note of the peasants. Peasant women in full-petticoated costume he admires, with the pleats of dark blue and red, so that when she walks "the red goes flash-flash-flash, like a bird showing its colors." Pretty they are, with a charm lacking in modern elegance, though the passion he feels for the peasant man is absent. These peasant girls and women are, he thinks, brisk and defiant, with straight stiff backs, "like little walls," and no nonsense about them. They dart along in a birdlike, alert way, and in them too, as in the men, he de-tects something defiant and un-get-at-able. Which is how it should be, he decides, this defiant, splendid split between the sexes. Not in the least like Italy, tender Italy, "so tender—like cooked macaroni—yards and yards of soft tenderness raveled round everything." None of that nauseating Madonna-worship here. Men and women "don't idealize each other" in Sardinia it seems.

Nothing escapes him: he is struck by the difference in eyes between those here and in Sicily. The big bright dark eyes in Sicily could be fascinating, with a little imp lighting them at the center, "the eyes of old Greece, surely." Here the eyes have no impudent imp: they are all velvet, their darkness curiously blank, remote, and he jumps in with his need to read meaning into them. These eyes have an older note, he feels, before Greece, "as if the intelligence lay deep within the cave," so that one searches in the gloom in vain. What is it about these eyes that gives a hint of an unknown lurking creature? Unlighted is the word he seizes on for this quality he can't pin down. "Sometimes Velasquez, and sometimes Goya give a suggestion of these large, dark, unlighted eyes."

Enough of eyes, enough of Cagliari and its shops, though not before Frieda succumbs to some peasant material she spies in the doorway of a shop, stripy cotton stuff. She buys enough for a dress. They decide to get on the narrow-gauge railway that penetrates the middle of the island, and buy third-class tickets to Mandas: it is either that or first—no second. They shoulder their knapsacks and climb into the wooden carriage, on the wooden seats, ahead of them a slow journey of sixty miles into unknown territory. Lawrence is always happiest on the move, and everyone around them in the fairly crowded open carriage seems in good spirits, "like being in a lively inn."

The train crawls into the first villages, and the thick-adobe houses, clay colored, look very foreign, like little colonies made of earth. Then into the hills, and they see how sparsely inhabited the interior of Sardinia is, much of it wild scrub, with grayish cleared areas of arable land for the corn. Lawrence is reminded of Cornwall, like the region around Zennor and Land's End where they lived during the war, with low, moorlike hills and glimpses of sea. Still prepared to like everything, he finds the landscape so different from dramatic, operatic Italy, full of scenic excitement. Sardinia has ordinary ridges of moor running away, giving a feeling of space "like liberty itself, after the peaky confinement of Sicily." Yes, he can imagine himself in a Celtic landscape as they puff through the wild heath.

THEY REACH MANDAS, and at the little station restaurant they can have a bed. It is after seven. Up the cold winding stone stair goes a woman with a candle to show the way. The bedroom smells sour, so they fling open the window on "big frosty stars snapping ferocious in heaven."

Hungry, they go down the stone stair to the dining room, sitting at a long table to eat soup in the stone cold room. The brown woman comes out of the kitchen and serves up smoking cabbage soup which has bits of macaroni floating in it, mixed with the cabbage bits. Afterward Lawrence has fried pork, and boiled eggs for Frieda. Three station officials come in, two of them wearing scarlet peaked caps, one in a black-and-gold cap, joining them at the table and tucking into the soup. To make conversation, Lawrence says good evening and remarks how cold it is. Yes, they say unwillingly, it is fresh. "An Italian never says it is cold: it is never more than *fresco*." Now Lawrence's comic style comes into its own, and no one, reading this passage, can say that Lawrence is without humor. One of the young officials they called afterward the *maialino* (the gay little black pig). "And never, from among the steam, have I heard a more joyful trio of soup-swilkering. They sucked it from their spoons with long gusto-rich sucks. The *maialino* was the treble—he trilled his soup into his mouth with a swift sucking vibration, interrupted by bits of cabbage. . . . Black-cap was the baritone, good rolling spoon-sucks. And the one in spectacles was the bass . . . sudden deep gulps. Suddenly the *maialino* cocked up his spoon in one hand, chewed a huge mouthful of bread and swallowed it down with a smack-smack-smack! of his tongue against his palate."

In the morning, the sun not yet up at seven, Lawrence is still amazed to find himself looking at a scene so like England, or the bleak parts of Cornwall, or Derbyshire, or a part of Ireland. The same old drystone walls, the same somber, dark grass under the naked sky. He feels back in time, "before the curtains of history lifted," a world bare and somber and open.

And going out on the frozen road he is intoxicated to his soul by the grass all bluish with hoarfrost. We realize again that he is on a quest and sees symbols and connections everywhere. Crossing the road over the frozen cowpats he is thrilled by the familiarity, and by the fact that his feet are on granite. This is where he belongs, not on limestone or marble; granite is "so live under my feet." And for once he and Frieda are in accord; as they head down the road to the village she too feels free, "as one does not feel in Italy and Sicily, where all is so classic and fixed."

They take the morning train and go on to the terminus, Sorgono. Though Lawrence harps still on Cornwall, on England, honesty compels him to say, for all his yearning to belong, that there is that strange note in the south and east as if the *depths* were barren, "sun-stricken . . . the heart eaten out by dryness." Frieda cries out sentimentally that she likes it, but asked if she could live there is unable to say.

Traveling to Sorgono they cross over the mountain knot at the center of Sardinia that is called Gennargentu. Rising up through the hazel thickets and out again on the myrtle scrub, Lawrence sees again in the distance the black-and-white flash of a peasant in his native costume, looking lonely and vivid on his pony. Proud mankind, how it once was. "But alas, most of the men are still khaki-muffled, rabbit-indistinguishable, ignominious."

To do justice to the "long tress of a waterfall" dropping into a small gorge, to the clump of naked poplars far below, to the nakedly gleaming silvery mauve fig tree, he would have to be a painter. "A fig tree come forth in its nudity gleaming over the dark winter earth is a sight to behold. . . . Ah, if it could but answer! or if we had tree-speech!"

The train bolts over a bridge, perilously high, then in sheer surprise they come to a station, linked to the main line by a post bus. Men pour aboard, workers of some kind: miners or laborers or land workers, the English traveler thinks. He is all eyes and ears, noticing the huge sacks they all carry, and their clothes. One old man dressed in the black and white he loves, though his costume is grubby and in tatters, others in "the tight madder-brown breeches and sleeved waistcoats," some wearing sheepskin tunics, and all in the long stocking caps, of black stockinette, that he finds so expressive, "like a sort of crest, as a lizard wears his crest at mating time."

And the smell they give off, of sheep and men and goat! This is what he has come to witness, what he has hoped for, these "rusé" medieval survivors. Their rank smell convinces him, though he can't wait to be convinced: these half-wild animal-like fellows are the real thing. One has his shirt unbuttoned, and he's back inside it like a black goat. This is real, this coarse life they give off. Democracy is lost on them, and so is Jesus, so are the *socialisti* and *fascisti* warring away in Italy. "One feels for the first time the real old medieval life, which is enclosed in itself and has no interest in the world outside. . . . I love my indomitable coarse men from mountain Sardinia, for their stocking caps and their splendid, animal-bright stupidity. If only the last wave of all-alikeness won't wash those superb crests away. . . ."

And now we come to the crux of this extraordinary book, half travel diary, half gospel, to the crucial peak on which dreams are shattered, where the dirty weather of realism blots out the view. They are drawing near to Sorgono at last, a weary journey of only sixty miles which has taken them seven hours. Even Lawrence has had his fill of shouting peasants by now. Here it comes in sight, magical little Sorgono, where they hope to rest for a day or two and find a pleasant inn. They climb down wearily in the little terminus station, no bigger than a halt, and an old man "fluttering with rags" asks if they are looking for the *Albergo*. Lawrence parts with his knapsack, and the old fellow leads them down a muddy lane to the high road, through glades of young oaks. How pretty! It could be the English West Country, Hardy country. They can hear the buzz of a sawmill and are in sight of the town nestling prettily among wooded hills.

Their ragged guide brings them up short before a blank, pink-washed building with its huge sign, Risveglio. Lawrence, depending on his Baedeker, has been expecting the Albergo d'Italia. They are told it doesn't exist anymore.

It is this place or nothing. Inside, a tin counter meant for a bar, and a youngish man in charge who looks disgusting, with unwashed hair and a dreary manner. He leads them down a passage as muddy as the lane outside, up a dirty flight of wooden stairs to a bedroom. Lawrence and Frieda stare at the sordid scene: a broken chair carrying a bit of candle, an abominable chamber pot, a bare wooden floor, dirty black, "and an expanse of wall charted with the bloody deaths of mosquitoes." Outside the window a yard with chickens, an ass, two oxen, and assorted smells. In the middle of the yard sprawls a bristly black pig. Lawrence brings himself to turn back the bed-sheets, decorated with the stains of previous guests. Asked if there is anything else, the dirty-shirted sullen host says, "Niente," and goes. Lawrence in a towering rage turns to his silent queen bee. "Dirty, disgusting swine!" he cries.

They go down to the open bar, "which seemed like part of the road. A muleteer, leaving his mules at the corner, was drinking at the counter."

A stroll through the village on this Saturday afternoon confirms their worst fears: they have landed in the dreariest of holes. In an open space where a great gray bus stands they ask the mournful bus driver about the next bus to the main railway. It goes at 7:30 the next morning. Well, at least they can make their escape. Meanwhile, nothing for it but to grit one's teeth.

And there is worse to come. Heading past a huddle of poor dwellings toward a lane rising steeply between banks they are appalled to find themselves at a place used by the villagers for a public lavatory. Lawrence explodes in disgust: "It is the immemorial Italian custom. Why trouble with W.C.'s? The most socially constituted people on earth, they even like to relieve themselves in company."

In the thick of one of these communal gatherings they scramble out the best way they can, up one of the earth banks and into a stubble field. So ignominious. In his temper, and refusing to endure that odorous lane again, he marches Frieda on a detour across a plowed field and down a cart track. The cold gathers over the hills, they are stared at by merino sheep with "their prominent, gold-curious eyes," walking and walking to avoid facing that benighted bedroom again so soon, until Frieda rebels. Swinging round to go back she attacks Lawrence for his self-righteousness. "Why are you so indignant? Anyone would think your moral self had been outraged! Why take it morally? You petrify that man at the inn by the very way you speak to him. Why don't you take it as it comes? It's all life."

Of course she is asking the impossible. His black rage won't go away because he has been fascinated by an illusion, an imaginary Sorgono. And reeling around inside himself he hits on the unpalatable truth. "If I had expected nothing I should not have been so hit." It is why Lawrence is so appealing, and sometimes so absurd. His saving grace is his willingness to show himself in a ridiculous light. Not knowing what else to do, he curses. "I cursed the degenerate aborigines, the dirty-breasted host who *dared* to keep such an inn, the sordid villagers who had the baseness to squat their beastly human nastiness in this upland valley. All my praise of the long stocking-cap—you remember?—vanished from my mouth. I cursed them all, and the queen bee for an interfering female. . . ."

Wretched though this experience is, Lawrence is not one to be cast down for long. Hope springs up in his breast at the least glimmer of light, and he is still vulnerable as ever to disappointment, still bent on his quest. The foul bedroom is endured. Frieda protects her head by tying around it a large white kerchief before risking the pillow. Somehow they sleep, feet pounding in the corridor outside, high-pitched, weird singing from below, then to punctuate the hours a cock lets fly in a series of demoniac screams.

Next morning they decide on a later bus, leaving at 9:30 for Nuoro. It is Sunday morning, a new day and a fresh start. The simplest things renew him: "seeing the frost among the tangled, still bushes of Sardinia, my soul thrilled again." In the remote places of Italy, in the Abruzzi, say, there was something wonderful, but then the bitter realization that the land had been "humanized, through and through," becomes known. Sardinia, he believed, was not all worked out, not over and done with. He formulated, there on the bus, his belief in the existence of "unknown, unworked lands where the salt has not lost its savor." And if he had been asked for evidence, where would he have pointed? To the frost on the bushes, no doubt.

When they come at last to Nuoro he is buoyed once more in his quest: this time a clean inn, a room that looks palatial, beds invitingly clean and white, and outside, down below their balcony rail, a band is playing raggedly, there is a carnival going on, with maskers jigging along. The river of life flows down there in the one street, and for the moment Lawrence has learned his lesson. The maskers are nearly all women and girls, no "hardy indomitable males" to admire, no masculine freemasonry of the kind men generate in their own company, that he would praise in his contests with Frieda.

But wait. Peering more closely he sees that most of these maskers are young men masquerading as women, with scuffles breaking out between them and the *actual* women, who lash out with clouts on the head. The proud split between the sexes is more complex than he had thought, and for once he has no answer. "Man is going to be male Lord if he can," so what is he up to here, mincing along with a stuffed bosom and a stuffed bustle? Better to praise the Sardinian landscape, wild, remote, with none of the castles one finds perching everywhere in Italy and Sicily. Here the dark hills rise untouched, "virgin-wild," standing outside of life, ignorant of the classical past.

They have liked Nuoro and are sorry to leave the inn and their host, *simpatico* like the town, a nice, capbale "human old woman." She gives them good coffee and milk, good bread, and they saunter through the town toward the bus. It is Monday, with detached men standing at street corners as if resisting the current of work, "rather sulky, forlorn males who insist on making another day of it."

Nuoro has no sights demanding to be seen, and to tell the truth:

> Sights are an irritating bore. . . . Happy is the town that has nothing to show. What a lot of stunts and affectations it saves! Life is then life, not museum-stuffing. One could saunter along the rather inert, Monday-morning street and see the women having a bit of a gossip, and see an old crone with a basket of bread on her head, and see the unwilling ones hanging back from work, and the whole current of industry disinclined to flow. Life is life and things are things. . . . I have had my thrills from Carpaccio and Botticelli. But now I've had enough. I can always look at an old, grey-bearded peasant in his earthy white drawers and his black waist-frill . . . just crooking along beside his little ox-wagon. . . . I wouldn't care a straw if Attila came and demolished every bit of art in Europe. *Basta la mossa*! The horrors of barbarism are not so fearful, I verily believe, as the horrors of strangulation with old culture.

They get on the bus and make for the steamer, over "a savage, dark-bushed, sky-exposed land," rolling into Orosei, a godforsaken little town, then into Siniscola, narrow, stony, crude, pelting along at a fearsome pace, the morning "of a bell-like beauty," on their last Sardinian drive, the slopes "sun-wild and sea-wild." The adventure is over.

RICHARD ALDINGTON writes that Lawrence's plans seemed always to have been in a state of chronic uncertainty. It is true. Back again in Fontana Vecchia, he asked himself the question: did he want to keep on for another year? Yes, he thought he did. A month later, on February 22, he wrote to the American Robert Mountsier, who acted as his agent there, to look into the possibility of a farm in America. Then on March 2 he wrote to his Russian friend Koteliansky to say that, warm though he now felt toward America—Thomas Seltzer had just sent him ten copies of *Women in Love*—he wasn't sure that he was meant to go. And "this house is very nice, the world is green and flowery . . . and there is a sort of Greek morning-world glamour!" If he loved nothing else, he loved Fontana Vecchia. As in his novels, flowers and sunshine and the sea were not merely pleasant, they were signals from the nonhuman world. The pagan gods were never far away.

The uncertainty was brought to an end by Frieda, who had had a telegram from Germany to say that her mother was very ill and needed her. Lawrence, hating to be left alone, took her reluctantly to Palermo for the boat to Naples. Suddenly the lovely Fontana Vecchia was an empty shell. "Don't like it at all." He tore into the writing of *Sea and Sardinia* and sent off volleys of letters to all and sundry. He broke with his agent in London, Pinker, and proposed to Curtis Brown that they take him on. Always his instinct was to act on the spur of the moment, and this was such a time. Suddenly he decided to stop sitting gloomily on his own in Sicily and make for Frieda in Baden-Baden.

Perhaps because going direct to Germany seemed too much like giving in to Frieda's will, he stopped en route in Capri and was introduced by Compton Mackenzie to two American expatriates in their thirties, a quiet, modest couple who remained loyal friends for the rest of his life. Earl Brewster was a Midwesterner, his wife Achsah from Connecticut. They had a small daughter with them and they were both painters. Aside from art, their passion was Buddhism. As it happened, they had been tenants of Fontana Vecchia ten years before. Unlikely though the friendship was, they hit it off with Lawrence at once. Brewster in his first impressions depicted this famous writer as "delicate . . . pale, his hands long, narrow, capable, his eyes clear-seeing and blue, his brown hair and red beard glowing like flames from the intensity of his life, his voice flexible . . . with often a curious plaintive note, sometimes in excitement rising high in key." Many had commented already on this voice jumping up in pitch, at moments almost squeaking in agitation.

In Baden-Baden he got on well, as always, with the old lady he called his "Schwiegermutter" who seemed genuinely fond of him, pressing delicacies on him when he came to tea at the nursing home where she now lived. He and his wife, he told his new friends the Brewsters, were staying in a small inn on the edge of the Black Forest a few miles from Baden. Germany he found tired and sad, a very different country, "life-empty—no young men." Not a uniform in sight, no evidence of authority, yet unlike the near anarchy of Italy the people obeyed the laws, and everything worked in an orderly fashion as it always did. He predicted an era of war ahead: "some sort of warfare, one knows not what. But Mars is the god before us. . . ."

Unlike Sicily, little children didn't beg here, and food was remarkably cheap. For about six shillings a day one could have "good German sausages and beer, *good* Rhine wine, *good* whipped cream, and the first strawberries. . . ." And to tease the vegetarian Brewsters and their Buddhism he added, "No sausageless Nirvana: no! no!" Enjoying himself thoroughly he tacked on a postscript: "Ah, the flesh-pots! We had asparagus (German, the best in the world), strawberries, and Rhine wine and Roast Pork for dinner. What did you have?" In the main body of his long letter he made a vehement declaration, apparently in response to a letter of theirs: "I here and now, finally and forever give up knowing anything about love, or wanting to know. I believe it doesn't exist, save as a word. . . . In fact I here and now, finally and forever leave off loving anything or anybody. *Basta la mossa!*" Provoked by Earl Brewster's praise of Buddha, he went on, "Leave me my tigers, leave me spangled leopards, leave me bright cobra snakes. . . . As for your Nirvana, my boy, paint stripes on it and see how it looks."

With misanthropy still dominating his mood he wrote to Koteliansky that "The world at large makes me sick. I never want to think of it. Thank God, I have no news and know nobody." Frieda, on the other hand, was happily consorting with German friends, to his increasing irritation. He took himself off to sit under a tree and work—he was finishing *Aaron's Rod*. Copies of his little book *Psychoanalysis and the Unconscious* came from America and cheered him up. What he called his theory of the unconscious would be developed in a second volume, *Fantasia of the Unconscious*, he informed Seltzer, and he wanted to make it more interesting than the first book. This it certainly is.

What Brenda Maddox calls "the pent-up yearning to be a parent, a psychic healer and a preacher" had produced the first book on psychology, that and his conviction that it was "in the air now." Published in New York in 1921, it was greatly disliked. Anticipating hostile reviews he had not yet seen, he waded into his defense, *Fantasia*, with immense verve and scorn. He had talked with Freudian friends in London and set about attacking the Freudian concept of the unconscious as a repository of everything outlawed and degraded. For Lawrence the true unconscious was the primordial principle of life itself. "We must discover, if we can, the true unconscious, where our life bubbles up in us, prior to any mentality . . . innocent of any mental alteration. . . . It is the spontaneous origin from which it behooves us to live."

Fantasia of the Unconscious is for Murry Lawrence's greatest book, his gospel. The reason for this curious judgment is strikingly obvious when we see how it reinforces his thesis that Lawrence was a sexually damaged man. It is great, claims Murry, because in this great effort he strives to save others from suffering his own fate. It is terrible, Lawrence would have said, to be agreed with by such a snake in the grass. The passages Murry seizes on of course have to do with mother-love: "A man finds it impossible to realize himself in marriage. He recognizes the fact that his emotional, even passional regard for his mother is deeper than it could ever be for a wife." Hence the birth of the "incest-motive."

This intense regard for his mother would change in his last years, when he swung over in sympathy to the careless vigor of his father. Even in *Sons and Lovers*, where he is in the full flow of his condemnation of his father, he shows sympathy for Walter Morel when he gets the worst of a crisis, and "his manhood broke." How important it was for Lawrence to achieve this manhood, and how terrible when it "broke." But let us not stray from his book *Fantasia*. Elaborating from his own history he says explicitly, in a long passage that Murry would seize on as incontrovertible proof of his case against Lawrence:

> If you want to see the real desirable wife-spirit, look at a mother with her boy of eighteen. How she serves him, how she stimulates him, how her true female self is his, is wife-submissive to him as never, never it could be to a husband. . . . And then what? The son gets on swimmingly for a time, until he is faced by the fact of actual sex-necessity. . . . Think of the power which a mature woman thus infuses into her boy. He flares up like a flame in oxygen. No wonder they say geniuses mostly have great mothers. They mostly have sad fates. . . . You will not easily get a man to believe that his carnal love for the woman he has made his wife is as high a love as that felt for his mother.

From this it follows that "in our day, most dangerous is the love and benevolence ideal." An insistence on the one life mode only, the spiritual mode, living from what he termed the "upper centers" only, could result in neurasthenia and consumption. So we are told in so many words that his mother, by loving her son too much, had given him tuberculosis, though that word would henceforth be struck out of his vocabulary. In this book he delivers a warning to the men and women of his generation who could suffer the fate he had narrowly escaped. This, Murry alleges, is the great lie. In reality Lawrence is talking about his own inability to be a whole man. "How precarious," Murry concludes, "was that necessary fulfillment in marriage, on which his creative mind must always build."

As far as finances went, Lawrence was still being careful with money, telling Lady Cynthia Asquith that "I've got about seventy-five pounds in the bank, and to hell with everybody." America was now showing a growing interest in his work, but he asked Robert Mountsier, about to visit them in Germany, to bring him underpants costing no more than three shillings and sixpence a pair, and to include some tea and three tubes of Kolynos toothpaste. He had liked being in Germany, it was such a relief from disorderly Italy, but now it was summer, and he could see Frieda looking admiringly at handsome young men with blond hair, in their hobnail boots and leather shorts. They went to Austria and stayed at Zell-am-See, and to escape the phenomenal heat of 1921 took trips into the mountains. The edginess between them is there in all its perversity in his novella *The Captain's Doll*, where Hepburn and Hannele are soon identifiable as Lawrence and Frieda. Climbing on to the mountains a squabble develops, ostensibly about Hepburn's hatred of mountains, but under it runs a fundamental hostility. Something about Hannele's delight in the high air makes him want to oppose her, just as his ridiculous anger fuels her determination to oppose him.

"If you don't like it," she says, rather jeering, "why ever did you come?"

"I had to try," he says.

"And if you don't like it," she says, "why ever do you try to spoil it for me?"

He makes no answer, but the reason is that for the moment he hates her and her ecstasy on the mountaintop. She is making the mountains bigger than him, and they are not bigger, "any more than you are bigger than me if you stand on a ladder." For the moment he is too wary of her wonder and ridicule, but his rage will soon spill out. "You must suffer from megalomania," she says.

But as we shall see again and again the row was not about his abomination of mountains and ladders, it was about bullying. The black passion he had worked himself up to was because he wanted her to love him, and she wouldn't. For Frieda, bullying was always at the back of these scenes. "He wanted to bully her, physically, sexually, and from the inside." If she was going to love him it would have to be on her terms, not his. "But a dark-eyed little master and bully she would never have."

So said Hannele to herself. But a blue-eyed little would-be master and bully was what Frieda did in fact have. Young Bert in Eastwood had always taken charge of things, from the country rambles to charades, and if he didn't get his way he bullied. Morel in *Sons and Lovers* bullied and blustered, but his son Paul bullied more subtly. Anthony Burgess says shrewdly that there were only three women in the whole of Lawrence's life who would stand no nonsense, and whom he therefore respected, and they were all mothers: his own, Frieda's, and Frieda herself.

He felt at a disadvantage in Germany among Frieda's relatives and friends; after all it was her homeland, not his. He wrote from Zell-am-See: "Everything is free and perfectly easy. And still I feel I can't breathe. Frieda loves it and is quite bitter when I say I want to go away. But there it is—I do."

By the end of August he had had enough. He hated the north, he loathed the very smell of snow, he would die "if I don't eat yellow figs within a fortnight." Again he said to a correspondent that after a winter in Taormina he might well go to America, though his knees went weak at the very thought.

The cause of Lawrence's inability to breathe was not hard to locate. Frieda's obvious closeness to her sister Johanna excluded him. The other sister, Else, now a widow but the companion of Alfred Weber, arrived from Munich with her three children. A childless

Lawrence, whose wife of forty was now unlikely to give him a child—even if that had been possible, and the doubt exists—must, suggests Murry, have been filled with misgivings "to find that the simple seal of fulfillment in marriage was denied him." More than ever he wanted to go south, if only to get away from these relatives. "One should never see one's relatives," he decided, "or anybody else's."

He had his way. They launched themselves at the hell of the railway journey from Zell to Florence on packed trains, traveling second class. In a flat over the diminished Arno in this hottest year of the century he saw a few friends. The empty flat belonged to their friend Nelly Morrison. Catherine and Donald Carswell called and were disturbed by the change in him. He seemed remote, withdrawn, ominously quiet, and uncertain. They hung about in this temporary abode for a few weeks above "that great stone rattle the Via de'Bardi," then pushed on south to Sienna and Rome, stopping briefly in Capri.

In Florence Lawrence must have got wind of the hostility aroused by *Women in Love*, published by Secker in June. It had come out in New York the year before, just ahead of *Ulysses* and *The Waste Land*. Accumulated mail with all its nastiness awaited him in Fontana, but he was pleased to see the Brewsters again in Capri. They were busily packing up to leave for the East on a kind of pilgrimage, and Lawrence said off the cuff that he might join them in Ceylon. Travel always meant adventure for Lawrence, and here was temptation in a most attractive form. He was now casting around for some reason to turn his back on a Europe that he felt coldly disliked him.

Women in Love was, he believed rightly, his best work. Certainly it was his most far-reaching. Called by Brenda Maddox his most Germanic book, it was influenced by the legacy of Frieda's German culture and teemed with ideas. Reaching Fontana Vecchia on September 28 in the dark and rain, he wrote to the Brewsters that it was even lovelier than he remembered, with "the great window of the eastern sky, seaward."

Setting aside his harsh words about Sicily he declared it *"much the best of any place in Italy."* He was trying to digest the foul news of the denunciation of *Women in Love*, the threat of a libel action and the attack by his erstwhile friend Murry. It seems he was all things evil. He wouldn't call his condition sorrow—*"merde! Mille fois merde!"* He waxed biblical in his exhortations to Brewster to flee the contagion of the modern world. "Let us go from the Sodom of angels like Lot and Abraham, before the fire falls." And how he wanted the fire to fall, on London in particular, but of course it wouldn't. Calming down, he wrote, "No, seriously, let us agree to take a way together into the future." He thought he would follow the Brewsters to Ceylon once the winter was over.

In the London periodical *John Bull* he read that *Women in Love* was a "Loathsome Study of Sex Depravity Leading Youth to Unspeakable Disaster." This was so stupid it could easily be dismissed, and the editor-proprietor, Horatio Bottomly, would soon be serving a prison sentence for fraud. More disgusting was the attack by Murry in the *Athenaeum*, saying of his great friend: "He would, if he could, put us all on the rack to make us confess his protozoic god: he is deliberately, incessantly and passionately obscene in the exact sense of the word." He had detected a caricature of himself in the novel, yet he clung on. After all, Lawrence was famous.

In the preface to *Fantasia* he made clear that his novels and poems were "pure passionate experience" that came "unwatched out of one's pen." To trust as he did to introspection, showing people not primarily as social beings but complexes in the sway of irrational nature, was to put the novel beyond the reach of the London critics of his day.

Lawrence's mail became worse, indeed worrying. Philip Heseltine, a young composer and admirer he had known in Cornwall, identified himself and his wife Puma in the novel. His solicitors were now pursuing a suit for libel. Lawrence was willing to make alterations to a future edition, but a frightened Martin Secker settled out of court, paying Heseltine fifty pounds and withdrawing remaining copies of the first edition. This did nothing for Lawrence's bile, who called the settlement "hush-money." In an effort to relieve his fury he told Koteliansky, whom he called Kot, "Well, they are both such abject shits it is a pity they can't be flushed down a sewer." Nonetheless he was worried now about his habit of drawing his characters too closely from real life, wondering whether he should do anything about Norman Douglas's spitting image in *Aaron's Rod*. Somehow, though, he managed to make his vile temper sound humorous in his letter to Brewster. One poor woman visitor crept about as if she had a dagger at her neck, and he believed "even the old goat doesn't have her belated kid for fear I pounce on her. . . . I've written such very spiteful letters to everybody that now the postman never comes." Yet still he wasn't done. "A curse, a murrain, a pox on this crawling, sniffling, spunkless brood of humanity." He withdrew his half finished *Mr. Noon* because of its autobiographical nature.

He tried to work off his spleen by writing *The Captain's Doll*. He had got the idea high up in the mountains of the Tyrol "and don't quite know how to get it down without breaking its neck." He asked Brewster to be sure to tell him how much a house cost to rent in Ceylon, and a pound of bacon and a dozen eggs. "Don't," he ended rudely, "be on a damned high Buddhistic plane: I'm in no mood to stand it."

Equally rancorous were his remarks on Jews. Offensive they indeed are, but contradictory, and were probably common parlance in golf clubs in the England of his day, as no doubt they were in the pubs of Eastwood. For instance, in Germany on June 21 he commented to a friend of Amy Lowell that "Nobody has any money any more except the profiteers, chiefly Jews." He asked his New York publisher Thomas Seltzer, "Are you a Jew?" and confided to Robert Mountsier that "if Seltzer deals decently with me then I don't mind if he is a Jew and a little nobody. I don't really like Jews." Yet in London he had a number of Jewish friends, and one of his closest lifelong friends, the lawyer Koteliansky, was Jewish, as was the painter Mark Gertler. Murry said of *Women in Love* that Lawrence made no attempt to conceal his worst traits, and the same can be said of his letters. In the letter to Mountsier quoted above, he went on: "I like still less the semi-gentleman, successful commercial publisher, who is always on the safe side: Duckworth, Methuen, Chatto all that crowd. They, the *bourgeois*, are my real enemy. Don't be too sniffy of the risky little Jew. He adventures—these other all-right swine, no."

3

Wyewurk

(1921–1922)

he serialization of *Sea and Sardinia* in *The Dial* in America brought him a letter from the United States in 1921 that would literally alter the course of Lawrence's life. A wealthy American patroness, Mabel Dodge Sterne (soon to be Luhan), had moved from a fashionable salon life in New York, divorced her husband, and begun a relationship with an Indian in the small town of Taos, New Mexico, where she was busily fostering an art colony and supporting the cause of the Indians. Impressed by Lawrence's descriptions of Sardinian peasants, she saw him as someone she ought to cultivate. With American generosity she offered him, sight unseen, one of the new adobe houses under construction in Taos, together with subsistence and the cost of his voyage. She enclosed with her letter a few leaves of *desachey*, an Indian herb said to make the heart light, and a little *osha*, a medicinal root.

She had set out in her letter to be at her most beguiling, and Lawrence, just risen from his sickbed of two months after falling ill in Capri, was in a mood to be impressed. Strangely, he had already written to Brewster in October that "my plan, ultimately, is to get a little farm somewhere by myself, in Mexico, New Mexico, Rocky

Mountains or British Columbia." For years he had thought of America as a possible destination, in 1915 being tempted by Frederick Delius's offer of a house in Florida. Now, after the appalling reviews of *Women in Love* and the threat of libel, he despaired of being properly valued in his own country. "I feel at the moment," he wrote Brewster, "I don't care where I live, that people are bloody swine—or bloodless swine everywhere. . . ." Suddenly, here out of the blue he was being offered the chance of a fresh start. He wrote back appreciatively the same afternoon, after chewing dutifully at the root, which had a licorice taste, and smelling the Indian leaves. With astonishing speed he came to a decision: "Truly, the q-b and I would like to come to Taos—there are no little bees."

Taos began with the same three letters as Taormina, which seemed a kind of omen. It might have occurred to him that the Chinese Tao, or way, could be another sign, but he was always dismissive of Eastern religions. Unwilling as ever to be beholden to anyone, he declined her offer of travel expenses. They would pay their own way, and once there their cost of living. They did their own housework, he explained, even the floor-cleaning, even the washing, because they disliked the idea of servants. And he *liked* doing things: preferred to wash his own shirt. So the answer was a positive yes, they would come.

Then he bombarded his unknown benefactor with questions. He would like to know—if she was practical enough to be able to tell him—how much it would cost per month to live there. Also, was there a sub-arty colony in residence in Taos? Indeed there was, with Mrs. Sterne its fulcrum, but even if there was, he added innocently, "it couldn't be worse than Florence." Was there a sad atmosphere of defeated, dying Indians? Most important, how did one get there? Which was the nearest port? He would look into the possibility of getting a cargo boat from Palermo.

Whatever he did, he was determined to have all his current work finished before leaving Europe, so as to have adequate resources behind him. His English royalties had been eaten into by the months spent in Germany with Frieda. At the beginning of December he was dispatching short stories and novellas to Curtis Brown in London and Mountsier in New York. Even laid up in bed he had kept working, finishing "The Ladybird," *The Captain's Doll*, "The Horse-Dealer's Daughter," and a longer version of *The Fox*. By the time he was awarded his only prize, the James Tait Black Prize of a hundred pounds for *The Lost Girl* in December, he knew that more than $1,500 was due to him from the United States.

To occupy himself before launching out on new work he had been reading the Sicilian novels and stories of Giovanni Verga, "the only Italian who does interest me." Later he would translate Verga's *Mastro-don-Gesualdo* and his *Little Novels of Sicily*, recreating Verga's difficult style in splendidly vigorous, sardonic versions of his own.

His "bit of flu" had abated by the time he broke the news to Earl Brewster about his new destination and fate, and about the formidable woman waiting for him with open arms in Taos. Seeking to inspire himself, and to overcome an instinct which made him "shrink" from the States, he wrote in his letter that Taos was a center of sun worship, or so he understood. "They say the sun was born there." He had been fascinated for years by the Aztec, the Indian, old Mexico whereas there was no magic for him in Buddha. The East was all fulfilled, but not the glamorous West. To tell the truth, he couldn't help hating Buddha: "I can't even help putting my spite and irreverence against him in this letter."

But if Mabel Dodge Sterne assumed, as she may well have done, that all was settled, she had yet to know her Lawrence. In his letter to Brewster of November 16 he said, "Of course I have not decided." Indeed he had not. Indecision soon set in with a vengeance. This period would become the most prolonged bout of dithering in his entire life. Not only did he fear the very thought of America, he was being made aware, in letters and cables, of a powerful woman whose will, even at that distance, had begun to bear down on him. He was especially fearful of New York, even of passing through it. Over Christmas he fell sick again, with a bronchial illness he called flu. Mabel Dodge knew of Lawrence's frail health. Gertrude Stein's brother, Leo, meeting the English writer in Florence, had told her, "I wonder which will give out first, his lungs or his wits."

He studied all the possible routes to America with the exception of New York. Finally he settled for New Orleans, sailing from Bordeaux on January 15. That was the plan. Not fit enough in time, he booked the Palermo-to-New York route instead, with deep misgivings. For once he was being wise when he also canceled this arrangement: a New York winter would have been dangerous for a man in his state of health. Writing apologetically to Mabel Dodge after Frieda had informed her on January 27 with characteristic tactlessness that "We were coming *straight* to you at Taos but now we are not," he made no mention of his health but blamed "a Balaam's Ass in my belly which won't budge, when I turn my face west. I can't help it. It just stubbornly swerves away in me. I *will* come. But I detour."

HIS DETOUR would take him to Ceylon and then Australia. Trying to fathom the reason for his endless vacillating, he confessed to Brewster, "Dio mio, I am so ridiculous, wavering between east and west." Was there ever, exclaims an exasperated Aldington in his biography, "such a weathercock of a man, or one more helplessly given over to self-torment?" It is easy to see as laughable someone so contradictory that he now, after deciding to make for Ceylon instead of America, had to try passionately to like aspects of Buddhism for his friend Brewster's sake. He somersaulted his way to an acceptance of "Life is sorrow," the least Lawrentian of mottoes, by seeing it as a first, not a last truth. What worried him now was the peace aspect of it all. "I am so much afraid that it means a sort of weakness and giving in." Still he weered about in his effort to be true to himself. People who knew Lawrence found his fits of fury most bewildering when they were followed swiftly afterward by an almost feminine tenderness.

Once decided on his purpose, his bilious temper was no more. This transformation, repeated so often, was extraordinary. Aldington believed that he should have punished himself less, taken more account of his frail physique and weak lungs, instead of subjecting himself to "the strenuous charlady's life" that he always insisted was good for him. Somewhere inside him was a blithe, happy disposition, naturally curious, bubbling with enthusiasm.

On February 19 he wrote briskly, tinged with regret at what he was about to give up, to his mother-in-law in Germany:

> My dear Schwiegermutter,
> We sit ready to travel: 4 trunks, one household trunk, one book trunk . . . and then two valises, hat-box . . . just like Abraham faring forth to a new land. Tomorrow, 10.34, we leave: eat in Messina, where we must change: arrive 8.30 in Palermo—and so to the Hotel Panormus, where our woman friend lives. Thursday night to Naples, by ship. Then Sunday morning on the S.S. Osterley, Orient Line, to Ceylon.

How he relished the details of travel. He enclosed his address in Ceylon and consoled himself with the thought that it was only fourteen days from Naples. Perhaps Frieda's sister was right, perhaps they would come back to Sicily and "our Fontana." He ruled nothing in or out. But he had not experienced ocean travel before and could not wait to get started. He was always an efficient packer but had to deal with the encumbrance of a decorated wooden panel, one side of a peasant cart, which a Sicilian friend had given them. Lawrence would have jettisoned it, but Frieda's sentimentality won the day.

The sea air stimulated his appetite, and he was full of praise for the ship, "so still, so quiet, so civilized and such a cleanliness." Lawrence was at his most charming, darting about with plenty to say, while Frieda, determined on a life of idleness, sat in a deck chair embroidering a rug. Lawrence, pleased with everything, the people on board so friendly, ice cream in the mornings and dances in the evenings, dropped his bottle of ink on the deck one day and left his black mark on the Osterley forever. Of course he was working on his translation of *Mastro-don-Gesualdo.*

Excited to be in the eastern Mediterranean, he saw Crete slipping past in the distance. When they reached Port Said, stopping for three hours to take on coal, he felt himself in the *Thousand and One Nights.* The women shopping were "little waddling heaps of black crêpe, and two houri-eyes between veil and mantle. . . . Came a charabanc, with twenty black woman-parcels." One of the women drew back her veils and spat in the direction of the infidels. And it was all unchanged from his childhood Bible-reading days: the beggars, water-carriers, the "scribe" at his little table writing letters, the old man and his Koran, the men smoking "chibouks" in cafés open to the pavement.

Crawling through the Suez Canal at five miles an hour was like traveling overland, the banks so near he could have thrown an orange at the working Arabs. Sandhills in the distance were rosy and sharp, the horizon keen as a blade. A thousand gulls whirled about, so many it was like a snowstorm. In the Red Sea next morning he saw Mount Sinai, "like a dagger that has been dipped in blood," the shores hot as an oven. "Behind lies at last Jerusalem, Greece, Rome and Europe—fulfilled and past, a great terrible dream. With Jews it began, with Jews it ends." The exit from the Red Sea into the Indian Ocean was for Lawrence an escape from ancient ideology. How good to see the fishes flying as gaily as silver butterflies and the joyful black dolphins that ran to and fro before them "like frolicsome little black pigs."

Many of the passengers were Australian, and they made the acquaintance of a Mrs. Anna Jenkins, a musician, who urged them to visit Western Australia when they went on to America. There and then Lawrence declared to a friend in Italy that Australia sounded promising, "full of life and energy."

On March 13, 1922, with a smell of cinnamon in the air, they docked at Colombo, to be greeted by their nice friends Earl and

Achsah Brewster and their daughter Harwood. The Brewsters had a pleasant, spacious bungalow overlooking Kandy in what had been a coconut palm estate, with accommodation in it already prepared for the Lawrences. A fortnight later Lawrence was registering his shock at the tremendous heat and humidity and the hair-raising night-noises of the jungle round the house. Aldington remembers being once asked if he had ever heard this tropical cacophony. Lawrence, a gifted and sometimes malicious mimic, then let out a series of howls, squawks, gobbling sounds, and "help-murder" shrieks.

The dry heart of Sicily had been hard enough for Lawrence to bear, but this climate of humidity and high temperature sapped all his energy. In an exceptionally hot year Ceylon positively steamed, and he hated it. He and Frieda had a quiet corner of the bungalow, with its own veranda, but the teeming life around him, not to mention the night howls and yells, was repugnant to him. One morning he went to put on his topee and was aghast to find it a home for a family of rats. Soon he was objecting as vehemently as ever to the passivity and lack of resistance, the sheer bonelessness of Buddhism, this time after confronting Buddha images everywhere. "Oh, I wish he would *stand up!*" he cried, raining abuse on the "hideous little Buddha temples, like decked-up pigsties." No, for him Buddhism was a "rat-hole religion."

In a letter to Robert Pratt Barlow in Taormina on March 30 he makes it clear that he had given up, not only on Ceylon but on the East in general. "I feel I don't belong, and never should." In this letter he executed one of his most spectacular U-turns. After turning his back on England in disgust for its treatment of *The Rainbow* and *Women in Love*, he now thought it a mistake to forsake England and move out into "the periphery of life," running away like Jonahs "from the place where we belong."

This visit to Ceylon had convinced him that "the most living clue to life is in us Englishmen in England, and the great mistake we make is in not uniting together . . . and so carrying the vital spark through." Being a renegade was no good. He even considered returning to England during the course of the summer. This impulse to stand up for England was no doubt inspired by the visit to Kandy of the Prince of Wales on March 23, though not in a way one might have expected. He had begun to suspect the four servants at the Brewsters of jeering at him behind his back, and thus identified with the Prince of Wales, who "seemed to be almost the butt of everybody, white and black alike. They all secretly hate him for being a Prince, and make a Princely butt of him—and he knows it." There Prince Edward sat, "a pale little wisp" high up on his gorgeously bedecked elephant, looking sad and forlorn. To his sister Emily, Lawrence conveyed his sympathy for the "poor devil . . . all twitchy." How worn out and disheartened he seemed. "A woman threw a bouquet, and he nearly jumped out of his skin." Lawrence, watching this representative of natural aristocracy and the divine right of kings in dismay, himself a skin short, feeling increasingly ill and blaming it all on Ceylon, could only express the outraged pride of his Englishness by refusing to let a rickshaw boy pull him uphill when he was scarcely fit to walk. The prince's visit is recorded in his verbose poem "Elephant," where his feelings fail to ignite—not to be compared with the splendid poems to animals he wrote while in Taormina, or the tender and elegiac "The Elephant Is Slow to Mate," written near the end of his life:

> The elephant, the huge old beast,
>   is slow to mate:
> he finds a female, they show no haste
>   they wait
>
> for the sympathy in their vast shy hearts
>   slowly, slowly to rouse
> as they loiter along the river-beds
>   and drink and browse . . .
>
> They do not snatch, they do not tear;
>   their massive blood

moves as the moon-tides, near, more near,
    till they touch in flood.

FAR AWAY from Eastwood, Lawrence was now regarding his parents in a new light. The reviled father in *Sons and Lovers* was, he told Brewster, "a true pagan" who suffered at the hands of his wife, a righteous woman who turned her children against him. "Never mind, my duckies," Walter Morel would say to his white-faced children, "you needna be afraid of me. I'll do ye na harm." The author would write that novel differently now if he could.

It was not only the impossible climate that condemned Ceylon as far as Lawrence was concerned. Afflicted with a mysterious illness the moment he arrived, he felt he would never be able to work there. Financial anxieties, imaginary or real, always lurked in his mind. The dollars awaiting him in America were reassuring, but they were not in his pocket. He had paid out 140 pounds to get them to Colombo, and when he decided to go on to Sydney via Perth he would have to pay 112 pounds more. He was sufficiently insecure to write to their old friend Mary Cannan that "If I cable you from some corner of the earth to lend me money, don't leave me in the lurch." He had no intention of doing so, but having her say she would was the comfort he needed.

Moving on, he wanted the Brewsters to know that he considered them his true friends, adding humorously, "therefore I shall tell you your faults." He could not resist a final swipe at Buddhism, telling his studious converted friend that it was "like a mud pool that has no bottom to it."

Just before he and Frieda departed from Kandy the rains came, "at exactly ten in the morning and four in the afternoon, timed to a minute." They embarked on the *Orsova*, the voyage taking ten days from Colombo to Freemantle. Uncharacteristically he wrote only one letter, four days out of Freemantle, saying they were somewhere in a big blue choppy sea with "flying fishes sprinting out of the waves like winged drops." On board was a Catholic Spanish priest playing Chopin very well, while the boat gently rolled. Needless to say, the illness that had afflicted him in Ceylon was no more, another reason for dismissing the place. The place, wherever it was, always became the scapegoat for what ailed him. While there he had predicted the decline and fall of the British Empire, and this prospect only strengthened his resolve to be "English in the teeth of all the world."

The *Orsova* docked at Freemantle on May 4, 1922. The Lawrences spent their first night in a hotel, then enjoyed the hospitality of Anna Jenkins, their shipboard acquaintance, in a suburb of the city. Mrs. Jenkins, eager to show off her find, introduced Lawrence and his German wife to the Perth *literati*, including William Siebenhaar, a poet and radical born in Holland and published in Australia. It was he who mentioned the guest house of Mollie Skinner, an unmarried nurse and local author who lived in the hills at Darlington, sixteen miles to the east of the city. Before moving to this new location, Lawrence was astonished to find a copy of *The Rainbow* on the shelves of Perth Literary Institute. No one seemed to know it had been banned in London.

Lawrence impressed all who met him for the first time by his combination of charm and frankness, though a number of these Australians were initially puzzled. Mollie Skinner herself, soon to be a collaborator with the Englishman on *The Boy in the Bush*, wondered, when the little party arrived from Perth, which of the two men was Lawrence. Mrs. Jenkins was gushing over a "frail little red-bearded man," but surely he could not be the author she had read about. Another of Mrs. Jenkins's friends, May Gawler, thought him a mixture of "a reddish bearded able-seaman and a handy man at the back door," and asked herself "how this rather shabby, slightly coarse, far from spruce and tidy little man could possibly have caused such a flutter" in the world.

At the back of the guest house, "Leithdale," the land swiftly became "the bush," and Lawrence went on some exploratory rambles through it. Already his intuition was telling him that this landscape was something totally outside his experience. He loved the Western Australian sky, "high and blue and new, as if no one had ever taken a breath from it, but the thinly scattered gum trees, looking pale and ghostly, made the land called the bush like a moor with trees." One night when he went out alone for a walk he was half frightened to death, caught under "the huge electric moon" near a clump of tall, nude, dead trees, "shining almost phosphorescent." A presence seized him, he went cold, "the hair on his scalp stirred," and hurrying back he felt behind him something gruesome that could have "reached out a long black arm and gripped him."

Jessie Chambers has left a graphic description of the effect on Lawrence of the full moon. With his uncannily swift intuition he was able to feel, without being told, the vast empty spaces of this land mass nearly as big as North America, its population of seven million clinging to its coastal fringes. (Oddly, almost the only reference by Lawrence to aborigines occurs in his novel *Kangaroo*, where tree trunks are likened to "naked pale aborigines among the dark-soaked foliage.")

At first the utter nothingness of the land defeated him. What to make of it? In a letter to his mother-in-law he called it "somewhat like a dream. . . . It is *too* new, you see: too vast. It needs hundreds of years yet before it can live. This is the land where the unborn souls, strange and not to be known, which shall be born in 500 years, live. A grey, foreign spirit." The spirit of place was never more alive in him than during his time in Australia. "Like Wordsworth," writes David Ellis in his biography of these years, "he was quite literally inclined to feel that a landscape lived with a special life of its own."

Richard Aldington says amusingly, with more than a touch of malice, that in Europe Lawrence had pined to be "a bit of a hermit (which bit?)," yet among these enormous Australian empty spaces, where he could have lost himself and been bothered by no one, there was no mention of a desire for a hermitage. It is noticeable, remarks Aldington, that in the places where he did settle, Florence and Taormina and Taos, there was no shortage of gossip—an essential ingredient, he might have added, for a novelist.

Though Mollie Skinner and her friends would have liked to hold on to Lawrence, it was soon clear that Lawrence had his eye on Sydney as a stopping-off place before sailing for America. He had been studying the shipping schedules and went into Perth to book passage to Sydney on Thursday, May 18. After they had gone, Mollie Skinner remembered that "The funny thing about the Lawrences was that they liked not being known as celebrities." They left behind a friend in William Siebenhaar, and later Lawrence did his best to find a publisher for Siebenhaar's translation of *Max Havelaar* by the Dutch writer E. D. Dekker, which had appeared in Holland under the pseudonym Multatuli.

ON THEIR WAY SOUTH aboard the *Malwa* they stopped briefly in Adelaide, which Lawrence may well have liked as Australia's most English of cities. They visited the art gallery there and did the same during an overnight stay in Melbourne. On board the *Malwa* were two Nottingham men migrating to Australia. Both hosiery mechanics, Denis Forrester and Bill Marchbanks had jobs waiting for them in Sydney knitting mills. One of them lent Lawrence money a few weeks later, so he evidently hit it off with them. Indian passengers aboard ship led him to speculate that "India will fall into chaos once the British let go. The religions are so antagonistic." He had no sympathy for the current agitation for liberty, and even less for the spread of democracy, as was seen in *Sea and Sardinia*. An egalitarian country like Australia was bound to provoke him to indignation, and it soon did.

The *Malwa* docked on the quay where the Opera House now stands, on May 27. It was 6:40 in the morning and the rain pelted down. They stayed for a few nights in a hotel in Sydney, then traveled by train to a small coal-mining town called Thirroul, forty miles south of the city on the New South Wales coast. Getting there with all the luggage they owned, plus the side of a Sicilian cart, must have been a trial, and long before they accomplished it Lawrence was expressing his distaste for "the hateful newness, the democratic conceit, every man a little pope of perfection." He was about to plunge into the writing of his novel *Kangaroo*, and in the opening pages introduces us to an English writer, R. L. Somers, with his "mature, handsome wife," endeavoring to catch the attention of taxi drivers squatting on the grass of the park beside Macquarie Street in Sydney. The couple were outside their hotel with their luggage, but the taxi drivers and workmen on the grass "had that air of owning the city which belongs to a good Australian." The couple were foreign-looking, the woman may have been Russian, and the little fellow with the beard was "A comical-looking bloke! Perhaps a Bolshy."

Why, asks an incredulous Aldington in his account, come thirteen thousand miles armed with letters of introduction that he might have presented in the city, to rent a bungalow in what was in effect an Australian Eastwood? The question is of course rhetorical. Thirroul had little in common with Eastwood, and Lawrence was a man who followed his instincts. Frieda says vaguely in her memoirs that she and her husband got on a train with all their trunks and got out again when the surroundings looked promising. But this was not the practical Lawrence's way. More than likely he would have scoured the newspapers and inquired at the hotel before setting out. In Joseph Davis's *D. H. Lawrence at Thirroul* the author suggests that Lawrence was considering Sydney's north shore before opting for the New South Wales coast.

Curiously, though Thirroul was indeed a mining town, it was also a small holiday resort. Because the holiday season was long over they were able to rent a large bungalow in red brick with a tin roof for thirty shillings a week. The account of Somers and Harriet in *Kangaroo* taking over the accommodation from a large family is shown by Frieda's memoir to be autobiographical to the last detail. Frieda loved it from the start, delighted to have her own place again. The spacious holiday bungalow was comically called Wyewurk. Lawrence would have found the name ironic, since he knew perfectly well why one had to work: he needed to survive. Nearby was a house called Wyewurrie. They were at 3 Craig Street, overlooking the roar of the Pacific.

Whenever they took over rooms or a villa, the accommodation was attacked with Lawrence's puritanical zeal, using plenty of water, carbolic, and elbow grease. Lawrence would have been down on his knees scrubbing out while Frieda dusted and tacked up the hanging rugs and dug out tablecloths and ornaments brought from Sicily and Ceylon. No doubt the side of the Sicilian cart would have been propped up somewhere, to complete their display of household gods. Lawrence mentioned to Achsah Brewster that the little black embroidered Greek bag given to them in Capri was hanging up on a nail.

In his novel, Wyewurk was changed to the equally banal Torestin. After his labors with the scrubbing brush, his alter ego Somers renamed it Toscrubin. His reward came when the dark jarrah-wood floors rose into view from the dirt. (He had experienced the same rapture in Italy, braces round his waist, seeing a dirty floor flushing crimson. "It was enough to make one burst forth in hymns.") Harriet-Frieda praised the arch brickwork of the fireplace.

There are so many parallels between the author and the protagonist that one has to keep reminding oneself that much of the action in the novel is fiction. What is certain is that a naked Lawrence was being exposed in the guise of Richard Lovat Somers, and that the battle between Somers and Harriet was a real battle. The Callcotts next door were probably fictional, though their name is borrowed from the name of the estate agents dealing with their bungalow. The estate agent's wife remembers picking a bunch of dahlias for Frieda, and this was transposed to an incident in the novel when Harriet admired the dahlias in their neighbor's garden.

In fact they probably knew no one, and in his letters Lawrence exulted in knowing absolutely nobody "for a vast distance around one." They bought food from tradesmen's wagons, and milk and butter from generous farmers nearby. Even in the Australian winter they could bathe in the sea daily, showering off the salt water under a makeshift shower attached to the place. Frieda caused a stir by doing her shopping with a basket, whereas the locals stowed everything into a suitcase. Lawrence was soon plowing away at high speed with his Australian novel, a book so close to reality and so embedded in the spontaneous living present that in some respects it resembles *Sea and Sardinia*. Episodes in the novel that were clearly based on actual events, such as Frieda's hysterical laughter at the sight of Lawrence's desperate struggle to save his hat which had blown into the sea, were juxtaposed with scenes of political conflict and conspiracy in order to explore his growing fascination with the nature of power. Yet all that has to do with the marriage difficulties of Harriet and Richard Somers we can read as being about Frieda and Lawrence and be certain that we are reading the truth, or at least Lawrence's version of the truth. And we can say with equal certainty that nowhere in all his writing is his treatment of his inner self so pitiless.

Meeting no one socially was, he maintained, wonderful. "For the first time in my life I feel how lovely it is to know nobody in the whole country: and nobody can come to the door, except the tradesmen who bring the bread and meat and so on, and who are very unobtrusive." He now appreciated the casual approach of the Australian people, as he did their dry humor, above all for the way they left him alone. The class hatred he had loathed in England was absent here. "Class makes a gulf, across which all the best flow is lost," he wrote, and in *Kangaroo* he attacked his own tendency to separateness and isolation. Above all he responded to the delicate beauty of the Australian mornings: "There was an unspeakable beauty about the mornings, the great sun from the sea, such a big, untamed, proud sun, rising up into a sky of such tender delicacy, blue, so blue, and yet so frail, that even blue seems too coarse a color to describe it, more virgin than humanity can conceive."

Kangaroo, chaotic though it is regarded by many critics, is an impassioned novel for all its quirky humor, and surely Lawrence's most confessional work of fiction. Middleton Murry pounces on it in his study because here is Lawrence admitting so much through the mouthpiece of Richard Lovat Somers. At one point Somers recounts a recurrent dream of which he is afraid. Lawrence, says Murry, was a great enemy of dreams, which he saw as weaknesses come to assail him when his guard was down. Somers, recovering when awake, reflects: "Two women in his life he had loved down to the quick of life and death: his mother and Harriet. And the woman in the dream was so awfully his mother, risen from the dead, and at the same time Harriet, as it were, departing from this life, that he stared at the night-paleness between the window-curtains in horror."

Lawrence had reached the stage in his marriage where he hated his dependence on Frieda but realized that without her he had nothing. In the novel Somers finds his wife in tears because she feels excluded from his thoughts and longings. Confronting this in his heart, but not before her, Somers admits that "At once his heart became very troubled: because after all she was all he had in the world, and he couldn't bear her to be really disappointed or wounded. He wanted to ask her what was the matter . . . but he knew it would be false. He knew that her greatest grief was when he turned away from their personal human life of intimacy to this impersonal business of male activity for which he was always craving."

Here, as honestly as he could put it, was the nub of the matter. When he does confess his longing to do something with living people instead of being simply a writer living alone, Harriet answers contemptuously, "Don't swank, you don't live alone. You've got *me* there safe enough, to support you. Don't swank to me about being alone, because it insults me, you see. I know how much alone you are, with me always there keeping you together."

This is ruthless, and the man writing it is Lawrence. Murry concedes that the candor of this confession is courageous, but goes on to question its reality. The real substance of *Kangaroo* for Murry is Somers's continual evasion of the truth about himself. It is difficult to see how this evasion manifests itself. For instance, the hero, Somers, is described again and again as "small" or "little," is called "little Richard," and seems to dwindle physically as the narrative unfolds. It is as if he is losing his footing as a man, depending on his wife as he once depended on his mother. As she becomes bigger, more substantial, warm and comforting in his imagination, he is "little Richard," tempted to creep back to her in his frailty.

David Ellis notices this too, and his scholar's detachment is more to be trusted than the vendetta being waged by Murry. Ellis comments that the authorial figures in Lawrence's earlier writings are not "little," then from *Aaron's Rod* onward the self-image changes. Why he was seen in Australia by May Gawler and Mollie Skinner as "little" is at first puzzling, given his average height of five foot nine. Photographs however show a slender man with narrow shoulders, and as he grew older he did, with the onset of periodic bouts of illness, dwindle physically. That he was painfully aware of his thin legs is made clear in "The Nightmare" chapter of *Kangaroo*, when Somers recalls being examined for call-up during the war, and "a fat fellow pointed to his thin legs with a jeer." In Derby the humiliation is repeated, having to stand in front of doctors "with his ridiculous thin legs." One badge of his manhood was threatened at Bodmin barracks by someone saying, "That'll have to come off tomorrow, dad." It never did. More than once in the novel Somers is intimidated by the sight of brawny males on the beaches. Ellis concludes that as a result of wartime experiences and illness Lawrence had begun to hold himself in a way that drew attention to his slight build.

Murry of course goes much further. Lawrence, he says damn-ingly, had ceased to believe in himself. He quotes Jack Callcott say-ing to Somers near the end, "When it comes to doing anything, you sort of fade out, you're nowhere." Richard Somers, pained beyond words by "the contempt of the confident he-man for the shifty she-man," is silent. Harriet, after one marital row ends, says, "I have to be the only man as well as the only woman." For Murry there is nothing more to be said, though of course he continues saying it with variations, and at great length.

Kangaroo was written on the spot at Wyewurk and was com-pleted in forty-two days, an astonishing tour de force. Wanting to celebrate, Lawrence invited his two Nottinghamshire acquaintances and their wives, the Forresters and Marchbankses, out to Thirroul for a picnic. Hiring a car and driver, they went off to a location on the rocks by the Lodden River. With his novel's problems solved and his book in the bag, he behaved for once like a spendthrift. Pho-tographs show him sitting at his ease during this outing, a rare sight. As he owned up to Brewster in a letter, "In truth, I sit easier in my skin here than anywhere."

The book is extraordinary on a number of levels. As well as ridi-culing himself, he pokes fun at the reader and dismisses the idea of the novel as a work of art. The novel form, he said once, is "inca-pable of the Absolute." When he is stuck he inserts actual extracts from the *Sydney Bulletin* in a chapter derisively called "Bits." Exas-perated suddenly in mid-flight with the whole enterprise he ex-claimes "If you don't like the novel, don't read it." The "lord-and-master stuff," which had incensed Frieda for years as idi-otic and a lie, is now finally torn down—though it will rise again as pure fantasy in *The Plumed Serpent*—by Harriet crying scornfully, "Him, a lord and master! How could one believe in such a man?" If Somers wanted to go off and be a man among men, then let him leave her and go. She knew perfectly well that he could not do it.

IT IS PROBABLE, from a letter to Koteliansky on July 9, 1922, that at the back of his mind Lawrence intended to write his idea of an avant-garde novel, though the disjointed narrative owes more to what Ellis calls his commitment to "a Romantic spontaneity." Koteliansky must have mentioned the recent publication of Joyce's *Ulysses*, for Lawrence replies that he will be able to read it when he gets to America. When he did look at it he saw at once that he and Joyce were poles apart. *Kangaroo* is not modernist in any serious sense. The narrative tells a story that has a discernible beginning, middle, and end in the traditional manner. The novel, however, is certainly original in its Lawrentian waywardness, its refusal to be art, its swerving between autobiography and contradictory aims of various kinds, including essay writing, travel journal, the intensity of high poetry, and an anatomy of modern marriage. It gets nowhere because there is nowhere to go, and it situates itself, as do his new poems, in the pure present. The occasional jokiness is meant to disarm and has nothing to do with nihilism, which he always rejected. Behind the humor of his handling of Harriet and Somers's marital ship lies the admission that the "perfect love" of their beginning has foundered, and in a passage canceled from the manuscript he says flatly, "Now I don't like love, and I don't like sex. . . ." and goes on to resurrect yet again his dream of a David and Jonathan "absolute" friendship, before spurning this too—though not his craving for "*some* living fellowship with other men."

Just as intensely serious, under the banter, are the issues raised in the "Nightmare" chapter of *Kangaroo*, with its valuable clues to Lawrence's continual rage. Many men during the war, muses Somers, were subjected to things a thousand times worse than he, yet "He was full of a lava fire of rage and hate, at the bottom of his soul. And he knew it was the same with most men. . . . He cared for nothing now, but to let loose the hell-rage that was in him. Get rid of it by letting it out. For there was no digesting it. He had been trying that for three years, and roaming the face of the earth trying to soothe himself with the sops of travel and new experience and scenery. . . ."

Only David Ellis seems to have speculated that the name Richard Lovat Somers could be an allusion to that other nomadic writer, R.L.S., a semi-invalid like Lawrence himself. Stevenson's novels were familiar to Lawrence when, in his early days, after succumbing to pneumonia in November 1911, he had gone to Bournemouth to convalesce, like Stevenson before him. Cursing his sick year of 1911 he wrote to Louie Burrows that he longed to escape to the warm south: "I swear I'll flee to the tropics first opportunity." He was aware of the Scottish writer's life and perhaps had Stevenson in mind when he said he thought of writing a "romance" while in Australia, before going on to the South Seas. Lawrence's long-held dream of buying a boat and sailing the world had been acted out by Stevenson when he leased a yacht and cruised over the Pacific for two years. In 1890 he had lived in Sydney for a month before settling in Samoa, and this too would have been known to Lawrence.

For all his objections to democratic Australia he came almost to love the place, even to the extent of wondering wistfully if he should stay. He loved being close to the ocean, like having "the Pacific in the garden," and sitting at their table the surf seemed about "to rush in under our feet." What scared him was the power of the vast impersonal wilderness there behind him. "It's too strong," he has Somers say. "It would lure me quite away from myself." He was bewitched, as he had never been in Europe, by a beauty that was remote, that had an "almost coal-age pristine quality. Only it's too far for me. I can't reach so awfully far. Further than Egypt. I feel I slither on the edge of a gulf. . . ." He tried again and again, in his novel and in letters, to grasp Australia's atmosphere and spirit.

To Frieda's sister Else he wrote, "I must say this new country has been a surprise to me." The anthropologist Sir William Flinders Petrie had said that new countries were no·younger than their parent country, but to Lawrence this place was older, unimaginably older. As soon as night fell it was as if he ceased to exist. "That is a queer sensation: as if the life here really had never *entered in*: as if it were just sprinkled over, and the land lay untouched . . . it all feels so slovenly, slip-shod, rootless and empty, it is like a dream. . . . Yet at the same time wonderful . . . and if one could have had a dozen people, perhaps, and a big piece of land of one's own. . . ." At which Aldington in his book snorts in disbelief: "How soon he would have loathed his dozen people if he had ever got them!"

About to leave, and like his hero Somers pining like a fool for "lovely, lovely Europe," he took delivery of a batch of letters from London and Europe. Instantly the very thought of Europe made him sick. "He wished that every mail-boat would go down that was bringing any letter to him, that a flood would rise and cover Europe entirely. . . . Never had he felt so filled with spite against everybody he had known in the old life, as now." The hell-rage that was in him had erupted again.

Kangaroo went off to America before Lawrence did. Running short of funds because money he had asked Robert Mountsier to cable had not yet come, he was obliged to do something he must have hated, borrow a small sum to pay off the remainder of his rent. He went into Camperdown, a suburb of Sydney, and got it from Marchbanks, one of his Nottinghamshire friends. As he drew near to the *Tahiti*'s sailing date for San Francisco he felt reluctant to leave, and so did Frieda.

It was August, the Australian spring. The bush was covered in sulphur wattle flowers, the national flower, a kind of mimosa. Harriet in the novel thought it the loveliest thing she had ever known. As David Ellis puts it, "Lawrence was always inclined to like a place best once the arrangements for leaving it had been finalized," but there is no doubting the genuineness of Lawrence's response to this wonderfully transformed land with its plumes and trees of wattle, "as if the angels had flown right down out of the softest gold regions of heaven to settle here in the Australian bush" with its uncanny stillness, the entire bush flowering all at once "at the gates of heaven."

Each letter of adieu he wrote sounded more regretful than the last. To an Australian author, Katherine Throssell, he wrote respectfully to say that he was sorry they didn't meet in Western Australia, and sorry too that he didn't know her books. She had sent him a newspaper clipping about the birth of her son. "I understand you are prouder of that little newspaper cutting than of all the yards you've had for books." He didn't want her to think he was bolting from Australia: on the contrary, "Australia seems to me a most marvelous country to disappear into. When one has had enough of the world—when one doesn't want to wrestle with another single thing, humanly—then come to Australia. . . . It is a land where one can go out of life, I feel, the life one gets so sick of." But, he implied, he was born or doomed to wrestle, and fight, and get sick of life as it was. His wife, he added, wanted a little farm more than anything else. "But how should I sit still so long?" In fact she was soon to have her heart's desire, courtesy of Mabel Dodge Sterne.

The *Tahiti* sailed on August 11, 1922, a day late, on its way to San Francisco with a first stop at Wellington, New Zealand. New Zealand was Katherine Mansfield's birthplace, and she was on his mind when they landed there briefly. He was unaware that she was dying when he sent her a postcard with the single word Ricordi ("Remembrances"). After the falling out with Murry, this was an attempt at reconciliation with them both.

From New Zealand they sailed for the South Seas made famous by Stevenson and Melville. After calling at Raratonga and Papeete, Lawrence amended his essay on Melville by agreeing with the American that these natives were like children, and there was no going back to that state. "Whatever else the South Sea Islander is, he is centuries and centuries behind us in the life-struggle, the consciousness-struggle, the struggle of the soul into fullness."

If Papeete was a great disappointment, so, this time, was ocean travel. "Travel," he wrote to Mary Cannan after two days on the island "seems to me a splendid lesson in disillusion—chiefly that." Not only these "earthly paradises" but the ship itself let him down. It staggered over the ocean like a big overcrowded boardinghouse. To begin with he wrote without rancor of a gentleman practicing the saxophone in the music room and Frieda proud of her victory at whist, but the closer he came to America the more he dreaded it, without quite knowing why. America, he had told Brewster, groping to decipher his own feelings, seemed "utterly things as they are not." So why was he going? Was America the future?

As always on board ship the Lawrences hit it off with fellow passengers, but the rot set in with a vengeance when they reached Tahiti and were joined by a mob of movie people, the actors and crew of a film to be called *Passions of the Sea*. The puritanical Lawrence, unable to stomach their lack of inhibitions, finally objected to their behavior and was laughed at. Even Frieda, no innocent, found their antics offensive. After twenty-five days at sea, their longest voyage so far, they landed at San Francisco on Monday, September 4. He had avoided entering America by the dreaded New York and he had fashioned from his experience of Australia a remarkable if wayward novel and one of his finest poems, "Kangaroo":

> Delicate mother Kangaroo
> Sitting up there rabbit-wise, but huge, plumb-weighted,
> And lifting her beautiful slender face, oh! so much more gently and
>   finely lined than a rabbit's, or than a hare's,
> Lifting her face to nibble at a round white peppermint drop, which
>   she loves, sensitive mother Kangaroo.
>
> Her sensitive, long, pure-bred face,
> Her full antipodal eyes, so dark,
> So big and quiet and remote, having watched so many empty dawns
>   in silent Australia.

Her little loose hands, and drooping Victorian shoulders.
And then her great weight below the waist, her vast pale belly
With a thin young yellow little paw hanging out, and straggle of a
    long thin ear, like ribbon,
Like a funny trimming to the middle of her belly, thin little dangle
    of an immature paw, and one thin ear. . . .

Brenda Maddox writes disparagingly that the antipodal animal
which this poem depicts was the one he saw in the Sydney zoo. Indeed, the "round white peppermint" tells us so. But what of it? The
alliance between body and soul for which Whitman had found a
magical new language is taken a stage further in these poems of animal identification that are such a triumph of Lawrence's astonishing
sensibility.

4

My Greatest Experience from the Outside World

(1922–1923)

C hecking in at the luxurious Palace Hotel after landing with twenty dollars in his pocket (the hotel would cost seven dollars a night), he telegraphed dramatically to Mountsier, "Arrived penniless." There was no cause for alarm. There was money in the bank somewhere, and *Hearst's International* offered what was for him the unheard-of sum of a thousand dollars for *The Captain's Doll*, twice the amount he had been able to earn during a whole year in England. Mabel Sterne was not there to greet them but made up for it handsomely by sending them their train fares to Lamy in New Mexico, twelve hundred miles south, as well as assuring them that they were to regard themselves as her guest.

Waiting for the money from Mountsier to arrive, the Lawrences spent a few days taking in the sights of San Francisco like two bewildered tourists. Confused by the self-service cafeterias, they went to a movie theater that had a "jazz orchestra and a huge and voluminous organ," and Lawrence thought he was in a nonstop Hades. Now with funds, on Friday, September 8, they set off on a rail journey of two days to Lamy, twenty miles south of Santa Fe. There on the afternoon of September 10 they were brought face-to-face with their host Mabel and her Indian lover Tony Luhan.

Mabel Dodge Sterne, as she was still called for the moment, had been born in 1879 to a wealthy banking family in Buffalo. She had known and dispensed with numerous lovers and three husbands. With her first husband, Karl Evans, she had her only child. His death in a hunting accident freed her to indulge her artistic leanings to the full. Her second husband, Edwin Dodge, a Boston architect, carried her off to live in the Villa Curonia on the outskirts of Florence, where she soon established a salon for writers, musicians, painters, and actors. Gertrude Stein and Bernard Berenson belonged to a circle of friends there that included Amy Lowell and the dancer Isadora Duncan.

Mabel returned to New York in 1912, ostensibly for her son to be educated, set up another salon, and involved herself (and her money) in radical politics. A grand pageant in support of a group of silk workers from Paterson, New Jersey, brought her into contact with John Reed, author of *Ten Days That Shook the World*. Her love affair with him was widely publicized, but when she divorced Edwin Dodge it was in order to marry Maurice Sterne, a painter. It was Sterne who introduced his wife to New Mexico, having gone there to paint Indians. Mabel, a syndicated columnist for the Hearst chain, gave up her journalism the moment she recognized that her destiny was to promote Indian culture in New Mexico. She abandoned the overcivilized Santa Fe for remote Taos, and when Sterne departed she began to live with Tony Luhan, a strapping Indian carpenter, whom she commissioned to build her a house. The Russian Jewish Sterne was divorced with an allowance of a hundred dollars a month.

New Mexico, with no rail link beyond Lamy, had in Santa Fe the oldest capital city in the United States. Because of its relative isolation it had remained Spanish in atmosphere. Becoming a state only in 1912, its governor's palace in Santa Fe had been built in 1609 for the viceroy of Spain. The spectacular beauty of the territory, its Taos Valley, Rocky Mountains, and reputation for healthy living, with its dry air, high altitudes, and hot springs, was attracting invalids and artists as it had done since the turn of the century. Lawrence would be stunned by his first sight of the Taos Valley and counted it his "greatest experience from the outside world that I have ever had. . . . The moment I saw the brilliant, proud morning shine high up over the deserts of Santa Fe, something stood still in my soul, and I started to attend."

He hankered after it even when he was near death, trying to believe that its healing powers could somehow save him, if he could only get back there. Brenda Maddox suggests that at the back of his mind when he accepted so swiftly Mabel's invitation was the thought that New Mexico would perhaps restore him to full health, but this could be said of anywhere that attracted him, as it could his rejection of cities and the north.

The woman waiting for him at Lamy station looked reassuringly calm and welcoming, her hair cut with bangs in an Indian style, but he had yet to encounter the force of her will. Shorter than Frieda, they were both forty-three, and in both their pasts was a Jewish disciple of Freud. A. A. Brill had sought to liberate Mabel's creativity during a course of analysis in New York, and Otto Gross in Germany had persuaded Frieda of the evils of repression. They had much to talk about, shared an admiration for Nietzsche, and felt at first they had much in common.

Mabel's voice was deceptively soft and melodious, her body small and square, determined-looking. She had a clear view of herself as a muse figure, and in this respect too she was like Frieda, though her aims were altogether more specific. Frieda, when she was in accord with Lawrence, saw herself as nurturing his genius. Mabel, as she makes clear in *Lorenzo in Taos*, had a definite plan in her mind as far as Lawrence was concerned. His intuition may have warned him of this in advance, sending him east at first instead of west. She had given Frieda an Indian necklace through the post because of its magic qualities, but Lawrence had proved resistant, blithely heading for Australia. Mabel was easy to dismiss in the abstract but not face-to-face. After only a few weeks he registered the power of her eyes, which he saw as "dangerous as the headlights of a great machine coming full at you in the night."

The man driving Mabel's Cadillac was her lover, Antonio Luhan. Lawrence, taken aback by this tall, noble, deeply impressive man who wore his hair in long braids and had an almost palpable inner serenity, had to swiftly revise his ideas about childish savages. Mabel was clearly devoted to him, but his silent nature frustrated her female passion for talk and what she called her need for a flow of ideas. Lawrence seemed the very person to satisfy this hunger that she described in her *Intimate Memoirs* as "unnameable."

Her first impressions of Lawrence were unflattering, as were those of the women at Perth and Darlington. She was startled by his "slim fragility besides Frieda's solidity, of a red beard that was somehow too old for him, and of a nervous incompetence. He was agitated, fussy, distraught, and giggling with nervous grimaces." It occurred to her that his nervousness was brought about by her relationship with Tony Luhan, which was evidently intimate. This may indeed have caused him some discomfort in view of his objection to miscegenation. More likely, however, was the sense of inferiority he had allowed Harriet in *Kangaroo* to expose so cruelly in her husband. Somers was so isolated, she alleged, that he was "hardly a man at all, among men. He had absolutely nothing but her." Mabel had certainly noticed Lawrence's awkwardness in front of Tony and the way he positioned himself away from Tony beside Frieda at the station café.

She and Frieda sat in the rear seats together for the journey to Santa Fe. Lawrence, sensitive to Frieda's open admiration for other men, had to sit in silence as he heard her telling Mabel that Tony with his broad back must be "like a rock to lean on." Not far from Santa Fe the car broke down. If Tony Luhan knew little about car engines, Lawrence knew less, and when Frieda urged him to get out and assist the Indian he said so. According to Mabel, he then said, in a tone she failed to specify, that he considered himself "a failure in the world of men." This could have been thrown over his shoulder sardonically at the woman who enjoyed gleefully needling him, but for Mabel it was a confession. The Lawrences were still an unknown quantity to her.

Tony Luhan, after blaming the car's failure on the malevolence of a roadside snake, somehow got them going again. Things went awry when they arrived in Santa Fe because for some reason the accommodation Mabel thought she had booked was not sufficient for four. She delivered the Lawrences to her friend Witter Bynner, who was only too pleased to offer them a bed, while Mabel and Luhan went to stay with others. Bynner, a wealthy American poet who was a little older than Lawrence, had traveled abroad for years and now lived in Santa Fe with a lover, Willard "Spud" Johnson. Bynner knew of Lawrence's explosive temper and was about to witness a demonstration. His first sight of the famous writer was of a painfully thin man trying to disentangle himself from luggage that included a Sicilian cart panel. Tony, trying to back the car into a courtyard, hit the panel and cracked it in two. Lawrence danced up and down in a rage, shouting, "It's your fault, Frieda—you've made me carry that vile thing round the world, but I'm done with it. Take it, Mr. Bynner, keep it, it's yours!"

Bynner's sympathy was for the abused Frieda, and from that moment his loyalty to her never wavered. As for the panel, it stayed where it was left, and was still there thirty-eight years later when a French writer came to interview Bynner. His adobe house was very small, and he gave up his only bedroom to his guests, sleeping with Johnson on couches in the living room. Next morning he was astonished to find that Lawrence had washed the dishes, swept the floor, and laid the table for breakfast, forestalling the arrival of Bynner's maid from across the street.

NEXT DAY the visitors drove north without incident, following an old road so precipitous as they neared Taos that Lawrence caught his breath, so Mabel claimed. It was September 11, Lawrence's thirty-seventh birthday. They reached her estate as darkness was falling.

Their host had a new adobe house prepared and ready for the Lawrences, only a short distance from her own. Lawrence was charmed by its bright interior of four rooms and a kitchen. He noted Mabel's queenly nature, and though he thought her "very nice" he was aware of the price: she expected him "to *write* this country up." Taos itself, when he came to look around, he found suffocatingly close, with its two thousand people grouped around a plaza cluttered with wagons and shops. The Big House belonging to Mabel with its cluster of corrals, guest houses, and servants' quarters was at one end, and at the other was the Pueblo, housing six hundred Indians in what Lawrence described as "a pile of earth-colored cube-boxes in a heap," made of adobe.

The five-roomed adobe allocated to the Lawrences was called the Pink House, and its Indian rugs, whitewashed walls, pine beams, and clay fireplaces adorned with pottery had the kind of uneven, natural simplicity they liked. But Mabel was a dynamo of organization: almost before they had properly unpacked she whisked her celebrity off to attend the Apache celebrations on the Jucarillo reservation, escorted by Tony Luhan and an old friend, Bessie Freeman. Left behind as she intended, she and Frieda were free to gossip and exchange confidences. Frieda, less experienced as a woman of the world than Mabel, was too open and guileless to resist Mabel's probing, and when Lawrence returned he would accuse his gushing wife of "giving the show away."

One difference between the two women must have quickly become clear to Mabel, who had held court at salons in Florence and New York and was therefore an experienced *Kulturträger*. As she listened to Frieda's confidences about Lawrence's relationship with the Cornishman William Hocking at Zennor and her love affairs in Nottinghamshire and Germany during her marriage to Ernest Weekley, Mabel realized that her knowledge of men was more extensive than Frieda's. As her book *Lorenzo in Taos* makes clear, she already saw herself as a rival for Lawrence's love.

For the moment, however, they chattered together happily as new friends. Mabel, as well as wanting secretly to draw Lawrence away from Frieda, was herself seduced away from Tony Luhan at the very beginning by the magnetism of Lawrence's conversation and the sheer charm of his personality. She adored his flow of ideas, was starved of talk, and equated his interests with hers in matters of the spirit, in theosophy and magic.

On his return from the Apache gathering, 120 miles across the desert, Lawrence seemed uncharacteristically reticent. It would in fact take him three years to finally decide on his stance vis-à-vis the Indians. Initially he felt it necessary to revise his essays on Fenimore Cooper in *Studies in Classic American Literature*. Five months later his impressions of the Apaches were published in the *Dial*. "Indians and an Englishman" made clear his ambivalence and spoke of a gap between him and them in spite of their shared tribal origins. Before that, drawn into Mabel and Tony Luhan's battle for Indian rights and John Collier's campaign against the notorious Bursum Bill (designed to settle the claims of squatters at the expense of the Indians), he signed a national petition, adding his name to the protests of Carl Sandburg, Zane Grey, Vachel Lindsay, and Edgar Lee Masters, and writing an article, "Certain Americans and an Englishman," which appeared in the *New York Times Magazine* in December.

Pleased though Mabel must have been, she would no doubt have liked his piece to have been more positive. But with his imperfect grasp of the situation he trod carefully, determined not to fall into the sentimentality that afflicted "highbrow palefaces" whenever they confronted the Indian question. "Let us try to adjust ourselves again to the Indian outlook," he wrote, "to take up the old dark thread from their vision . . . without forgetting we are ourselves."

Later, when he came to write the essays collected in *Mornings in Mexico*, he was altogether more forthright. Even anthropologists, he argued in "Indians and Entertainment," were afflicted with what he called the creeping note of sentimentality which made him automatically dismissive: "You've got to de-bunk the Indian, as you've got to de-bunk the Cowboy. . . . But the Indian bunk is not the Indian's invention. It is ours. . . . The common healthy vulgar white usually feels a certain native dislike of these drumming aboriginals. The highbrow invariably lapses into sentimentalism like the smell of bad eggs." For the truth was, the Indian direction was totally different from ours. "The consciousness of one branch of humanity is the annihilation of the consciousness of another branch. . . . And we can understand the consciousness of the Indian only in terms of the death of our consciousness."

Their round dances around the drum, for instance, were almost incomprehensible to us, since there were no words to the singing, and no spectacle, no spectator. "Yet perhaps it is the most stirring sight in the world, in the dark, near the fire, with the drum going, the pine trees standing still, the everlasting darkness and the strange listing and dropping, surging, crowing, gurgling, aah-h-h-ing of the male voices."

So it was, he maintained, with the idea of God. There was no Indian god in our sense of the word, no great mind directing the universe. "Yet the mystery of creation, the wonder and fascination . . . shimmers in every leaf and stone, in every thorn and bud, in the fangs of the rattle-snake and in the soft eyes of a fawn. Things utterly opposed are still pure wonder of creation, the yellow of the mountain lion and the breeze in the aspen leaves." As for commandments, the pure Indian has only three, two negative and one positive: "Thou shalt not lie. Thou shalt not be a coward. Thou shalt acknowledge the wonder."

THESE BRILLIANT ESSAYS lay ahead. For the time being he was glad to enjoy the inspiring landscape and the novelty of learning to ride under Tony Luhan's direction, as he did his contact with the friendly Pueblo Indians. And looking up, wonder of wonders, he could see the Rockies. He and Frieda were instructed patiently by an amused Tony in the art of mounting and controlling a horse. Frieda was too lazy to ride for long, but Lawrence spent many hours in his Mexican saddle. Quick to learn, he dressed for the part in white riding breeches, a blue shirt, and a cowboy hat, fulfilled at last—in his imagination at least—as a man in the world of men, though aware too that he was playing a game. Dining in the Big House as he sometimes did, he and Frieda would take part in Mabel's Indian evenings in the dining room after the meal, and the whole company would join in, dancing to the drum in an attempt to enter the spirit of the occasion, with Lawrence yelling at the top of his voice as he hopped round in a circle with the others.

But of course he was no more integrated here in the West than he would be anywhere else. As well as experiencing pangs of nostalgia for Australia, feeling that he hadn't extricated all of himself from that country, he was observing at close quarters Mabel's association with Tony Luhan. "Generous and nice" though Mabel admittedly was, he told Brewster that he didn't feel free, living on someone else's property and accepting their kindnesses. "I can't breathe my own air and go my own little way." What he felt about the Indians would be delayed for some time, but his thoughts about Mabel and Tony went straight into his revised essay on Fenimore Cooper, and were hardly "nice." "Supposing," he would soon write, "an Indian loves a white woman, and lives with her. He will probably be very proud of it, for he will be a big man among his own people, especially if the white mistress has money. . . . But at the same time he will subtly jeer at his white mistress, try to destroy her white pride. He will submit to her, if he is forced to, with a kind of false, unwilling childishness, and even love her with the same childlike gentle-

ness, sometimes beautiful. But at the bottom of his heart he is gibing, gibing at her. Not only is it the sex resistance but the race resistance as well. There seems to be no reconciliation in the flesh."

In the revised version he would also change the language of his
essay (and all the others in the book), making it altogether more sardonic and slangy. Living in America entailed what were for him
necessary amendments to his enthusiasm for books like *Deerslayer*.
In 1919, when the first version of his tremendous admiration for
Cooper led him to spurn Tolstoy, Turgenev, Dostoevsky, and
Flaubert in favor of the "lovely, mature and sensitive art" of Cooper
and Hardy. Now he felt obliged to alter his opinion of *Deerslayer* as
a perfect novel, "flawless as a jewel," to "a gem of a book. Or a bit of
perfect paste. And myself, I like a bit of perfect paste in a perfect setting, so long as I am not fooled by pretence of reality." The new
tone was regretful, mocking, and one that gave him room for ma-
neuver, now that he was confronted with the Indian in all his com-
plexity, not to mention the theme of blood brotherhood which had
so attracted him to Cooper in the first place.

By the time he had begun to feel settled in America he was more
confident of paying his way financially. Scrupulous about paying off
loans, he wrote to Koteliansky in warm appreciation of past generosity, telling him not to hesitate if he needed money himself.
Eddie Marsh received the twenty pounds lent ages ago, and on September 22, uncomfortable with Mabel's largesse, he sent that other
grande dame, Ottoline Morrell, the fifteen pounds she had forked
out during his desperate hard days in England. By October 19 he
heard from Seltzer that *Women in Love* had sold out its three thousand trade edition. Then on October 25 came news from his sister
Ada that Sallie Hopkin, the wife of his old Eastwood friend and
mentor Willie Hopkin, had died.

He was moved to write of his indebtedness to them both when
he was a youth and a student teacher, and the Hopkins had "led me
over some frontiers." "If you or I have to go on over queer places,
further, well, the rest of the journey she goes with us like a passen-

ger now. . . . Nevertheless, one uses words to cover up a crying inside one."

The news had affected him deeply. Here he was, the aspens on
the mountains were yellow, donkeys and horses wandered over the
pale desert, the nights were cold, the days hot. He and Frieda, he
said proudly, rode every afternoon till sundown. He seemed so far
away yet weirdly near to the Hopkins home in Devonshire Drive.
The thought of another grave in the cemetery down Church Street
made him feel he was growing old. He sent a love "that belongs to
the old life."

As well as revising his essays on classic American literature he
wrote new poems. Four of them were inspired by first impressions
of New Mexico, but a strange long poem, "Spirits Summoned
West" was a meditation on the death of women, and seems to have
been triggered by the news of Sallie Hopkin's death. The poem's
first line repeats exactly the last sentence of his letter of condolence,
"England seems full of graves to me." The love "that belongs to
the old life" which closes the letter is taken up as a theme in the
poem:

> Women who were gentle
> And who loved me
> And whom I loved
> And told to die. . . .
>
> Women of the older generation, who knew
> The full doom of loving, and not being able to take back.
> Who understood at last what it was to be told to die.

He calls these spirits of women to join him in the West where he
sits "with dark-wrapped Rocky Mountains motionless squatting
around in a ring / Remembering I told them to die . . . the gentle-
kneed women." Suddenly these unspecified virgin women become
his mother:

> Come back, then, mother, my love, whom I told to die.

It was only I who saw the virgin you
That had no home. . . .
I didn't tell you to die for nothing.
I wanted the virgin you to be home at last
In my heart.

Murry is quick to claim this as a key poem, giving the clue to Lawrence's "intolerable and final yearning" for a manhood he could never have. Whether he is addressing only his mother, or women like Sallie Hopkin, he is apparently asking "You whom I loved for gentleness, the wife and mother and mistress," all of them "overlooked virgins," to live in spirit in his heart where he could love them. For Murry this means one thing: Lawrence could only fear and hate living women. With astonishing presumption he goes on to mourn his friend's lack of courage, which he finds "pitiful and tragic," in not taking the leap in order to separate himself from women completely and live alone.

Certainly this poem is intensely private and disturbing, yet Lawrence allowed Murry to publish it in his *Adelphi* magazine. Writing to Edward Garnett ten years before, he had deplored the tendency of personal, lyrical writers like himself to betray themselves "to a parcel of fools." But this poem, clear as its message may have been to Murry, was deeply introspective and far from clear to most readers.

On the other hand there is transparent self-exposure in the trenchant essays of *Studies in Classic American Literature*, providing, of course, one takes for granted that Lawrence is talking nakedly about himself, expressing, says Murry, "the secret desire of his soul." Deerslayer, in the Fenimore Cooper essay, was right, says Lawrence, "not to give in to the temptations of sex. Rather than be dragged into a false heat of deliberate sensuality he will remain alone. . . . So he will preserve his integrity, and remain alone in the flesh."

Murry sees the essay on Hawthorne as crucial, since *"The Scarlet*

Letter is to Lawrence one of the greatest allegories in all literature. It is to him an allegory of the destruction of man by woman." In other words it is the allegory of himself.

But Lawrence is saying something different, that this great book is an allegory of the triumph of sin. And what is sin? Lawrence the supreme explainer is ready with his definition. "It isn't the breaking of divine commandments. It is the breaking of one's own integrity."

So far so good. Then come the pronouncements that have infuriated feminists ever since, like the statements in *Aaron's Rod*. *The Scarlet Letter* shows plainly, says Lawrence with absolute conviction, that "Unless a man believes in himself . . . unless he fiercely obeys his own Holy Ghost, his woman will destroy him. Woman is the nemesis of doubting man. She can't help it. . . . Unless a woman is held, by man, safe within the bounds of belief . . . she becomes subtly diabolic. . . . If a woman doesn't believe in a *man*, she believes, essentially, in nothing. She becomes, willy-nilly, a devil." And so on. This, says Murry, is Lawrence protesting too much. He is really talking about his inability to inspire belief in the women who profess to love him because in the last analysis he cannot believe in himself. Therefore the women are vengeful Furies, as in the upsetting dream in *Kangaroo* when a woman something like Harriet, something like his dead mother, fuse together in repudiating Somers. "He cried tears from his very bowels, and laid his hand on the woman's arm, saying: "But I love you. Don't you *believe* in me? Don't you *believe* in me?" What Murry calls the self-deception is manifest. Woman was to blame, though this excuse was becoming threadbare. "The great dark God, who will sustain us in our loving one another," was being sought as a solution in the second half of *Kangaroo*, and the search would be taken up again once more in *The Plumed Serpent*.

THE SMOTHERING that Lawrence had complained about to Mountsier had not exactly let up, but with his financial independence at least temporarily secure he was finding it less irksome, and "Mabel Sterne is learning to leave us alone, and *not* be a padrona."

This was naive of him, notwithstanding his perception of her dangerously powerful will, though he was unaware of her hidden agenda, confessed in *Lorenzo in Taos*. No sooner had the Lawrences arrived than she saw Frieda as an obstacle to Lawrence's genius, rationalizing this by casting herself in the role of spiritual mother, a role she thought Frieda incapable of fulfilling. We only have her word for his complaint that he felt "the heavy German hand of the flesh" bearing down on him when he was ill, or his condemnation of her as "inimical to the spirit." Ridiculous though it reads, Mabel's criticism of Frieda to him, telling him she was a bad mother, did indicate that his bitterness had to do with something her psychoanalyst would have called oedipal, and she was made aware of it.

Excited beyond measure by Lawrence's company, by the force of his personality and the flood of brilliant talk, spending hours with him on rides over the desert, she broached the subject of her *Intimate Memoirs*, on which she wanted him to collaborate, and her dream of a book about the region that she hoped he would write. Naturally she imagined a central role in such a book for herself. Lawrence responded favorably, as always when it came to collaborating with women. Jessie Chambers had been his sounding board and more during the writing of *Sons and Lovers*, and Frieda's influence on *The Rainbow* and *Women in Love* is everywhere apparent. He was given Mabel's poems to read, and with his teacher's thoroughness gave her a list of episodes in her life that she should jot down and expand with absolute frankness. At some point the two projects, her memoirs and a novel with her as the central figure, seemed to merge. Her preliminary jottings, he told her sternly, had to include memories she didn't want to remember. His ability to instill confidence and belief in others with his intense curiosity, his belief in himself as a liberator, and his way of listening with endless patience and devotion, as if hearing something profound, would hove been immensely flattering to her.

He soon got as far as visualizing the novel-collaboration as a work in progress, judging by his letter of October 6 to Mountsier. "Am doing a M. Sterne novel of *here*, with her Indian. Wonder how we shall get on with it. I don't let her see my stuff." Frieda scribbled a postscript that shows her, at this stage at least, definitely in favor: "It's very clever the beginning, it will be rather sardonic!" The hours he had begun to spend in consultation with Mabel in her study and when riding would soon lead to friction, but for the moment all was well.

It was not that Frieda disliked Mabel. On the contrary, she saw her at first as an ally against Lawrence, who had persuaded his patron to jettison her fashionable clothes in order to dress in pinafores like Frieda. Mabel must have said that Frieda was too bulky to suit pinafores, tied round the middle with a ribbon, because Frieda replied cheerfully, "Lawrence likes fat. He says my stomach is like a big loaf of bread."

Mabel for her part had a good deal of sympathy with Frieda. She understood that her longing for spiritual intimacy with Lawrence was abhorrent to Frieda. This distaste west back a long way. Hermione-Ottoline's desire in *Women in Love* to care for the unstable Birkin's spiritual health produced this vitriolic outburst from Ursula (and we must remember that the author, by recording it, knew only too well that it was justified): "You go to your women—go to them—they are your sort—you've always had a string of them trailing after you—and you always will. Go to your spiritual brides—but don't come to me as well, because I'm not having any, thank you. . . . You will marry me for daily use, but you'll keep yourself well provided with spiritual brides in the background. I know your dirty little game."

It is ironic that we find Frieda, in these early days of the women's relationship, confiding in Mabel when her grievances against Lawrence overcame her. "He tears me to pieces," she complained once, in tears. He would be loving and tender, then react violently with anger and blows, saying she was making him her servant. Mabel even recorded in her memoir Frieda's wish to leave Lawrence because she thought he was mad. There is no reason to doubt these exchanges, since they had been witnessed in public fights many times before.

The half-dozen penciled pages of a novel about a wealthy American woman who leaves industrialized America to fulfill her destiny in the West describes Sybil Mond on a train from New York as "a sturdy woman with a round face, like an obstinate girl of fourteen . . . naive-looking, softly full and feminine. And curiously heartbroken at being alone, traveling alone." This girlish woman was at the same time "heavy with energy like a small bison." Not long before the situation in Taos deteriorated he wrote to Mountsier that he was abandoning the novel attempt. "I think if I wrote the MS novel, and the Indian, it would be just *too* impossible."

It had been made impossible by Frieda's vehement objections to his and Mabel's morning sessions of work. Mabel stated bluntly in her memoir that Lawrence did not attract her sexually, but for all that she had taken to dressing provocatively on these mornings, wearing only a housecoat and moccasins. Mabel noted wickedly that he looked uneasily away from her unmade bed on his way through her bedroom to her study.

In letters he was now talking disparagingly of "Mabeltown," and told Mountsier that he would soon have to make a move. "She arranges one too much as if one were a retainer or protégé of hers. . . . I won't be bullied, even by kindness. I won't have people exerting their wills over me."

As the first stage of the Lawrences' entanglement with Mabel came to an end, with furious notes flying to and fro between all three, it is clear that Mabel was defeated in her eagerness to replace Frieda and dominate Lawrence herself. He could deal ruthlessly with people on paper but not face-to-face, and after sheepishly telling Mabel that their morning sessions would have to stop he sank back into himself, allowing the battle to rage over his head.

By late October an escape route had been found. They had visited two log cabins on the Del Monte Ranch, seventeen miles from Taos in a beautiful spot among the Lobo Mountains. The run-down property belonged to Mabel, and the plan was to rent it from her. Lawrence was no longer short of money. Sales of *Women in Love* had reached fifteen thousand, which mystified the author, though of course he was pleased. "Why do they read me? But anyhow they do read me—which is more than England does."

Appearances were deceptive where Lawrence and Frieda were concerned, and the bond between them was a fact, for all their difficulties. When the work on the Mabel novel was transferred to the Pink House, with Frieda noisily present in the background, the book fizzled out in a matter of days.

Before they departed for their mountain retreat, Lawrence issued a manifesto in answer to one of Mabel's, in which he defended himself against her charges, whatever they were, leveling nine of his own. He had already shown Frieda one of the long intimate letters he was now receiving from Mabel, and was out to "make everything square and open" by setting the record straight. In short, he accused her of trying treacherously to drive a wedge between him and his wife.

> You are *antagonistic* to the *living* relation of a man and his wife: because you only understand a sort of bullying. . . . I believe that, at its best, the central relation between Frieda and me is the best thing in my life, and as far as I go, the best thing in life.

He repudiated any future collaboration on books by saying, "I will *never* help you to think and flow as you want," and threw in an insult, equating Tony with her dog Lorraine, which one could see as a measure of his own humiliation in accepting her "generosity": "I don't believe in the lie of your 'submission' to Tony," he wrote, with the waspish malice he sometimes exhibited. "As well say you 'submit' to Lorraine." Discouraging though this must have been to Mabel, she was not so easily dismissed. In a sense she would have been gratified by the acknowledgment of her as a force to be reckoned with.

In the event, the log cabins owned by Mabel were not available after all, but the Hawk family a short distance away had a large log cabin to rent, with a smaller one nearby that Lawrence wanted for two young Danish painters he had met in Taos, Knud Merrild and Kai Gotzsche, who happened to be broke. It was fortunate that they all liked one another and that the Danes were happy to help them survive the coming winter in the wild. Lawrence, now that he was in funds, paid the rent for both cabins and for once enjoyed being the provider.

By the time they were ready to pack at the end of November the Lawrences had made their peace with Mabel after a fashion. Lawrence thanked her courteously for the loan of the Pink House, but Mabel's chagrin was such that she left for Santa Fe rather than face having to wave her lost writer goodbye. Lawrence had done his best in letters to entice Mountsier and Bessie Freeman to join them, but this little foursome comprised all the community he had been able to muster. They headed bravely into the unknown with their luggage in the Danes' ancient Ford.

Knud Merrild's memoir, *A Poet and Two Painters*, tells the story, in simple direct language, of that winter near the Del Monte Ranch. Lawrence liked the Danish painters because they had none of the affectations of so many of the art colony residents, and because Mabel had snubbed them as nonentities. Also their car would be useful for keeping them all in touch with Taos. And he was shrewd enough to realize that they were physically strong, would be able to help him with the heavy work, and would do nothing to fray his nerves by opposing his philosophy of separation from a corrupt civilization. They could play the flute and the fiddle, and they did genuinely admire this fiery little man's spirit. Soon they were appreciative of his generosity too: as well as paying their rent he provided their food, taught them to ride, tutored them in Spanish, and encouraged them to design jackets for his books. He went out of his way to assist them in arranging shows of their work in Taos, and told them to use his name wherever it was profitable for them.

AN ADDITION to this group of pioneers was a little black bull terrier, Bibbles, a pet acquired by Lawrence. It was one of Mabel's pups, and it was a bitch—two strikes against her. In the New Year it would provoke Lawrence into one of his ugliest ungovernable rages, but before that explosion took place he wrote a long poem, "Bibbles," that was full of his affection for the creature, as well as comic exasperation at her indiscriminate fraternizing nature. With his gift for identifying himself with animals he gives us the funny little beast in quick free lines that bring the pup instantly to life:

> So funny
> Lobbing wildly through deep snow like a rabbit,
> Hurtling like a black ball through the snow,
> Champing it, tossing a mouthful,
> Little black spot in the landscape!

She was the first pet he'd "owned" since the lop-eared rabbits of his boyhood that his father had brought home on his way from work across the fields. How he observed her, amused by all her antics, and—since he was in the midst of revising his book on classic American writers—how rapidly she became a symbol for everything he was ambivalent about in America. Whitman, with his exultant message of the Open Road, had meant so much to him, but he hated his chanting of Democracy, En Masse, One Identity, and here was this little "black love-bird" running round in its eagerness to love all and sundry.

> Believe in the One Identity, don't you,
> You little Walt-Whitmanesque bitch?

He had lost her in Taos plaza, and after searching endlessly came on her prancing fondly after the skirts of an old Mexican woman

"who hated you, and kept looking round at you and cursing / you in
a mutter"

> Yet you're so nice,
> So quick, like a little black dragon.
> So fierce, when the coyotes howl, barking like a whole little lion,
>   and rumbling,
> And starting forward in the dusk, with your little black fur all
>   bristling like plush
> Against those coyotes, who would swallow you like an oyster.
> And in the morning, when the bedroom door is opened,
> Rushing in like a little black whirlwind, leaping straight as an arrow
>   on the bed at the pillow
> And turning the day suddenly into a black tornado of *joie de vivre*,
>   Chinese dragon.

There was no doubt that Lawrence loved his fastness on the
Lobo Mountains. It was like a repeat of Zennor in Cornwall, except
that now he had achieved the seemingly impossible and found two
people who were able to live with him at close quarters without
undue strain. They were young, tolerant, humorous, and, best of all,
nonliterary. As winter closed in and snow fell he worked side by side
with the two painters, felling trees for log fires and clearing paths.
In Taos the Indians had nicknamed him Red Fox because of his russet coloring and his watchful eyes. This hardly pleased him: he
would have preferred something more savage.

He would be at his most difficult during the heavy snowstorms
which kept them pinned indoors for days at a time, the Danes joining them in their cabin for extended talks and folk singing. Knud
Merrild in his memoir records many instances of Lawrence in a
black corrosive fury with Frieda, his blue eyes blazing. Yet the
Danes refused to take sides, and in fact had taken a liking to the
easygoing Frieda. When the storms eased and the three men went
tramping through the snow, with Frieda content to lie on her bed
smoking cigarettes, Lawrence would struggle to match the pace of

his more robust friends, finding excuses to stop and catch his breath. Merrild describes one occasion when they were climbing to reach a high ridge, turning to see Lawrence far below them, forlornly trying to keep up.

What Lawrence especially liked, apart from the camaraderie of laboring at common tasks with members of his own sex, as he had done in his youth during hay-making with the Chambers family and again at Higher Tregerthen with William Hocking, when he had literally reverted to his working-class roots and become a farm laborer, was the satisfaction of living rough and feeling more real. David Ellis makes the point that, given his imaginative nature and feeling as he did something of an outlaw in the world, he was "in need of frequent confirmation that the external world was really there."

It was in Cornwall that the battle of wills between him and Frieda moved into another, deadlier phase. The Danes' bafflement as they saw Lawrence's fury rise and subside might have been eased if they could have read in *Aaron's Rod* of the deadlock Aaron and his wife Lottie had reached in their terrible game of wills. For "She became the same as he. Even in her moments of most passionate desire for him, the cold and snake-like tension of her will never relaxed. . . ." As for him, he realized at last that

> he had never intended to yield himself fully to her or to anything: that his very being was pivoted on the fact of his isolate self-responsibility, aloneness. His intrinsic and central aloneness was the very center of his being. Break it, and he broke his being. . . . It was the great temptation, to yield himself: and it was the final sacrilege. . . . By the innermost isolation and singleness of his own soul he would abide though the skies fell on top of one another, and seven heavens collapsed.
>
> Vaguely he realized this. And vaguely he realized that this had been the root cause of his strife with Lottie: Lottie, the only person

who had mattered at all to him in the world: save perhaps his mother.

Most of his literary work while on the Lobo had to do with the making of poetry, and magnificent many of these poems are. "The Blue Jay" is eloquent with his admiration of the creature's electric aliveness, and its independence. "Turning his back on everything," as he felt he himself was doing up there on his mountain, its strident laugh of ridicule echoing his own inner laughter:

The blue jay with a crest on his head
Comes round the cabin in the snow.
He runs in the snow like a bit of blue metal,
Turning his back on everything . . .

It's the blue jay laughing at us,
It's the blue jay jeering at us, Bibs . . .

The days were often sunny, but at night the temperature dropped ferociously. During the day water would be carried into the cabins, but keeping clean was a problem they had to solve by visiting the Manby hot springs. They rode there on the horses Lawrence had hired from the Hawks nearby. These likable neighbors, twenty-five-year-old Bill Hawk, his wife Rachel, and Bill's younger sister Elizabeth sometimes had Bill Hawk's parents living with them, but not now: they had retreated to warmer regions for the winter.

Lawrence's poem "Mountain Lion" has become justly famous. The four of them encountered two Mexicans at the entrance of the Lobo canyon. The strangers were carrying something yellow, a deer perhaps. No, it was a mountain lion, "A long, long slim cat, yellow like a lioness," trapped that morning:

Her round bright face, bright as frost,
Her round, fine-fashioned head, with two dead ears;
And stripes in the brilliant frost of her face, sharp, fine dark rays . . .

His identification had never been so passionately expressed, his bitterness at the world so clearly stated, as with this poem of mourning for the beautiful dead cat in which he chose to read his own fate.

> And I think in this empty world there was room for me and a
> mountain lion.
> And I think in the world beyond, how easily we might spare a
> million or two of humans
> And never miss them.
> Yet what a gap in the world, the missing white frost-face of that
> slim yellow mountain lion!

AS THEY NEARED Christmas, Lawrence's thoughts turned to problems of accommodation and transport for his first guests since his move. His publisher and literary agent had both decided to come, and this in itself was a problem, as Mountsier and Seltzer had reached a stage where they cordially detested each other. But Lawrence now felt able to think of other things besides roofing, felling timber, fixing doors, and putting up shelves. Life was still rough and primitive, the three fires the Lawrences kept going in their big five-room cabin had to be constantly stoked, and water, in the depths of winter, would always be a preoccupation. For Lawrence, who even saw his soul-life in terms of battle, these conditions were nothing to complain about.

He tried first to approach Mabel regarding his publisher's visit, telling him in a letter that she was quite friendly, now that misunderstandings between them had been cleared up, "only somewhat *blind* to anything except her own way." Mabel replied that her son's forthcoming marriage meant that her rooms would be filled with guests, and suggested a friend, Elizabeth Harwood, who could put up both the Lawrences and the Seltzers over Christmas. This for Lawrence was a veiled snub, and in her memoir Mabel admits she acted out of resentment. Rumors that she and her son had been encouraging, according to her own account, hinting that she had forced the Lawrences to move out because they were using her, came to Lawrence through his contacts with Taos.

Merrild recalled an evening when they were snowbound and the talk flowed wildly. Lawrence's misanthropy reached a new pitch of intensity as he insisted that some killing was necessary and that they should not flinch from it. He for one would like to kill "some of the beastly bankers, industrialists, lawyers, war makers and schemers of all kinds." Merrild, as a devil's advocate, asked if Lawrence was proposing to start this personal slaughter at once, and who he intended to kill. Lawrence thought a moment, then said slowly and with emphasis, "I will kill Mabel first."

He had been looking forward to seeing the Christmas dance of the Pueblo Indians in Taos, but now that Mabel was to be avoided he gave up the idea—only to turn up after all with Frieda as the guest of Nina Witt, a childhood friend of Mabel's from her Buffalo days. The Seltzers lodged there too for a night, before transferring on Christmas Day to Del Monte. Lawrence's growing importance as a literary figure accounts for the fact that both publisher and agent were prepared to undertake the arduous train journey from the East to visit him on his mountain retreat. Russian-born Thomas Seltzer, a small publisher whose firm was only three years old, had published *Women in Love* in 1920 when no one else was interested, triumphing against an attempted prosecution of the novel, and was now the publisher of a number of Lawrence's books, including *Sea and Sardinia*.

Adele Seltzer was small but her husband was tiny, only five feet tall. No wonder Adele wrote later that "Lawrence is a Titan, and I go about with an ever-present wonder that we, Thomas and I, little, little Jews, should be the publishers of the great English giant of this age. Not because with Jewish shrewdness we outwitted some other publisher, but because . . . we had faith in him as a writer." This belief would stand them in good stead with Lawrence for some time to come. They enjoyed the atmosphere of the Del Monte ménage during their week, admired the boyish Danish artists, saw the Lawrences with touching innocence as a harmonious couple, and as for meeting their author in the flesh, it was "a stupendous experience." Adele in her letter to a friend later went on: "He loses nothing by being seen at close range. As for his wife, she's a Norse goddess. . . . Lawrence is a captivating personality, always flashing sparks. When he's in the mood to sing and make fun he is utterly charming, with an elfish grace. . . . Like the elements, he can be fierce and wild, tigerish, bearish (but not brutish)."

They lent a hand willingly with the chores, which Frieda frequently dodged, chopping wood and carrying water from the water hole "at a distance equal to three city blocks." Seltzer recalled later in a letter to Merrild that New Year's Eve was still memorable, with Lawrence singing carols in his "small but sweet voice."

The day after Mountsier arrived the Seltzers pointedly left, Adele to go home and Thomas on a venture to California, where he tried without success (losing heavily in the process) to sell the film rights of *Women in Love* to Warner Bros. If not quite as enamored as his wife, Seltzer later insisted that Lawrence was "at bottom, sane, for all his losses of control. Follow him in the kitchen when he cooks, when he washes and irons his own underwear, when he does chores for Frieda. . . . When he walks with you in the country . . . in his conversation he is almost always inspiring because of his extraordinary ability to create a flow, a current between himself and the other person. So many people dwell only on his fierce outbreaks. . . ."

5

Down on the Dark,
Volcanic Earth
(1923)

I f there was a current between Lawrence and Mountsier at the start of his visit, it soon short-circuited. Reporting to Seltzer on January 4, 1923, that the agent-journalist was "being very nice," he soon changed his mind when the American complained that his breakfast of porridge served up by the Danes was inadequate, as was his cold room in the Danes' cabin. His business letters to his client the previous autumn had been unpleasant, arrogant in tone and hostile to Seltzer, so that Lawrence, with his "distaste for Yankees," was prejudiced in advance. Mountsier for his part was prejudiced against Jews, and against Seltzer in particular, whom he saw as inefficient in his business dealings and a block on his approaches to others who would publish his now-famous author on more generous terms. Lawrence, no fool, realized that Mountsier was probably right, but had made his choice. He liked the tiny Jew, calling him "one of the believing sort," and objected to Mountsier's criticism of both *Aaron's Rod* and *Kangaroo*. Mountsier stayed for most of January, even after taking a fall from his horse and breaking a wrist, finally moving down to Taos before leaving for good. On February 3, after receiving a bill for $300 to cover Mountsier's return railway fare from New York, Lawrence wrote to say that he had decided to handle his own affairs. To Seltzer he said on February 7 that he had broken the connection: "Mountsier didn't believe in me, he was against me inwardly."

Asked by Seltzer to respond in an essay to Meredith Starr's *The Future of the Novel*, he waded into the subject in what an American critic of *Studies* called his "coal-heaver style," deploring the cerebral ultra-self-consciousness of Proust, Joyce, and Dorothy Richardson, and the fact that philosophy and fiction had become split. "They used to be one, right from the days of myth. Then they went and parted, like a nagging married couple, with Aristotle and Thomas Aquinas and that beastly Kant. So the novel went sloppy, and philosophy went abstract-dry. The two should come together again—in the novel." A convulsion or cataclysm was needed, and he called his essay "Surgery for the Novel—or a Bomb."

In February 1923 Murry broke a long silence by writing to tell him that Katherine Mansfield, her struggle against consumption at an end, had entered Gurdjieff's establishment at Fontainebleu. It was a forlorn last hope of a cure. She was given instruction in spiritual dogma derived from the East and put in a bed in a loft above a cow stall to inhale the animal odors. Then came the shock of her death, reported in Murry's second note.

Lawrence and Katherine had always shared a curious, unspoken affinity of spirit in spite of their quarrels. Whenever she thought of wild flowers she thought of the Lawrences, of that unhappy time in Cornwall when the wild foxgloves were out everywhere, that the Cornish called "high poppies." Foxgloves for Katherine meant peering through the yellow curtains of the cottage next door to see "the great sumptuous blooms" arranged in pitchers against the rough whitewashed walls, Lawrence and Frieda seated between them "like blissful prisoners." She clung to memories of him when "his black self was not. Oh, there is something so lovable about him and his eagerness, his passionate eagerness for life—that is what one loves so." In the July before her death, feeling her own grip on life slipping away, she wrote in a letter to Koteliansky that she would love to see Lawrence "in a sunny place and pick violets." After being let down so often by Murry's shifty promises and neglect of her, she was one of the few people to appreciate the insistence in *Aaron's Rod* on a separate life, and felt "as if the book was feeding me."

Murry and Lawrence were now so out of touch that Murry sent the note about Katherine's death via Koteliansky. The news frightened him, not least because of the disease which had killed her. "Dear Jack," he wrote, in an attempt to mend the rift between them, "Yes, it is something gone out of our lives. Yes, I always knew a bond in my heart. Feel a fear where the bond is broken now. Feel as if old moorings were breaking. What is going to happen to us all? We will unite up again when I come to England. . . . Still it makes me afraid. As if worse were coming. I feel like the Sicilians. They always cry for help from their dead. We shall have to, cry to ours: we do cry." He ended miserably, "I wish it needn't all have been as it has been: I do wish it."

The Danes, as the Rocky Mountain winter wore on, were having to come to terms as best they could with the devil in Lawrence, liable to leap out without warning in his intermittent war with Frieda. If she was indeed a devouring mother, he would not let her devour him. Once, as she was about to show the Danes photographs of her children, Lawrence pounced and ripped them to bits, just as he destroyed her carton of cigarettes in a fit of spite. Not that she was incapable of retaliation: far from it. She ridiculed his schoolmaster's pedantry when he gave the Danes lessons in Spanish, and laughed with devastating mockery at his discomfort when a girl artist friend of the Danes hitchhiked the seventeen miles of frozen snow to see them, and then stayed overnight with them. Catherine Carswell has written of Frieda: "She was mindless Womanhood, wilful, defiant, disrespectful, argumentative, assertive, vengeful, sly, illogical, treacherous, unscrupulous and self-seeking." What

Lawrence had chosen for a wife was, she thought, "rather a force of nature—a female force—than an individual woman . . . a healing rain or a maddening tempest of stupidity. . . . There were things she jeered at in him and things in her that maddened him—things that neither would consent to subdue."

The prudery of his protest about the girl from Taos, slight in itself, could be seen as a prelude to the savagery of the ugly scene that followed soon afterward, when his little bitch Bibbles was suddenly in heat. Many biographers have recoiled from this incident, the truth of which has been verified by Knud Merrild's unbiased account. It is all there in any case in Lawrence's poem about the dog with its sharp immediacy, except that the murderous rage is left out. In it are his disgust at Frieda's "indiscriminate love," his own tendency to form uncritical friendships, and his announcement to Frieda that he was finished with sex and love, and wanted only "Fidelity! Loyalty! Attachment!" He had been humiliated enough times by her infidelity and her willingness to flirt with any attractive male she fancied, and now it was all being heaped on this "miserable little bitch of love-tricks" who was, he said, crawling to him for protection from the "great ranch-dogs" belonging to the Hawks who had got her scent.

He rejected out of hand the practical suggestion that Bibbles should be kept on a leash or locked in for a while. No, she had to be taught to obey her master. Instead the ungrateful little creature shot away into the woods and disappeared. When she came back he whipped her with a juniper twig and she ran off again, this time to the cabin of the Danes, to

> Fawn before them, and love them as if they were the ones you had *really* loved all along.
> And they're taken in.
> They feel quite tender over you, till you play the same trick on them, dirty bitch.

Suddenly Lawrence burst in to the Danes' shack, white and trembling with murderous rage. It was noon. He knocked the dog off Gotzsche's lap and rushed after her into the snow, aiming kicks at her in such insane fury that Merrild placed himself between Bibbles and Lawrence, fearing for the dog's life. Off went the yelping dog into the woods and safety. The men stood toe-to-toe, with Merrild convinced that if he had not been the stronger, Lawrence would have attacked him too. Fortunately these insane rages were of short duration, and Lawrence, whose pride would not allow him to lose face by apologizing, baked bread and a delicious cake for the Danes and was "very, very nice."

Merrild in his memoir had to try to make sense of a man who so revered the birds and beasts of his poems and yet could act so viciously. "There is, of course, no denying," he reasoned,

> that Lawrence was at that moment cruel to the dog, grossly so. But he was so to us, to his wife, and to everybody for that matter, at times, and mostly so to himself. He could be the very devil. Nevertheless, in spite of this, or because of it, we liked him just the same—the dog episode included. Lawrence loved animals and humanity more passionately than most of us do, and he who loves much shall be forgiven much. . . . Honestly, I don't think there is any reason to try to defend him.

Soon after this murderous eruption, or perhaps because of it, his weak lungs forced him to take to his bed, insisting as always that he had only "a slight cold" and would soon be on his feet. Bibbles, the "dirty, false little bitch" he had screamed at hysterically in a stream of violent curses, came in one day from the Danes' cabin where she had been living and jumped on his bed as she was accustomed to do, while he sat in pretended disgust, watching her "roll your head like a canary"

And show a tiny bunch of white teeth in your underhung blackness,

Self-conscious little bitch,
Aiming again at being loved.

That Lawrence was extremely fond of the little dog is obvious
from Adele Seltzer's comment that it was "wonderful to see how attached the two are—dog to man, man to dog, Lawrence sitting on a
low stool" beside the fire at Christmas with Pips—another of his
names for Bibbles—on his knees. He had told Seltzer soon after he
had departed that Bibbles had no loyalty. "To me, loyalty is far before love. Love seems usually to be just a dirty excuse for disloyal-
ties," and behind the outburst could well have been one more
protest at Frieda's past betrayals. When the decision had been taken
to leave Del Monte for Mexico in March, along with Bynner and
Johnson, he said meekly to Bynner, "I would awfully like to take the
little black dog with us. Could we do it, do you think?" and said to
Seltzer in a letter that same day how hard it was to leave "the Bim-
sey."

One remembers in the "Harriet and Lovat at Sea in Marriage"
chapter of *Kangaroo* the ridiculing of his ludicrous "lord and master"
beliefs by Harriet-Frieda: "Why, he was not really lord and master
of his own bread and butter," she is made to cry, and then, devastat-
ingly, "as it was, he was the most forlorn and isolated creature in the
world, without even a dog to his command." Well, he had acquired
a dog but was unable to command it. Was this what the maniacal
frenzy was all about? What Aldington calls his most cherished pre-
tences were seen through pitilessly by the man himself, as here in
Kangaroo, and yet to jettison them was another matter entirely: that
was the most extraordinary thing. No one was more obstinate and
perverse, or so liable to astonishingly rapid changes of mood which
contradicted everything he had shown to be absurd.

IT WAS HARD to break up the little encampment in the Rockies,
because in spite of Lawrence's lapses it had been for him a success.

Lawrence was pleased with the degree of self-sufficiency they had achieved. Frieda had been a mother figure to the Danes, knitting woolen caps for them and providing them with pillows and fresh bed linen, while Lawrence excelled himself with his cooking. They all gathered on Sundays in the Lawrences' cabin to eat together, and the cockily bossy Englishman who could be delightfully playful must have been encouraged to feel that his long-held dream of Rananim was at last within reach. On the cabin wall hung Lawrence's copy of Piero di Cosimo's *Death of Procris*, which Merrild and Gotzsche both thought was faulty. Not that this criticism dented his self-confidence in the slightest, and when he tried to show Merrild where his own painting was going wrong the Dane had to fight to retrieve his brush. "If you *have* to paint pictures, paint your own," he told the writer, not knowing that in a few years he would do so. For most of their stay at Del Monte the four lived a life of uninterrupted isolation. Bynner came once on a short visit, bringing his mother and his partner Spud Johnson. Merrild makes clear in his honest but rather amateurish book that he disliked the homosexual couple. Lawrence was more tolerant, being more aware, suggests David Ellis, of the complexities of his own sexual nature.

A vivid picture of Lawrence's physical condition comes across in Merrild's memoir when he gives an account of a visit with Lawrence and Gotzsche to the hot springs. Sitting in the crudely made bathhouse, the naked Lawrence with his arms outstretched reminded the painter of "a medieval woodcarving of Christ on the Cross." In 1923 he was not aware of frailty, though Lawrence was white and thin, giving an impression of sinewy strength. In other words, he did not feel he was gazing at a sick man.

Entering the country on a six-month tourist visa as the Lawrences had done meant that they would either have to leave the United States or seek an extension. They would have liked the Danes to come to Mexico with them, but the painters' Santa Fe exhibition was due to continue beyond March, and besides they were still broke. Lawrence turned to Bynner, who had some knowledge of Mexico, but had misgivings when Bynner and his partner seemed keen, chiefly because they were American and "I feel sore with all Americans for the moment." By "all" he meant Mabel, who had also expressed interest, but Mountsier would also have been in his mind. His vague plan was to go to England in the autumn, now that Murry had renewed contact following Katherine Mansfield's death. There was also his glowing review of *Aaron's Rod*. It was, thought Murry, a great book, presumably because of its repudiation of women, a path he believed Lawrence should follow in order to end the uncertainty of his "divided soul."

Although Lawrence and Frieda were probably nervous about adventuring in Mexico with its political unrest, not to mention the ailments they might pick up, in the event they had to go on to Mexico City ahead of Bynner and Johnson, who on March 20 were not ready to leave. They arranged to meet three days later. The Lawrences traveled "in an unkempt Pullman for two nights" and registered at the Hotel Regis in clothes that were far from smart. Feeling uncomfortable in this luxurious establishment they moved after one night to the Monte Carlo, a modest hotel run by Italians. The residents of the first-class hotel had looked immoral, thought Lawrence with his puritanical eye. The Monte Carlo, on the contrary, was friendly and real, and they liked its atmosphere.

Witter Bynner's account in *Journey with Genius* is a mixture of liveliness and malice, for he disliked Lawrence and sympathized with Frieda, as did his mother. In his memoir he mentions a troupe of vaudeville performers accompanied by trained apes and dogs and cockatoos, Italian women residents sitting down in the dining room with "long damp hair drying loose on towels across their shoulders, and the large print of Garibaldi on the dining room wall."

It is perhaps curious that Lawrence should have chosen Bynner and his much younger partner to accompany them, but, like the Danes in the Rockies, they were no threat. Frieda had mothered the young painters and seemed amused by the homosexual pair. Spud

Johnson she called "nice but such a 'jeune fille,'" and joked that Bynner was an old lady and Johnson a young one. Lawrence for his part never criticized their relationship in letters. Bynner's comments about them in private to Johnson were a good deal less charitable, and when he published his account of their travels in 1951 his waspish hostility to Lawrence would be revealed. All the same, the insights of even hostile witnesses can be enlightening.

MEXICO CITY seems to have seen more instances of Lawrence's public fury with Frieda than anywhere else. Bynner records one of his "flare-ups" in the Monte Carlo hotel, and it occurred to him that wine made him worse. He was sipping his Chianti while Frieda smoked. "Her cigarette began to slant downward in the left corner of her mouth," giving her the look of a gangster's moll. Her husband, outraged by the impropriety, yelled at her to remove the dangling stub. "There you sit with that thing in your mouth and your legs open to every man in the room! And you wonder why no decent woman in England would have anything to do with you!" Throwing the last drops of his wine at her he shot out into the street.

Frederick Leighton, an American importer in Mexico City, was another witness appalled by streams of coarse abuse heaped on Lawrence's wife, and wondered that "anyone's body, to say nothing of a sick, fragile one, could withstand such berserk bursts of passion." Lawrence was not, it appears, conscious of the degree of Bynner's dislike, and though they argued frequently it was good-humored. Bynner was a keen amateur photographer, and one of his portraits of Lawrence at Chapala so pleased the Englishman that he sent copies to several friends. Frieda is framed in an open window, and her husband stands before her out on the ground, smiling and jovial, looking in reasonable health. Carleton Beals, a Mexican expert, met Lawrence in Mexico City and described an entirely different being: "He was a thin man, with a body that seemed about to fall to pieces: his face was pasty, expressionless, but his greenish eyes glared from out his pale red beard with curious satyr-like luster . . . everything sent him into convulsive loss of self-control, quite un-English. . . ."

One could depend on Lawrence hating any city he happened to find himself in. The first pages of *The Plumed Serpent* have the heroine, Kate Leslie, in a voice that is clearly the author's, expressing her fear of the city's repulsiveness, its wide dismal streets of asphalt and stone, men selling pulque and sweets, cakes, fruit, greasy food, little soldiers in washed-out cotton uniforms, pinky drab, hanging about aimlessly. "She had been in many cities of the world, but Mexico had an underlying ugliness, a sort of squalid evil, which made Naples seem debonair in comparison. She was afraid, she dreaded the thought that anything might really touch her in this town, and give her the contagion of its crawling evil."

The four engaged in a month of sight-seeing before making for Chapala, a small village on the lake about thirty-five miles from Guadalajara. From Mexico City they made sorties out to Puebla and the Orizaba. Lawrence's tendency to vacillate was never more acute than during this month. An ominous symptom of this was a cold or something worse. On short trips to Cholula and Atlixco both the Lawrences were unwell.

Bynner noted on April 19 that Lawrence had revived somewhat "but cursed the land and despaired of its people. . . . If ever there was a sick soul it is his. . . . Poor Frieda!" He concluded that this man was a mass of superstitions, and to think of him as an intellectual was ludicrous. Postcards were being shot off in all directions. "Had enough of the New World," he wrote to Murry, asking him, "Have you thought of a house for me in the country? I want to come back." A letter to the Danes admitted sadly, "When I feel sick I want to go back. When I feel well I want to stay." Whatever it was that ailed him, and whether or not he was beset by superstition, he had somehow to be true to himself, to his feelings. On April 22, back in the city after visiting Teotihuacán and being deeply im-

pressed by the pyramids and the Temple of Quetzalcoatl, with its series of sculptured heads, one representing the "feathered serpent"
Quetzalcoatl himself, he told Eddie Marsh, "We are still in Mexico,
I tip-toe for a leap to Europe, and then hold back—don't quite
know why."

Frieda thought she knew. "When he finds a place by himself he
always likes it," she said to a skeptical Bynner. "He will be writing
again there. He will be happier."

So it turned out. He went off reconnoitering by himself, and on
May 1 cabled them from Lake Chapala. It was paradise, he said. He
had rented a *hacienda* and would wait for them there.

Before that, there had been the disastrous visit to the bullfight in
the Mexico City stadium, which in due course was written up in all
its gory horror in the opening pages of *The Plumed Serpent*. Bynner,
pilloried as Owen, "a born American, and if anything was on show
he had to see it" (because it was Life), was hardly likely to write the
subsequent account of his journey with Lawrence objectively, and
by 1951 his reputation as a poet had dwindled and Lawrence was in-
ternationally famous. Villiers in the novel, the young partner of
Owen, "was out after a thrill," but coldly. Even Kate is at first keen
to see the spectacle. "Like most modern people, she had a will-to-
happiness." This soon changes for her when the audience, "already
a mob," begins the game of grabbing hard straw hats and skimming
them away down the raked seats to jeering shouts from the mob as
more and more join in. The democrat in Bynner-Owen wants to see
it as fun, though secretly "he hated common rowdiness" just as
much as Kate now did. "I really hate common people," she says angrily. Owen, a champagne socialist, has to disagree with her, though
he is now uneasy. Then oranges and banana skins are being thrown.
"How I detest them!" says Kate.

Nevertheless she had come half expecting to be impressed by the
age-old ritual of bull sacrifice, derived from ancient rites. Instead
she gazes down on the four precious toreadors, looking like eunuchs
"with their rather fat posteriors and their squiffs of pigtails and their

clean-shaven faces." So these are the heroes, the darlings of the mob! But there is worse to come. An old blindfolded horse bearing a rider who shoves his lance into a bull's shoulder is suddenly gored. "Down went the horse, collapsing in front, but his rear still heaved up, with the bull's horn working vigorously up and down inside him. . . . And a huge heap of bowels coming out. And a nauseous stench. And the cries of pleased amusement from the crowd." Kate has had enough. Feeling a real pang of hatred against the Americanism of her companions "which is coldly and unscrupulously sensational," she walks out into a crashing rainstorm.

When they meet later at the hotel, Owen tries to tell her that though some of it was indeed awful she had missed some really pretty feats by the toreadors. Kate tells him what she thinks. "It's just a performance of human beings torturing animals. . . . Dirty little boys maiming flies—that's what they are. . . . Oh. I wish I could be a bull, just for five minutes. . . . Call that manliness? Then thank God a million times that I'm a woman, and know poltroonery and dirty-mindedness when I see it."

A FORMER poetry student of Bynner's from Berkeley lived in Guadalajara, and she was Lawrence's contact when he ventured off by himself to find somewhere remote but safe in the turmoil of a Mexican society torn apart by the revolutions and civil wars of 1911 and 1920. The country was still unstable, teetering on chaos, bandits roaming at will in certain areas. Near Guadalajara, northwest of Mexico City, was Mexico's largest lake, Lake Chapala.

Idella Purnell, a young woman living with her father, met Lawrence for the first time and found him delightful company. He entertained her with his mimicry, ranging from an imaginary bicycle rider, running round squeaking "Ting-a-ling-a-ling," to a presentation of Ezra Pound with his bemused mother and father from the Midwest trying to cope with the London literati.

In *The Plumed Serpent* the little lake resort of Chapala is called

Sayula. Kate Leslie, arriving by boat, sees first the white fluted towers of the church above the pepper trees: beyond lie the corrugated
mountains of Mexico. She thinks how peaceful it looks and delicate,
almost Japanese. "As she drew nearer she saw the beach with the
washing spread on the sand; the fleecy green willow trees and pepper trees, and the villas in foliage and flowers, hanging magenta curtains of bougainvillea, red dots of hibiscus, pink abundance of tall
oleander trees: occasional palm trees sticking out." Clearly it is a resort, with a few seats, a booth selling drinks, a little promenade,
white boats drawn up on a sandy beach, and several women sitting
under parasols; even a few bathers in the lake. On the stone jetty is
daubed in black letters an advertisement for car tires. Kate thinks it
not too savage, yet not overcivilized, somewhat down-at-heel but in
contact with the world, just about. It would suit her purposes, and
Lawrence evidently thought the same.

His book, begun around May 10, was written in two parts, broken off when it was half finished and not taken up again for eighteen
months, after he had been to Europe and come back again. Critics
in general have found the novel the hardest to swallow of all his
works, some judging it to be his biggest failure, others admiring his
audacious attempt to create a fictional Mexico transformed by the
resurrection of the ancient Aztec gods, in a land ruled by a military
dictatorship. None disputed that it was an intensely religious book,
notwithstanding its fascist overtones, with hymns and rituals all
imagined by the author. When you have read it, wrote Katherine
Anne Porter in the *New York Herald-Tribune*, "you will realize the
catastrophe that has overtaken Lawrence." Needless to say, he
thought it his most important book to date. And it exhausted him
more than any other. What is certain is that if he had written his expeditions in Mexico as a travel book it would have been acclaimed as
one of his finest, with its descriptive passages of unsurpassed beauty
and subtlety.

To prepare for it he read widely, though he was already familiar
with Prescott. Idella Purnell provided him with Bernal Díaz's *True*

History of the Conquest of Mexico, and he obtained the Everyman edition of Frances Calderon de la Barca's *Life in Mexico*. Some of the most attractive aspects of the novel were drawn from his surroundings and experience of life in Chapala, living as he did in a house which came complete with a native family. Getting to know them intimately, he was able to root his novel in a reality that was far removed from the fantasia of his vision.

In the novel the housekeeper, Juana, lives in a sort of den at the back of the Calle Zaragoza with her two daughters and two sons. Juana, a widow is about forty, short, her face dark and full, "with centerless dark eyes, untidy hair and a limping way of walking." Slovenly she might be, but Kate has been assured by the hotel owner that she is honest. At the outset she insists on addressing the white woman, Kate, as Nina—child. Soon Kate is fond of the "limping, untidy Juana, and of the two girls. Concha was fourteen, a thick, heavy barbaric girl with a mass of black waving hair which she was always scratching. Maria was eleven, a shy, thin, bird-like thing with big eyes that seemed to absorb the light round her." Jesús, the eldest son, lives and works mainly at the hotel. "And though, to order, he wore a black Fascisti shirt, he had the queer animal jeering of the socialists, an instinct for pulling things down." Ezequiel is different, a finer type. "He was slender and so erect that he almost curved backwards. He was very shy, *farouche*. Proud also, and more responsible to his family. . . . Shyly greeting Kate as he passed. He was a gentle man in his barbarism." At night the fear in the house is almost palpable. Ezequiel elects to sleep on a straw mat on the brick veranda outside Kate's door and guard her from possible robbers. He is seventeen but proud as a lion with his new duty. His tremendous snoring on the first night startles her, but she is comforted by the wild strength of the noise.

At Chapala, Lawrence and Frieda lived at the Calle Zaragoza, with Bynner and Johnson close by in the hotel. Lawrence could now get down to work, and his routine was a familiar one. Living barefoot in shorts and trousers, he sat under a pepper tree with a view of the lake and wrote. Afternoons were a time for them all to meet on the beach, and sometimes Bynner would entertain them in his room at the Hotel Arzopalom, serving up martinis. They went in a group or separately on excursions up the lake, and there are passages of hypnotic beauty in *The Plumed Serpent* describing late evenings on water that was so "frail-rippling, sperm-like."

From observing day by day his acquired family he extrapolated with his usual rapidity the basic sardonic attitudes of the Mexican Indian,

> careless about the past, careless about the present, careless about the future. They had even no interest in money. Whatever they got they spent in a minute, and forgot it again. . . . Without aim or purpose they lived absolutely *à terre*, down on the dark, volcanic earth. So in the black eyes of the family lay a certain vicious fear and wonder and misery. The misery of human beings who squat helpless outside their own unbuilt selves, unable to win their souls out of chaos, and indifferent to all other victories.

And if they were soulless, so were white people now. "But they have conquered the lower worlds of metal and energy, so they whizz around in machines, circling the void of their own emptiness." This was Kate, a fusion of Lawrence and Frieda, but to Baroness Anna von Richthofen on May 31 her English son-in-law was saying much the same:

> They are half civilized, half wild. If they only had a new faith, a new hope, they would perhaps be a new, young, beautiful people. But as Christians they don't get any further, are inwardly melancholy, live without hope. . . . Yet they are also good, can be gentle and honest, are very quiet and are not at all greedy for money. And I find that wonderful . . . where the whites are attached only to money and possessions. But not the peon. He really hasn't got this fever to possess, that is the remaining, actual world weariness with us.

He promised to send her a lovely *serape* for her birthday.

Meanwhile he sat down under a pepper tree to imagine a new faith and a new hope that would enable them to cast off their indifference and be reborn, a young, beautiful new race. It was an extraordinary task, and he was alight with it.

Kate was learning, as was Lawrence, that her servants "were the clue to all the native life. . . ." Juana, like Lawrence's own maid-of-all-work, after she had accepted the Lawrences as part of her family, seems to bear them no grudge as white foreigners. It was the *gringos*, the Americans, who took everything away from Mexico. In fact the grudge went deeper, against all white people, rich people, superior people. They exempted the *Niña*, but Juana protests too much, thinks Kate. They want to drive her off, too, "they couldn't help it. Like the Irish, they could cut off their noses to spite their face."

AFTER THE ASSASSINATION of Emiliano Zapata in 1919 (the murder of that other legendary figure, Pancho Villa, would happen during Lawrence's time in Chapala), Mexico now had a coalition and a socialist president, Alvaro Obregón, and programs were under way for the redistribution of the land and a campaign to attack mass illiteracy. Lawrence in Mexico City had seen the frescoes of Diego Rivera and José Orozco and thought them ugly. He had arguments with Bynner who believed there should be a reform of Mexico along Russian lines. These ideals, Lawrence said, were simply imports, like Spanish Catholicism itself, and yet another example of "the great paleface overlay."

As he got down to work on *The Plumed Serpent* he sought to fashion an alternative that would be true to Mexican-Indian culture. Only too aware of the more grisly aspects of Aztec history with its repulsive violence and cruelty, he created a leader of the Quetzalcoatl movement who was a living reincarnation of this most humane of the Aztec gods. David Ellis refers to Lawrence's trip to the pyramids and temple at Teotihuacán, twenty-eight miles from Mexico City, and comments, "This ancient site of what is likely to have been in its time the world's greatest theocracy would have impressed a visitor such as Lawrence in any circumstances."

Kate Leslie in the novel wonders at the separation of the sexes, so different from her own culture. Watching them on the beach, in the village, and in her own house, she sees there was none of the mingling that takes place at home. For one thing, "the men and women never walked their sex abroad, as white people do." The men have strangely fluctuating moods, working in fits and starts, sitting on the ground in groups "like Arabian nights," laughing together. Then suddenly under a cloud, relapsing "into numb gloom." Men and women "seemed always to be turning their backs to one another, as if they didn't want to see one another. No flirting, no courting. Only an occasional quick, dark look, the signal of a weapon-like desire. . . ."

Most astonishing is the behavior on the beach. The native women, wearing their chemise or small skirt, will be occupied in bathing at one end of the beach while the men absolutely ignore them. "They didn't even look the other way. It was the women bathing, that was all." There the women sit in their isolation in the shallow water like waterfowl, dipping gourd scoops into the lake and pouring water over their heads. The men are clearly dominant but the women seem in no way downtrodden, going their own way, wrapped in their *rebozos* "as in their own darkness." So far as marriage is concerned, the men seem to hold back from any real giving of themselves. They are gentle and protective to the small children. Then they forget them.

"Often a single man would stand alone at a street corner in his *serape*, motionless for hours, like some powerful specter." If they stand together in loose groups they are mostly silent, hardly ever touching each other. On the benches of the *plaza* they will sit for hours impassively, saying nothing. "Each one isolated in his own fate, his eyes black and quick like a snake's, and as blank."

Marriage, thinks Kate, will always be a casual thing here. Perhaps some powerful relationship of man to man might happen. And here we see Lawrence moving toward the dramatizing of his main theme of a religion calling for new men, with at its head two leaders, Ramon and Cipriano: the reincarnated god in living form, and the enforcer of a new order. One of the written hymns of Quetzalcoatl, distributed as a leaflet, proclaims:

> The stars and the earth and the sun and the moon and the winds
> Are about to dance the war dance round you, men!
> When I say the word, they will start. . . .
> They are saying to one another: Let us make an end
> Of those ill-smelling tribes of men, these frogs that can't jump,
> These cocks that can't crow
> These pigs that can't grunt
> This flesh that smells
> These money vermin.
>
> Let us have a spring cleaning in the world.
> For men upon the body of the earth are like lice,
> Devouring the earth into sores. . . .
> So tell the men I am coming to,
> To make themselves clean, inside and out.
> To roll the grave-stone off their souls, from the cave of their bellies,
> To prepare to be men.

Kate, baffled, cannot understand why there is no energy, no sign of passionate life. Strength there is in plenty. "She had seen an Indian trotting down a street with a piano on his back," supporting it by a band round his forehead. The women carry large burdens with a band round the breast. If there *is* passionate life, it leaves out the individual, she concludes. "Sex itself was a powerful, potent thing, not to be played with or paraded. The one mystery. And a mystery greater than the individual."

Bynner in his memoir commented—however unreliable his testimony was as to detail—that when Frieda, Bynner, and Johnson swam from the beach in the afternoons, Lawrence hung back, unwilling to expose his poor physique. A group of young boys whom the two Americans had gotten to know would invariably gather round, and in Bynner's narrative Lawrence objected that his friends were acting idiotically in romping with them. "Don't you realize how dirty these little chits are?" he is said to have protested. "They begin early down here doing everything." Far from suggesting that the Americans might be pederasts, he did no more than warn them of diseases these boys might be carrying. Bynner, as he completed his memoir in 1949, wrote to Idella Purnell that "I do not think the term homosexual, with its loose applications, should be applied to him."

IT WAS FRIEDA, with her fears of being in a village guarded by a squad of soldiers and having a young boy with a revolver sleeping outside her door, who called a halt to the novel and insisted they return to Europe. Their battles were intensifying, she had no occupation to absorb her as he did, and she wanted to see her children and her mother. Intimations of a new uprising in the country did not seem to bother Lawrence. He wrote airily to Adele Seltzer that "The place is a sort of no-man's land as far as security goes," and told Merrild with false bravado, "If I can't stand Europe we'll come back to Mexico and stick knives and revolvers in our belts."

With their quarrels worsening by the day, Frieda would take no account of her husband's reluctance to leave Mexico. His soul may have been like Balaam's ass, as he was fond of saying, but when Frieda dug in her heels there was no one more stubborn. Whether he liked it or not, she was going to Europe. After saying to Mabel in Taos that she should leave Lawrence for good if she was going to survive, she was now saying it to Bynner.

They were distracted by Bynner's illness, an infected anal fistula that needed surgery in a Guadalajara hospital. In Chapala again after visiting the American in hospital, his "thoughtful tenderness" appreciated by the patient, Lawrence left with Frieda on July 9 to begin the tortuous journey north. They had planned originally to go to New York by sea from Veracruz but changed direction because of the threat of dock strikes. Crossing the frontier at Laredo they went on to San Antonio and then New Orleans, which Lawrence found a "steaming, heavy, rather dead town."

Again their plans changed. Unwilling to join a ship to New York packed with holiday-makers, they got on a train to Washington. Lawrence, when he wrote to Knud Merrild, had expected to be at his destination by July 15, but he was still four days away. His tone veered between gloom and hope. He didn't expect to like the East. As for England, "It is no good, I know I am European. So I may as well go back and try it once more." He made no mention of the fact that he was going under duress. The comparative success of the communal experiment at Del Monte encouraged him to hope that they would all live together again somewhere. "The 'world' has no life to offer. Seeing things doesn't amount to much. We have to be a few men of honor and fearlessness, and make a life together. There is nothing else, believe me."

Once in New York they moved out to rural New Jersey, to a cottage near Morris Plains that his publisher had rented for the Lawrences and themselves. While the Seltzers commuted to their New York office, Lawrence and Frieda walked about in the country and waited for vacancies on the heavily booked ocean liners. The holiday season was in full swing, New York impossibly hot. Even before leaving Chapala they had apparently agreed that Frieda should go to Europe alone, but as late as August 7, having bought tickets for them both, Lawrence was still changing and unchanging his mind. His letter to Catherine Carswell at this late date said, as definitely as he was able, "I'm not coming to Europe after all. Find I just don't want to—not yet." He had discussed with Frieda his vague plan of going west again, perhaps to join up with the Danes in Los Angeles, perhaps to sail the Pacific, an old dream that refused to lie down.

Still waiting for a liner, he was dragged into literary luncheons and dinners by the Seltzers, who thought it was important for him to be visible. At one dinner, asked by Garrison Villard, owner of the *Nation*, what he thought should be done about the world, he said through gritted teeth, "I thought, Mr. Villard, you understood that I hoped it would go to pieces as rapidly and completely as possible." Later, with Frieda gone, giving an interview to the *New York Evening Post*, no doubt with his wife in mind, he said that women's inertia had probably saved the world from destroying itself. As for himself, his quest for a thread of belief was a religious one.

Finally on August 18, 1923, he saw Frieda off on the *Orbita*, after what Catherine Carswell claimed (though she was not there) was perhaps the worst quarrel of their life together. If this did happen on the quay it seems strange that neither he nor she referred to it specifically. There was no doubt that Frieda was sick of their eternal warring, as she was of his mulish obstinacy, and her letter to Adele Seltzer, whom she felt was an ally, confirms this. "I feel so cross with Lawrence, when I hear him talk about loyalty—Pah, he only thinks of himself— I am glad to be alone and will not go back to his eternal hounding me, it's too ignominious! I will not stand his bad temper any more if I never see him again—I wrote him so—he can go to blazes, I have had enough."

This was a week after she had sailed. On the day of her sailing he wrote to Amy Lowell, "I ought to have gone to England. I wanted to go. But my inside self wouldn't let me. At the moment I just can't face my own country again. It makes me feel unhappy, like a terrible load." He said he felt jeered at by New Yorkers. "But that is literary." His old dream surfaced again: he would go out West, and if he could get a sailing ship of some sort, out to sea.

To Murry he was more specific about his reasons for staying, aware of Murry's objection to Frieda: "I ought to come, but I can't. . . . F. wants to see her children. And you know, wrong or not, I can't stomach the chasing of those Weekley children." A week later he was asking Murry, as well as Koteliansky and Catherine Carswell, to look after his wife in London. Behind Lawrence's reluctance to accompany her may have been the fact that Frieda's elder daughter had turned twenty-one and was legally free to see her mother whenever she wished.

Those biographers who have seen the separation as potentially permanent find the letter he wrote to Frieda in November especially significant. In it he says, "Don't bother about money—when I come we'll make a regular arrangement for you to have money if you wish. I told you the bank was to transfer a hundred pounds to you." The improvement in his financial position made it feasible for them to live separately or not, just as they wanted. But they had told each other they were through many times before, and a hundred pounds would not have taken her very far. She depended on him for money, and on his assistance in helping her mother and other relatives in a Germany bankrupted by the war. Any separation would have to wait for his return. "When I come" could be seen as giving in to her will, in spite of all his efforts to get her to submit to him.

6

Some Strange Raw Splendor

(1923–1924)

As he said goodbye to the Seltzers and began roaming westward alone on the morning of August 22, he seemed determined to make the best of things and enjoy his freedom. He was entering one of the strangest periods of his life. For a decade he and Frieda had been together as a couple more or less continually, and the picture of him living alone on a daily basis for the foreseeable future is one hard to envisage. Curious this period certainly was.

On his way to join up with the Danes he made first for Buffalo, where he was a guest for five days of Bessie Freeman, Mabel's childhood friend. Mabel's mother too lived here, and he reported to Seltzer that he was lunching with her before a trip to Niagara Falls. He was a tourist, out to enjoy himself as tourists were supposed to do. "You would hardly know me," he wrote with wry self-mockery, "I am so well-behaved. A perfect chameleon." But inside, the same sphinx looking out. What surprised him was the town itself, which he felt to be genuinely American as New York never was. Being there was an odd feeling, like walking around in the books of Elizabeth Gaskell, and yet the old-fashioned feeling was somehow nice, nice middle-class, "BOURgeois." He walked about in a state of wonder, wrapped around in nostalgia, in a town that was like Manchester sixty years ago—"or Nottingham." He signed off with "*Vamos*" ("Let's go!"), a call to himself, and on August 27 he was on the move again.

He reached Chicago and changed trains, glad to leave a city where it "rained and fogged . . . and floods of muddy-flowing people oozed thick in the canyon-beds of the streets," heading on the Union Pacific through Salt Lake City to Los Angeles. There his two artist friends met him at the station, where they had parked their old Ford. Merrild put him up for a night in his rooming house on West Twenty-Seventh Street, before he moved on August 31 into the Hotel Miramar in Santa Monica. He learned from his young friends that after some work at the film studios and a spell of house painting they were getting by with the help of a patron, a geologist in Brentwood who had commissioned them to paint murals on the wall of his library.

To combat the new aimlessness of his days and nights without Frieda he turned to his solution for many ills, work. As well as reviews for the *Nation* and Murry's *Adelphi*, he had with him Mollie Skinner's manuscript of her novel *The House of Ellis*. It had arrived from Australia a few days before he left New York, and he wrote to the author from the Miramar to say that he had read it carefully, found it full of good stuff that needed pulling together, and would rewrite it and publish it as their collaboration if she agreed. "If you give me a free hand I'll see if I can't make a complete book out of it." If not, he would do his best to find a publisher for it as it stood, "but I'm afraid there isn't much chance." Instead of waiting for her agreement he set to work at once on what would become *The Boy in the Bush*. He badly needed an occupation for the three weeks he was in Los Angeles. On the eve of departure he told Adele Seltzer that people were very nice to him there but he found Southern California "a very selfish place." People cared about "*nothing* but just the moment. But also that can be pleasant."

"Restless and lonesome" he may well have appeared to Merrild at this time, but he was still able to indulge in caustic fun at the expense of *A Second Contemporary Verse Anthology*, which he reviewed for the *New York Evening Post Literary Review*. And for all the derision, the old insistence on allowing the demon inside one to have its say was still there:

> *Why do I think of stairways*
> *With a rush of hurt surprise?*

Heaven knows, my dear, unless you once fell down.

"My heart aches," says Keats, and you bet it's no joke. The element of danger. Man is always, all the time and for ever on the brink of the unknown. The minute you realize this, you prick your ears in alarm. And the minute any man steps alone, with his whole naked self, emotional and mental, into the everlasting hinterland of consciousness, you hate him and you wonder over him. Why can't he stay cozily playing word-games around the camp fire?

THERE IS SOMETHING comic and sad about his attempt to lend a hand with the Danes' mural painting, simply because, one suspects, he always hated to feel excluded. At a loose end in spite of his work on the Australian novel, he went on a trip with Merrild and Gotzsche to look at a total eclipse of the sun from a vantage point near Carmel. He organized a visit for them all to see a production of *Aida*, including in the party a Danish couple his friends knew. This was so uncharacteristic that it could only have been a result of his loneliness, as was his appearance at a Hollywood reception for an actor. For his last fortnight in Los Angeles he rented a room on Grand Avenue, close to the Danes.

He was still there when Bessie Freeman forwarded a cable for him from Mabel, who was now married to her Indian, Tony. If this was an attempt at a reconciliation, it produced no response. He was hanging on for news from Frieda, hopefully to say that she would soon be joining him. When only one brief letter came, her plans were too vague for him to include them in his own. Perhaps because of his bitter disappointment he came up with the bizarre idea of joining a ship as cook, with his Danish friends signing on as seamen. When this fell on stony ground, he aimed once more for Mexico, vaguely intending to look for a farm to rent there. Here he hit a new snag. Merrild, objecting to Lawrence's bossiness and believing he would soon change his mind yet again and return to England, preferred to stay where he was. The more relaxed Gotzsche, who was nearer Lawrence's age, agreed to go, and the "odd couple" set out on September 25 in the old Ford, making a detour on the way to the border to call on Bessie Freeman in Palm Springs. The day before they left the city Lawrence had told his wife that he could not see himself going to Europe in any case. "I've turned in my return ticket to New York, to get the money back," he wrote, ending, "I wish I heard from you again before I left—Don't stay longer in Europe if you don't want to." Under the apparent defiance was a forlorn acknowledgment that he missed her badly and needed her with him.

With Gotzsche as his chauffeur, no doubt wondering how long it would be before he was also the writer's nurse, they drove down California to Palm Springs through "pale whitish desert—a bit deathly," then after missing Bessie Freeman pushed on through the "broken, lost, hopeless little towns" of lower California, and by September 27 came to the Mexican town of Guaymas on the west coast, en route to Guadalajara.

Wandering "slowly and hotly" with Gotzsche down the wild west coast, he must have seen it as an outward expression of the dismal, desolate season he was living through. At Navojoa he found its empty hopelessness hard to bear. "It makes one feel the door is shut on one," he wrote to Bynner. Under the blazing sun of October in a vast hot sky stood big lonely green hills and mountains, "a flat blazing earth—then little towns that seem to be slipping down an abyss." The two nomads went to look at haciendas—Lawrence still toyed with the idea of buying a place—and hated the weird, brutal atmosphere of a cattle ranch. "Many of the haciendas," he reported, "are in the hands of Chinese, who run about like vermin down this coast." Ending his letter, he mentioned a circus with lions roaring at night. He asked to be greeted to the Spoodle, Bynner's name for Johnson. "Don't take any notice of my intermittency."

Their travel plan was to take a boat from Mazatlan to Manzanillo, and so on to Guadalajara, but at Mazatlan they abandoned thoughts of a boat and headed inland via Tepic. The conditions became steadily more hazardous. A "stage," in fact a Ford car, took them on October 14 to Ixtlan. Next day they rode muleback over the mountains and down the barranca to La Quemeda, a beautiful ride but grueling, nine hours in the saddle. At La Quemeda there was no train because of a landslide which had carried away the track. The place was a railway camp. "A lot of ill-bred hounds who think they are engineers: louts and canaille. The S. Pacific is American, and a hateful concern. I was glad to get off it. It trails a sort of blight all down the west coast." He told Seltzer, not for the first time, that "Americanism is a disease or a vice or both."

With no accommodation available they slept in a shed and got up at dawn to clamber on more mules and ride for another six hours to Eyzatlan. Here they were able to climb aboard the Mexican National Railway and proceed in what must have felt like luxury, reaching Guadalajara on October 17, an epic journey of twenty-two days from Los Angeles.

Coming at last into the upland country he knew, he recovered his pleasure in the splendid landscape. "And I like so much the real Mexico again, where the Americans haven't canned all the life. At the depths of me," he said to Seltzer, "I hate the Americans. There is still some strange raw splendor in Mexico."

He collected mail from Idella Purnell's father which had been forwarded from Los Angeles, including one from Frieda canceling his request for her to join him by saying she wanted him to come to England. But now that he had reached his goal he thought he would stay at least for the winter. He was done with *The Boy in the Bush* and thought it should be published before "Quetzalcoatl," as *The Plumed Serpent* was still called. But the Mexican novel was the one he must finish now.

In his letter to Seltzer he wondered if *The Boy in the Bush* should be published under his name and Miss Skinner's jointly, or with a nom de plume. The ending, which he mentioned as "a bit startling," was his entirely and a complete departure from the original manuscript. Mollie Skinner would be dismayed by it. Jack, the hero, in a quandary because he is split between a wife and a mistress, proposes to have two wives. This from a writer who had no woman at all, and for a companion a worried Danish artist writing a week later to his fellow countryman, "I am avoiding Lawrence as much as possible at present, because considering all things he is really insane as he is now." And it is true that he was behaving weirdly, reluctant to go to Chapala now that Frieda was not there, writing in the mornings and then hanging about on a bench or drifting over to the marketplace like a lost soul. The word adrift would seem exactly right for his wifeless state.

Reiterating to the Purnells that in his opinion California was "a queer place—in a way it has turned its back on the world, and looks into the void Pacific. It is absolutely selfish, very empty, but not false," he was living now with his temporary partner in the Hotel Garcia in Guadalajara, and still harping on the idea of a place to live in. "Perhaps I shall find a little ranch here. Put a peg in the world, a new navel, a new center."

For Gotzsche the words no longer carried conviction. Lawrence was ominously subdued, not even quarreling with the Dane, who was left groping for communication with a man usually happy and excited when traveling. A snapshot reveals a Lawrence changed into a drab, shabby, melancholy figure. He did in the end consent to go to Chapala and the lake he had found so beautiful, but it had altered in a bewildering way. "Somehow it becomes unreal to me now," he told Gotzsche. And of course the missing element of reality that would have made all the difference was Frieda. Gotzsche, more perturbed than ever, wrote to Merrild, "You know his ways and how he bends his head far down, till his beard is resting on his chest and he says (not laughing) 'Hee, hee, hee' every time one talks to him. A cold stream always runs down my spine when he does that."

His deeply troubled state seems to have run straight into the penultimate chapter of *The Boy in the Bush*, in which the hero Jack Grant soliloquizes:

> They would like to destroy me, because I am not cold and like an ant, as they are. Mary would like me to be killed. Look at her face. . . . Even Monica, though she is my wife. Even she feels a judgment ought to descend on me. Because I'm not what she wants me to be. . . . And because she can't get beyond me. . . . It has always been so, ever since I was born.

It was easy to see, Jack concluded, that they all hated and wanted to kill the "non-conforming me. Which is me myself." Yet "they all love me extremely the moment they think I am in line with them." Their obtuseness baffles him. "I thought they would know the Lord was with me, and a certain new thing with me on the face of the earth." This messianic streak was being encouraged by Murry in London, who kept Lawrence posted with copies of his *Adelphi* and claimed that the journal existed chiefly to promulgate Lawrence's work. Work by him was in fact appearing in it with some regularity, together with references to him as "incomparably the most important English writer of his generation." In the October issue Murry published poems from *Birds, Beasts and Flowers* and hinted in his editorial on a change of direction for the magazine connected with the return of a "friend." Murry wrote to say that England had need of his leadership, and in terms that made it appear that he and Frieda, recently so opposed to each other, were now in full accord. If

Lawrence was being given an honorable way back, he was nevertheless wary of what lay behind it. On September 22 he had written to
Frieda, "I had your letter from London. *Don't trust 'em*—that's my
perpetual warning."

Gotzsche, still trying to fathom Lawrence's wavering instability,
reported that he and Lawrence had gone with the Purnells to look
at a small house Dr. Purnell owned in Ajijic, a village on the lake
near Chapala. Again Lawrence was put off by something he either
couldn't define or wouldn't admit. Somehow the lake had "gone
alien to me." Gotzsche was touched by Lawrence's moods of sweetness, when he was so overwhelmingly good and reasonable, yet in
other moods "he seems to be absolutely nuts . . . and to have a hard
time with himself. He is afraid Frieda will avoid him: he says that
she can have a house in London and have her children with her,
then he can travel alone. 'She will hate it before long,' he says, biting his lower lip and nodding small, quick nods. The fact is that he
is afraid she will like that arrangement only too well. Nevertheless
he has a large heart and means well, but his ideas are so impractical
that it is doubtful he will get anyone to accept them."

This was a shrewd assessment by a man genuinely concerned
and alarmed by someone he had come to value as a friend. Ironi-
cally, on the very day he was writing to Merrild of Lawrence's spasmodic reasonableness, Lawrence wrote on November 10 to his
mother-in-law in terms that were, on the face of it, utterly unbend-
ing and bellicose. Perhaps, thinks Aldington, he was sounding Teu-
tonic in an attempt to flatter the old lady, though she was in fact as
much French as German. He fumed that it was stupid of Frieda to
say and keep saying that she loved him in spite of how he was. "I am
after all no Christ lying on his mother's lap. I go my way through
the world, and if F. finds it very hard to love me, then, dear God, let
her give love a rest, give it a holiday." His mother-in-law understood, as did his mother, "that man does not need, does not ask for
love from his wife, but strength, strength, strength. . . . And the stupid woman always sings love! love! love! . . . England is so *peaceful*,

writes Frieda. Shame on you, that today you ask for peace. I want no peace: I go about the world fighting. Pfui! In the grave I will find my peace. First let me fight and win through." Signing off as the "half-hero," he enclosed Christmas money for herself and Frieda's sister Else, and for the son of her younger sister, Johanna, or "Nusch."

Idella Purnell, though only in her early twenties, had started a novel incorporating the visit of the Lawrences with Bynner and Johnson to Chapala after they had left in the summer. When he returned in October she presumably sought Lawrence's advice, for the title "Friction" was suggested by him. In her novel the Lawrences appear as Edmund and Gertrude. The disoriented Lawrence she observed on his second visit led her to see him as helplessly in thrall to his wife. She writes in her novel that Gertrude "knew that her beloved man had become her beloved child, and that he could never leave her. . . . She felt however that she should leave him, for such a shock might make him finally draw himself together and become self-dependent."

Far from strengthening his self-reliance, Frieda's absence was bringing him to the point of acquiescing in his defeat, even if he was not about to admit it to her. Nor was he likely to admit that Jack Grant in *The Boy in the Bush* had the manly health he would have wished to enjoy himself. Before setting off with Gotsche for Mexico City and then the long journey to rejoin her, he would only say that he would rather be "staying the winter on a ranch somewhere. . . . I still don't believe in Europe, England, efforts, restfulness, *Adelphis* or any of that. The egg is addled. But I'll come back to say how do you do to it all."

Again the parallel with Stevenson is striking. Lawrence's English friends saw London as the center of the literary world, with him lost in the wilderness, wasting his talent in "out of the way places." In fact he had already left them behind, a world writer with seven books published in America and translations under way in many foreign languages without effort on his part. If England was to lead the world again, he told one friend, "she's got to pick up a lost trail. And the end of the lost trail is here in Mexico."

Before leaving Mexico City he received a conciliatory letter from Mabel, forwarded from Guadalajara, to which he replied with a friendly letter of his own. He was just packing to leave the following morning. He welcomed the change in her that she mentioned, and said he had changed too. Who was deceiving whom? As for the hostile world, he was more cunning than she, and "one must be a serpent as far as the world is concerned." He was being naive: whatever else had changed in Mabel, one could be sure that her cunning had not. But here she was pledging her loyalty, and he was grateful to have her standing behind him. He was thinking no doubt of Frieda's disloyalty in deserting him. "I need someone to stand behind me, badly." The important thing for him was that the way was clear for him to return to New Mexico if that was what he wanted.

Having made it up with Mabel, he was ready to leave for England on the *Toledo* on November 22, 1923, from Veracruz. Though he sounded detached in his letters to Frieda, it was a humiliating moment. For years he had preached that the husband should lead and the wife be prepared to follow. Crushed by her intransigence and now returning in response to her summons was, as David Ellis puts it, "one more consequence of that overly dependent temperament for which, with increasing bitterness after 1919, he was always inclined to hold his mother responsible."

APPROACHING PLYMOUTH in damp and fog, an English December about to pounce, he stood in the cold darkness of the winter evening remembering the day, four years ago, when he had departed. After what seemed a decade away, he stood in the prow of the *Toledo* as it entered the English Channel approaches and saw, like a message, the faint spark of the Land's End light.

He had made up with Murry as well as Mabel, but "making up" did not mean that he trusted Murry. He preferred not to think of what might have taken place during his absence. He knew Murry's character, and that he was now, since Katherine's death, unattached. As recently as April he had seduced the reclusive deaf painter Dorothy Brett, described by Lawrence in a letter to his mother-in-law as "a little simple but harmless." She carried a comical-looking ear-trumpet for her deafness and was the daughter of Viscount Esher. Lawrence had met her in his wartime London days. Murry's evasiveness told Brett that Murry had no intention of marrying her, but she was in love and in the habit of confiding her feelings to her diary in the form of letters to her dead friend Katherine Mansfield.

Many women found Murry attractive, including Frieda, who had spoken years ago of his "dangerous mouth." Catherine Carswell, never an admirer of Frieda, thought the attraction was bound up for Frieda with the fact that he was "somebody" in literary London. When Frieda arrived in England alone she lived in a one-room apartment on Pond Street, in a house where the Lawrences' friend Mark Gertler also lived. Gertler, himself consumptive, had no more love for Frieda than had Koteliansky, and wrote spitefully to the Russian lawyer that "She is worse than she might be because she apes Lawrence and his ideas coming out of her large German body sound silly and vulgar."

He was clever at mimicking her gutteral enthusiasms: "The country is so Real, the land is so *Real*, and the people are so REAL!" And after months of treatment in a sanatorium in the north he had no time for Lawrence's refusal to admit that he himself was probably tubercular. Frieda, he thought, was complicit in this, never urging him to take more care of himself. He would have been confirmed in his belief that Frieda was stupid if he had known of her reaction to Katherine Mansfield's death. Katherine's death had been brought about, Frieda declared to Adele Seltzer, because "she chose a death road and dare not face reality."

Gertler, positioned in the house where Frieda lived, was able to tell Koteliansky that Murry's coming and going made him wonder what else was going on. When Frieda left to visit her mother,

Murry, supposedly on his way to Switzerland, traveled with her as far as Paris. A disgusted Koteliansky at once suspected the worst. He had advised Frieda to wait for Lawrence in Germany, and evidently informed his friend in America that Murry was accompanying her. When Lawrence heard from Murry in Switzerland he could only answer, "From Frieda not a word—suppose Germany has swallowed her."

Whatever happened on the Continent between the two travelers has remained unclear. At the age of sixty-six Murry was writing nostalgically to Frieda in New Mexico to ask "for my own private satisfaction—it shall be buried afterward—did you love me as much as I loved you in those queer days? It drove me crazy—really crazy, I think—wanting you so badly: the comfort and delight of you, and then feeling Oh God, but Lorenzo will never get over it. I musn't, I must *not*." So it seems that he did hold back, whether for Lawrence's sake or to avoid taking his place is hard to say. Everyone knew that the Lawrences were at a crossroads and she was perhaps casting about for a new provider. Those who knew Murry would not have believed him capable of having the nerve for it. And whatever misgivings Frieda had about her husband's rages, she knew he was the last person to be unfaithful. And after all, he had been tested enough.

Whatever had or had not quite happened, Frieda was not someone to have regrets. She went unashamedly with Murry to meet her husband off the boat train. In a letter to Koteliansky with his implied criticism of her behavior, she blazed that "When you say Lawrence has loved me I have loved him a thousand times more! And to really love includes everything, intelligence and faith and sacrifice—and passion!" There was not only a world of men, she went on, but another world, "a deeper one, where life itself flows, there I am at home!"

Lawrence with his famous intuition saw at once that something had changed, and that there was a new relationship between his wife and Murry. Murry has described Lawrence's "greenish pallor" at

Waterloo Station, which Aldington interprets as "livid jealousy." His feelings can be guessed, but what he said was, "I can't bear it."

Almost at once he was ill and in bed, gazing at Morris wallpaper and drinking tea from willow pattern cups. To Bynner in Santa Fe he sent a message in telegraphese: "Gloom—yellow air—bad cold—bed—old house . . . D.H.L. perfectly miserable, as if he was in his tomb."

Once back on his feet, he could not believe how England had shrunk when he looked around, the mild English voices filling his ears with their complacency. Here he was on an island "no bigger than a back garden, chock-full of people who never realize there is anything outside their back garden, pretending to run the destinies of the world. It is pathetic and ridiculous."

And for all his personal animus against America when he was there, he was maddened by the anti-Americanism he heard. "These poor 'superior' gentry, all that is left to them is to blame the Americans. It amazes me, the rancor. . . . Just because the republican eagle of the west doesn't choose to be a pelican for other people's convenience. Why should it?" He unpacked the gifts in his luggage—a snow leopard skin, a belt of plaited horsehair, and a Mexican pot—and sat down in 1924 to write a group of virulent anti-Murry short stories, the finest of which, "Jimmy and the Desperate Woman," is devastating in its deadly accuracy.

Dorothy Brett, eager to be included in Lawrence's circle, invited Murry, Koteliansky, Gertler, and the Lawrences to Christmas dinner at her little Queen Anne house in Hampstead. In January 1924 she was entertaining Lawrence and Frieda in her sitting room and was a witness, perhaps for the first time, to one of his frightening outbursts of violence. It may have been brought on by him holding forth about Ramon, the Mexican leader in his half-finished novel who identified himself with Quetzalcoatl. Frieda, unable to stomach what she saw as his preposterous egotism and his utter foolishness in making "a god of himself," told him to shut up. Her husband, enraged, snatched up a poker and demolished the cups and saucers, abusing Frieda in the broad dialect he sometimes used in these quarrels and saying, "Beware, Frieda, if you ever talk to me like that again it will not be the tea things I smash but your head."

Frieda, knowing he would do no such thing, looked suitably contemptuous. Instead she swept up the debris and threw it in the refuse bin, then asked Dorothy Brett how much they owed her. Lawrence, his mood already changed, patted their host's hand and murmured that Frieda shouldn't make him so angry.

In his work at least he could exercise real power. There is no need to wonder about the model for Jimmy in "Jimmy and the Desperate Woman." Aldington describes the story as a masterpiece of ruthless satire, which makes it sound cold and heartless. For all its efficient and total demolition of the hero, it is instinct with subtle feeling and superbly sardonic insights. Murry is immediately recognizable in the story's opening which describes Jimmy as "editor of a high-class, rather highbrow, rather successful magazine, and his rather personal editorials brought him shoals, swarms, hosts of admiring acqaintances." Needless to say, these fans are nearly always female.

Even physically there is no mistake. Jimmy is handsome, his face endowed with a strong chin and slightly arched nose, the dark-gray eyes quite beautiful with their long lashes under the thick black brows. Now thirty-five, he is on the lookout for "the right sort of woman." In his circumstances he meets plenty of women of the sophisticated sort, but he has a dream, an ideal of the kind of simple, womanly woman to whom he would be "a sort of Solomon of wisdom" with his worldly experience. This woman would certainly be unsophisticated, and in the reaches of his imagination wild-blooded. Someone who might cancel out his clever ex-wife, whose words still ring in his ears and taunt him. She has forecast that he will soon fall on some woman's bosom. "That's the worst of him. If he could only stand alone for five minutes. But he can't."

Into the net of his mail swims Mrs. Emilia Pinnegar, who writes from a mining village in Yorkshire. His eye for talent tells him that she is the genuine article. He sees, reading between the lines of her poems, that she is of course unhappily married, and he comes alert. Could this be she? "The Coal-miner" says it all:

> The donkey-engine's beating noise
> And the rattle, rattle of the sorting screens
> Come down on me like the beat of his heart,
> And mean the same as his breathing means. . . .

> That is the manner of man he is.
> I married him and I should know.
> The mother earth from bowels of coal
> Brought him forth for the overhead woe.

Jimmy, who has scarcely been north of Oxford, corresponds and then comes out with it. He is off to lecture in Sheffield—may he call on her? He had already begun insinuating his way into the woman's confidence, until she tells him, "You ask me about myself, but what shall I say? I am a woman of thirty-one, with one child, a girl of eight, and I am married to a man who lives in the same house with me, but goes to another woman."

So the coast is clear: he sets off. He understands from her grim, dignified poems that his dream of a Tess of the d'Urbervilles will have to be amended. This woman has something desperate about her, tragic even. As well as altering his view of her he now changes his view of himself to that of a rescuer, riding in nobly to carry her away from the darkness of her valley life.

Tracking down her house in the gruesome mining village in February, with fires burning on a nearby pit-hill, frightens him to death. Stumbling up a black lane he sees a light on in the backyard and knocks on the door. Mrs. Pinnegar, tall, passive, and angry, makes him conscious of his own smallness.

She gives him tea, and the mother and daughter watch him in absolute silence. Unnerved by the grimness, he blurts out almost at once that the woman ought to get away, and before he can stop himself, says, "Why don't you come and live with me?"

He asks after her husband and is told he is on the afternoon shift. When she considers and seems to accept his offer, she adds that he had better see Mr. Pinnegar first. He goes out to arrange for a bed somewhere, and then returns. Introduced to the husband, he then has to submit to witnessing the ritual washing before the fire of the miner's gray back. The pungent dialogue between the squirming London editor and the unbelieving "real" man is brilliantly judged. When Jimmy declares his intentions, and the man says coarsely, "She does as she pleases," he goes off feeling "really scared, and really elated. He was doing something big. It was not that he was in *love* with the woman. But, my God, he wanted to take her away from that man." Why then does he feel horribly diminished by the motionless, lean figure of the collier with his bony head, who has somehow put a spell on him? "The very silent unconsciousness of Pinnegar dominated the room, wherever he was." Would she come with him now, today? No, she says abruptly, "I can come on Monday."

He goes back to London, appalled by what he has proposed but determined to see it through. When he meets her at the station with her child on Monday, a sickly grin is on his face as he holds out his hand. He realizes, too late, that the husband is there too. "The woman moved in his aura. She was hopelessly married to him."

This new vein of fiction for Lawrence, blending biting satire with the uncanny, is developed in three further stories during the next two months. They all, in one way or another, pursue a Murry figure, in two stories literally killing him off. "The Border Line" begins by introducing Frieda as Katherine Farquhar, "no longer slim but attractive in her soft, full, feminine way. . . . Fifteen years of marriage to an Englishman—or rather to two Englishmen—had not altered her racially. Daughter of a German Baron she was . . . ," and this was how Lawrence used to introduce Frieda in his letters. Katherine's first husband, Alan Anstruther, was red-haired, with "a weird innate conviction that he was beyond ordinary judgment"— another example of Lawrence seeing through his own flaws and recording them for all to read. The action takes place in Germany, in the presence of Strasbourg cathedral. Katherine's husband dies and is replaced by Philip, who has the insidious sexuality we recognize from "Jimmy." "This look of knowing in his dark eyes, and the feeling of secrecy that went with his dark little body, made him interesting to women." And damned him, of course, in Lawrence's eyes. In Paris, "Suddenly she seemed to feel Alan at her side again, as if Philip had never existed. As if Philip had never meant more to her than the shop assistant measuring off her orders."

The ending is unbelievable, yet somehow we are bewitched. Philip falls ill, and Katherine is rejoined by her dead husband, who arrives triumphantly, back from the dead. He was posted missing in 1915, so perhaps he has never really died. We are told only that Philip, dying from a chill that is literally murdering him, convulses on the bed in throes of death. "And on his face was a sickly grin of a thief caught in the very act."

"Smile" is a very short and grisly story. Matthew's wife has died after he has received a telegram saying "Ophelia's condition critical." We know by the man's features—his dark, handsome, clean-shaven face with thick black eyebrows—that here is yet another version of Murry, this time traveling with more than a little reluctance to the home of the Blue Sisters, where Ophelia has chosen to die. When he gets there she has just died. Her description, "so pretty, so childlike, so clever, so obstinate, so worn," together with their inconclusive relationship, indicates that we are meant to think of Murry and his dead wife Katherine. The husband, afflicted with hysteria, cannot help smiling when he should be mourning, and then, as the nuns look down, they see "the faint ironical curl at the corners of Ophelia's mouth. . . ." As for Matthew, "never was a man more utterly smileless."

The most bizarre story of the four is "The Last Laugh." Dispensing with a guise for himself, Lawrence introduces himself on the first page as Lorenzo in this macabre wintry tale set in a Georgian house in Hampstead. "Below was the yellow, foul-smelling glare of Hampstead tube station." Here is Dorothy Brett with her deaf-aid machine as Miss James, looking at her own paintings, her self-portrait in particular, with its brown hair and "its slightly opened rabbit mouth and its baffled, uncertain rabbit eyes." March-banks is easily identified as Murry, even to the cruelly noted bald spot among his dark, thin, rather curly hair, his face with its beautiful lines "like a fawn, and a doubtful martyred expression. A sort of fawn on the Cross."

Lawrence was enjoying his revenge. For the coup de grâce he gave himself occult powers, invoking Pan—"Snatches of wild, gay, trilling music and bursts of naked low laughter"—in order to strike down Marchbanks, who lies suddenly dead as if struck by lightning, and give a young policeman a club foot. "There was faint smell of almond blossom in the air." And even this preposterous tale has its visionary, apocalyptic touch, the moldering London sky "rolled back, like an old skin . . . leaving an absolutely new blue heaven." Jimmy in the story of the desperate woman has a face that reminded his men friends of Pan, a goaty gleam in his gray eyes. Here as Marchbanks he is being killed by the god he resembles "at his best."

The story lived on in Murry's memory to such an extent that he recalled it in a letter thirty-one years later to Frieda. It was she in fact who reminded him, writing that "for me you are always the old god Pan." Murry, now sixty-six, with two more grandchildren, replied that it was funny she should call him Pan. "Lorenzo, you remember, used Pan to kill me off in one of his short stories—a queer one which I never quite understood—all about me and a policeman in snowy Hampstead." Affecting bewilderment he wrote that he didn't and "don't understand quite what, *in the story*, I was supposed to have done that deserved death at Pan's hands." But what he had done in Lawrence's eyes was something he did simply by being himself.

These damning stories were published after October 1924, with the exception of "The Border Line," which appeared in *Hutchinson's Magazine* for September 1924. By then the Lawrences, together with Dorothy Brett, were in Mexico. But early in the year Lawrence had already begun to doubt the declarations of his erstwhile lieutenant to Frieda concerning his plans for the *Adelphi*. Murry's review of *The Lost Girl* in the *Athenaeum* in 1920 still rankled, with its heading "The Decay of Mr. Lawrence," as did his opinion in 1921 that *Women in Love* was "subhuman and bestial." To cap it all, Lawrence's article "On Coming Home" was rejected on the grounds of its unsuitability for the *Adelphi*. One can see why. The return of the native makes scathing reading. In one sense, he wrote:

> one's fellow countrymen . . . are the nicest and most civilised people in the world. But there they are: each one of them a perfect little accomplished figure, enclosed first and foremost within the box of his own self-contained ego, and afterward in all the other boxes he has made for himself, for his own safety. . . .
>
> England was such a brave country, for so many years: the old brave, reckless, manly England. . . . Too brave and reckless to be treacherous. My England. Look at us now. Not a man left inside all the millions of pairs of trousers. A host of would-be amiable cowards shut up in his own bubble of conceit. . . . My own, my native land just leaves me flabbergasted.

SOON HE WAS eager to be off, out of England, anywhere, but preferably to Taos, where his winter in a tiny community of four had revived the dream of Rananim in him again, a colony of friends who would create a new, clean life together. Frieda too was in favor, writing to Mabel on February 10 from Germany that it would be good to experience the spring there, "and I don't see why with some good will on all sides we shouldn't live near each other." She had accomplished her victory over Lawrence and was now ready to join forces with him once more.

There followed the infamous dinner at the Café Royal, to rouse spirits and if possible enroll recruits. Lawrence's enthusiasm went beyond anything Frieda had envisaged, and she sat well back as her evangelistic husband caught fire by asking his guests one by one if they would come with him to New Mexico. Donald Carswell, Koteliansky, Mark Gertler, and Mary Cannan demurred, though mildly and apologetically. Murry and Dorothy Brett accepted there and then, and Catherine Carswell agreed in principle. Lawrence toasted them and himself with port, and no one except Frieda knew how ill he was. Murry is supposed to have said within earshot of the others, "I love you, Lorenzo, but I won't promise not to betray you." Koteliansky made a grandiose speech, declaring that Lawrence was a great man and no one realized how great. The great man found either this or the port too much, fell forward, and passed out, vomiting on the tablecloth. Catherine Carswell recorded a chastened Lawrence saying to her the next day, "Well, Catherine, I made a fool of myself last night. We must all of us fall at times. It does no harm so long as we first admit and then forget it."

It was now that he met Frieda's younger daughter Barbara for the first time. He struck her as trustworthy, though she saw how frail he was and thought he had an odd, high-pitched voice in which she could hear a Midlands accent. As far as looks went, she liked Murry better, and his suave manner was familiar to her.

On a short visit with Frieda to see her mother he was prompted to write "A Letter from Germany," intended for Spud Johnson's magazine *The Laughing Horse*. It was dashed off swiftly, like all his journalism, but has proved to be strikingly prescient. He had a sense of strange things stirring in the darkness of postwar Germany, in this "still-unconquered Black Forest. . . . Out of the very air comes a sense of danger, a queer, *bristling* feeling of uncanny danger." He took note of the gangs of Young Socialists, youths and girls "with their non-materialistic professions, their half-mystic assertions." They struck him as primitive, "like loose, roving gangs of broken, scattered tribes." There was something barbaric about it all. The Ruhr occupation had brought it about, and an English "nullity." It was something the Allies had done, and now it was happening.

While in Baden-Baden he wrote to Murry in the brutalist manner he always used now to vent his exasperation and in an effort to stiffen his friend's backbone. He still had some feeling for him, after his fashion, but suspicion never left him, and he must have wondered if his attempt to prize him away from his precious *Adelphi* was a waste of time. From Murry's point of view, why should he grub away in primitive New Mexico when he enjoyed his comfortable literary life in London? He was, it seems, congenitally unable to commit himself outright to anything. Lawrence ordered him angrily to "Move for yourself alone. . . . I don't want any pact."

He had clearly ceased to believe in Murry's allegiance. "Let us clear away all nonsense. I don't *need* you. Neither do you need me. If you pretend to need me, you will hate me for it." And he went further, as he always did once he was worked up emotionally. "I don't care what you think of me, I don't care what you say of me, I don't even care what you do against me, as a writer." As we have seen already, Murry would do plenty, once Lawrence was safely in his grave.

Returning after this short visit to the mother-in-law he called "Dearest Little Mother," he wrote in the spirit of cheerfulness induced by being on the move to say that they were in Paris, after having visited Versailles, and how stupid it was, "so frightfully large and flat, much too large for the landscape." He said wittily that Marie Antoinette yearned to be a simple perfect peasant, with her "nice, somewhat common Austrian blonde face. Finally she became too simple, without a head." Then on briskly to domestic details: Frieda had purchased two hats, and they had bought three lovely blouses for Nusch. One more excursion, Chartres, and then to London. Sentimentally, for Lawrence, he told her that they were all traveling together, in spite of separation. "Such is life."

He may have summarily dismissed Murry, but communication with anyone he knew intimately was hard for him to give up, and on Monday, March 10, we find him writing to "Dear Jack" on the *Aquitania*, a day away from America. As often, he enjoyed the ocean voyage, even on this immense ship that was like being in a town. Brett, insatiably curious like a child, was having tea with the ship's doctor. Frieda found ship travel difficult, the motion upsetting. Needless to say, her husband liked to feel himself traveling. "And it's good to get away from the doom of Europe."

Through the struggle of customs, treating Brett in the stern, fatherly manner he often fell into with her, mad with passport officials for calling her "this girl," he bumped up to 100th Street in a taxi with all their luggage in the middle of a blizzard, "snow and rain on a gale of NE wind. New York looking vile." Nor did he like that woman, the Statue of Liberty, "clenching her fist in the harbor."

On the wharf was Seltzer waiting to greet them, though his author hadn't told him he was coming. He had got the news from Curtis Brown, who had no doubt acquainted Lawrence with the publisher's financial straits. Lawrence's first thought was how diminished he looked standing there pluckily with his bad news. Business had gone badly, partly because of the times, and because he had published too many "Montparnasse Americans." Poor Seltzer, in the red, was unable to pay Lawrence his royalties at present. He begged the Englishman to be patient, and Lawrence stoically agreed. He felt sympathy and a certain gratitude toward the little avant-garde publisher who was more creative than efficient, and had, after all, gambled on him in the first place. "Damn it all and damn everything. But I don't care terribly." But he levered enough out of Seltzer to buy their tickets westward and settle his outstanding federal tax. And after all he was not badly off, with 300 pounds in the bank in England and $2,285 in America. He accepted that he would never be a money-spinner. "You're not born for success in the Knopf sense," he lectured Seltzer, "any more than I am."

He had met the Honorable Dorothy Brett in 1915, never dreaming that she would turn out to be his only true disciple. Now in 1924 he felt oddly responsible for her, masking his protectiveness in the face of Frieda's resentment by talking harshly and impatiently to her, and when talking of her to others. Before knowing her as well as he was soon to do, he modeled Hilda Blessington on her, a character in *The Boy in the Bush* described as "one of the odd border-line people who don't and can't really belong." As he informed the Brewsters, she was "a painter, very deaf, about as old as I am, has a modest but sufficient income and is daughter of Viscount Esher." More cruelly, he compared her looks to those of an animal, part bird, part squirrel, part rabbit: "never quite a woman." She did have prominent rabbity teeth and a receding chin, and gave an impression of gawkiness.

Her apparent total lack of confidence could be misleading, as could her shyness, and anyone reading her memoir, *Lawrence and Brett*, written in 1933, will realize how shrewd and observant she could be. She was no simpleton, and her faux naive way of calling everything "little" concealed a person of surprising toughness and resilience who could be slyly malicious in the privacy of her diaries, usually at Frieda's expense.

7

On Being a Man

(1924–1925)

Brett had lost her mother when she was very young, leaving her to the mercy of her father, the second Viscount Esher, a Liberal MP. Elaine Feinstein in her biography deals with him severely, saying that he was in fact bisexual, had married for convenience, and made his daughters feel stupid by his cold treatment. One of his friends, says Brenda Maddox, sexually molested Dorothy: consequently she feared men. Handicapped by deafness, she made herself a laughingstock by calling her metal ear-trumpet "Toby." Discarded heartlessly by Murry, she now attached herself to Lawrence with a transferred, newly awakened ardor. Lawrence was bound to have known of the brief affair with Murry and was aware too of her unhappy childhood.

Her memoir addressing Lawrence throughout as "You," is adoring but enlivened by the sharp eye of a painter and by her own sometimes wicked humor. To avoid being married off by her family she had entered the Slade School, a contemporary of Gertler, Stanley Spencer, and Dora Carrington, and like Carrington was always called by her surname.

The Lawrences and their lone recruit embarked for New Mexico after being entertained in Willa Cather's rooms in New York. Willa Cather irritated Lawrence with her overserious approach to art. In his best knockabout style, eyes twinkling, he said he hated literature and literary people and their fuss about art. "I hate books and art and the whole business." The more indignant Willa Cather became, the more pleased he seemed, and what fun it was, Brett noted in her memoir, always from now on the recording angel on the sidelines. She heard Mabel Sterne referred to by Lawrence as the little black buffalo and looked forward eagerly to meeting her.

On they went to Chicago, a city bolted into a frozen winter, and then at Santa Fe there were two men to greet them, strangers to Brett, "nearly pulling your arms off, hugging you and shouting." One was tall, in a big hat and colorful shirt, the other small and thinner, his hat inconspicuously flat: they were Witter Bynner and Spud Johnson. Brett was much amused by The Spoodle, as Bynner called his partner. Next day the travelers said goodbye to their hosts and squeezed into the "stage" (a Ford) for Taos. Lawrence inquired about the road as they neared the precipitous approach and was told by the driver, "All right, but slippery." As they climbed higher and the road turned into a narrow ledge, a sheer drop on one side, Brett felt sick with fear and pinched Lawrence's knee. "This makes you furious." They climbed still higher and now could see far below the small ribbon of river foaming. "It's all over now, Brett," Lawrence reassured her. He had said that the skyline of Taos was the most beautiful of all he had seen in his travels: now here it was. Mabel was not at home, but here they were at Mabeltown, expected and welcomed by Mabel's Mexican cook Amelia, who had big glowing fires burning.

Writing to Koteliansky from New York, Lawrence had spoken in praise of Brett's detachment, blithely unaware or determined not to notice Frieda's sense of grievance with the arrangement. He even, after a fashion, saw some virtue in New York. Stiff and machine-made as it was, nevertheless he found it stimulating and without the deathliness of Europe. Worried about Seltzer's parlous state, he blamed the publisher's wife but took comfort from the fact that Curtis Brown's man there, Arthur Barmby, seemed decent and reliable, "a north of England man."

Now it was springtime in the Rockies, and Lawrence brimmed with hope. He and Frieda had been allocated one of Mabel's houses, and Brett had a studio close by. Mabel, who had been wintering in New York with Tony, was expected any day. Coming in from a walk the trio saw a big car on the patio, and Lawrence and Frieda went up to greet her, the "vileness of 1923" seemingly forgotten. Brett, being introduced, felt nervous and shy but was soon admiring of this woman she had heard much about, who now stood before her and was so different from anything she had imagined. Shorter than Brett, she was square, sturdy, her thick brown hair having a chestnut gleam, "bobbed like a Florentine boy." Taking in details as if she intended to paint a portrait, she saw that her fringe was cut in a curve, her gray dark-lashed eyes curiously alight, the well-shaped lips unpainted. She gave an impression of a rich, forceful personality, and as she walked "her arms swing and some of the force and strength behind the charm reveals itself."

One can see from these initial comments how astute the docile, overlooked Brett could be. With Mabel was a friend, Ida Rauh, an actress, deeply tanned, who looked amazingly like Sarah Bernhardt. Embarrassed by her Englishness before these confident Americans, Brett lapsed into one of her awkward silences that gave those who met her such a false impression.

Loving Taos unreservedly, with its painters and Indians, she was soon rigged out in Western style with her culottes, sombrero, and a dagger in her belt. It all delighted her, though in her memoir she soon begins to mention an undercurrent of emotional strain that had, she felt sure, nothing to do with her and was beyond her understanding.

Soon all this would change, the lunches at Mabel's, the charades with Lawrence and Ida as the luminaries, everybody at ease and first-rate except herself. She liked far better cantering on horses and marveling endlessly at the Indians in the Pueblo, old men with charming faces and young men with long-braided hair whose beauty—as beautiful as girls—took her breath away. The days were getting steadily warmer, touches of green pushing up in the fields around the houses, and Brett's vivid account of an excursion to the Ranchos Hot Springs reads like the description of a painting. The three women, Lawrence, and Tony went separately into little cubicles and undressed, Brett with her painful shyness aware of the lack of privacy, the gaps in the plank walls. Coming out, she was last in the water, in the dark light patterned with big splotches of sunlight.

This was her first glimpse of the naked Lawrence. "You are white like ivory, but oh, so thin; Frieda fat and jolly, like a Reubens: Mabel square and thick. Tony large, a pale, glistening light brown." Entranced by the clear water, she slipped in and joined them. There was horseplay between Lawrence and Frieda, and then he was standing in the shallow water up to his waist, water dripping from his beard, "looking wicked and Pan-like."

Brett was hampered by her deafness from understanding the curious undercurrents of emotion, but with her intuition and her sharp eye she was able to pick up clues. It was clear that "a vague discomfort hangs around us all." Mabel's powerful will was again making itself felt. Sitting around in the Lawrences' living room one evening, Frieda launched suddenly into the story of a quarrel in Cornwall in which she hit Lawrence over the head with a heavy plate, breaking it in pieces, relating it with such exuberance that Brett remembered her own violence at fourteen, throwing china candlesticks at the head of her governess. Frieda, in a confiding mood, said, "He is much stronger than I am, Brett. Sometimes I am really frightened of him: sometimes I think he is mad. When he is in one of his rages I am frightened of him." Lawrence, sewing a button on his pants, said warningly to her, "You had better be!" This was banter, the trio temporarily united in laughter. Another time, Lawrence asked Brett suddenly what she thought of *The Boy in the Bush*. She said she liked it, except for the ending. The hero should have died, she thought. The author agreed, saying it was how he wrote it—"only Frieda made me change it." Frieda said that she couldn't stand the superiority of the man, "always this superiority and death." Brett stuck to her guns, with Lawrence sighing in agreement. "The Brett always agrees with you, always sticks up for you," Frieda said challengingly, her eyes darting about. It was a foretaste of things to come.

They went on for some time in this false holidaylike atmosphere, until Mabel took the initiative and proposed giving the Lawrences the use of a mountain ranch two miles beyond Del Monte, where they had lived with the Danes. It was generous of her, but was this Mabel up to her manipulative tricks again? Lawrence thought so, but Frieda, eager for a place of her own, accepted it anyway, and suggested presenting Mabel with the manuscript of *Sons and Lovers* if she would let them own the property. In the event the broken-down ranch was worth less than a third of the value of the manuscript.

They went to survey the place. A little farm in the Rockies had been a dream of Lawrence's for years, though he was not going to say so. The road ceased to be a road and became a narrow track through pines. Nestling among big pines in a field was a little group of cabins, all of them dilapidated. One was choked with cow dung, the second one a possibility, and while the third was decent it seemed too small even for a bed. Mabel thought that with two Indians to do heavy laboring the place could be fixed up. Frieda jumped up and down with delight at the prospect of independence, while Lawrence hung back, uncertain. The magnificent view hypnotized them all.

On May 5, two months after starting from England, with Lawrence now excited at the thought of change and movement, they left Taos in early morning for the ranch. Lawrence had already named it Kiowa. The wagon with their belongings and stores was driven off ahead with two Indians in charge. The Indian called

Trinidad rode one of the horses provided by Mabel, leading the other two. The trio of pioneers followed in the car driven by Tony.

THEY WERE NOW the proud possessors of a hundred and sixty acres of unfarmable land dotted with pine trees. The cabins had to be literally rebuilt, helped by the Indians and a Mexican carpenter. Scrubbing them out was the kind of filthy job Lawrence seemed to relish. Before long he was overworking himself dangerously with hard manual labor. An irrigation ditch was dug, bringing water from the Gallina Canyon nearly a mile away. The Lawrences needed the largest cabin for themselves, while the second in size would be a guest cabin for when Mabel and others called. The Cinderella-like Brett, whom Mabel thought "a holy Russian idiot," beginning to resent her as yet another rival for her celebrity's attentions, meekly said she would be happy to live in the smallest cabin. Lawrence thought that with a new roof and a stove it should be all right, and turned his attention to another formidable cleaning job, the corral. At one time it had been the home of five hundred goats. "It was a healthy smell," he said without enthusiasm.

The Indians, now three, camped further up in a teepee, sitting at night in the open around their fire, beating a small hand drum and chanting softly. Now and then they were joined by Lawrence and his two women, who were content to sit under the pines wrapped in blankets, "caught and held by the Indian rhythm, as if the very earth itself were singing."

Brett did her full share of the unpleasant work, shoveling out goat dung and piling rocks, chopping wood for Frieda's stove, and carrying water from the stream while Frieda lay on her bed and smoked, and when the spirit moved her cooked huge meals for them all and made her own clothes. Lawrence rode long distances, sometimes with the submissive Brett, set about cleaning the well, and built an adobe oven, baking the bread himself. In his element now, he bought a cow, Susan. "I don't write—don't want to—don't care," he said. As had happened in Cornwall, he was regressing, allowing himself to lapse into a workingman like his father.

The renunciation did not last long. With the backbreaking work done, he sat against the big pine tree outside his cabin every morning and wrote, paying tribute in the essay "Pan in America" to the guardian spirit represented for him by the tree. "Long, long ago the Indians blazed it. And the lightning, or the storm, has cut off its crest. Yet its column is always there, alive and changeless, alive and changing. The tree has its own aura of life. . . . It vibrates its presence into my soul, and I am with Pan."

He and Brett were drawing closer, though he teased her endlessly. He was curious about her inner self, not prying but with his writer's need to be let in. One day as she was writing letters, she shuffled her letter away hastily as he approached. "How like a woman to hide her letters," he exclaimed. "Why do women always do that?"

The extent to which his time in New Mexico affected him, the deep love he felt for his wilderness life and the privilege it bestowed on him is clear from the majesty of his prose when paying homage to it:

> There are all kinds of beauty in the world, thank God, though ugliness is homogeneous. How lovely is Tuscany, with little red tulips wild among the corn: or bluebells at dusk in England, or mimosa in clouds of pure yellow among the grey-green dun foliage of Australia. . . . But for a *greatness* of beauty I have never experienced anything like New Mexico. All those mornings when I went with a hoe along the ditch to the Canyon, at the ranch, and stood, in the fierce, proud silence of the Rockies, on their foothills, to look far over the desert to the blue mountains away in Arizona, blue as chalcedony, with the sage-brush desert sweeping grey-blue in between, dotted with tiny cube-crystals of houses, the vast amphitheatre of lofty, indomitable desert, sweeping round to the ponderous Sangre de

Christo mountains on the east, and coming up flush at the pine dotted foothills of the Rockies! What splendor! Only the tawny eagle could really sail out into the splendor of it all. It had a splendid, silent terror, and a vast far-and-wide magnificence . . . way beyond mere aesthetic appreciation. Never is the light more pure and overweening than there, arching with a royalty almost cruel over the hollow uptilted world. Those that have spent morning after morning alone there pitched among the pines above the great proud world of desert will know how unbearably beautiful it is, how clear and unquestioned is the might of the day.

On occasional visits to Taos as Mabel's guest, matters now tended to become farcical, culminating in an acquaintance Lawrence formed with one of Mabel's protégés. Clarence Thompson, blatantly homosexual, was a young aspiring writer who had left Harvard and come west, encouraged by Mabel. His clothes were even showier than Bynner's, and he set out at once to cultivate Lawrence. At a dance toward the end of June in Mabel's large studio, Lawrence, who disliked dancing, refused to join in. Finally Frieda and Clarence disappeared into the night. Mabel in her memoirs said that Frieda had told Clarence while they were in the plaza that Lawrence wanted Mabel dead. It seems more likely that this absurd allegation had sprung up in Mabel's mind after Lawrence left his manuscript of "The Woman Who Rode Away" for her to read before leaving next morning for Kiowa with Frieda and Brett. One evening at the ranch he had said that the Pueblo Indians called Frieda "Angry Winter." What Brett was called no one knew, but one can be sure that Frieda would have had suggestions. Brett's adoration of Frieda's husband was becoming tiresome, either "a silly old habit" or detestable, according to her mood. Nevertheless she still in certain moods turned to her as an ally.

Back at the ranch he was preoccupied with his hens and with his "amiable but wayward" black cow, Susan, of whom he became fond, milking her and feeling tied, but liking the obligation. "I have no desire to go out. I hate motoring these long distances here," he told his sister Ada Clarke. Susan's "queer, jerky cowy gladness" had more appeal. The cow would disappear into the timber and stand "block still like invisibility itself, while I walk past her and on and on. She's a black blossom."

THAT SUMMER he completed two of his most substantial works of fiction. "The Woman Who Rode Away" is a long short story, and "St. Mawr" is in effect a novella. The first seems to have Mabel as its heroine. She believed the cave in it to be one near Taos, and suggested in *Lorenzo in Taos* that he had drawn on her account to him of her psychic experiences. In the story the woman rides into the mountains with her Indian servant, ostensibly to visit her daughter in a half-deserted convent five miles away. In a grove of trees she sits and waits, this woman who has become indifferent to people, to men, who takes her sunbaths every morning and "knew the sun in every thread of her body." Her heart, as she lies there, "that anxious straining heart," seems to disappear altogether like a falling flower in the sun. And though this sun shines on the whole world, she feels that when she lies unclothed "he focused on her alone." Waiting in the grove, they are joined by wild Indians, and she realizes gradually what is happening: she is now a captive. "The woman was powerless. And along with her supreme anger there came a slight thrill of exultation. She knew she was dead."

The story has a language that is cumulative in its slow inevitability, trancelike and hypnotic. The nameless rich woman is taken to a secret place, dressed and prepared with great gentleness, and laid on a large flat stone for sacrifice. Without anything being said explicitly, we are given to believe that this is something the woman wants. While she lies waiting as the sun sinks and the naked priest waits with a knife, she knows that this is the shortest day of the year, and her last day. As in ancient Greek tragedy, the act of violence is withheld from us. The tale concludes with a phrase that has infuriated feminists to this day. "The mastery that man must hold, and that passes from race to race."

Brenda Maddox, in a biography not noted for its finesse, has the ingenious idea of turning the story on its head, with the woman in Lawrence being killed in order that he can become a man. Now she is able to interpret it as "a powerful expression of inner torment," and refers the reader to the short essay "On Being a Man." Lawrence did indeed believe that manhood was not given but had to be fought for, and in his case the struggle was lifelong. In his essay he writes poignantly:

> Today men don't risk their blood and bone. They go forth, panoplied in their own idea of themselves. . . . Their unknown bodily self is never for one moment unsheathed. All the time, the only protagonist is the known ego, the self-conscious ego. And the dark self in the mysterious labyrinth of the body is cased in a tight armor of cowardly repression. . . .
>
> All the suffering today is psychic: it happens in the mind. The red Adam only suffers the slow torture of compression and derangement. A man's wife is a mental thing, a known thing to him. The old Adam in him never sees her. She is just a thing of his own conscious ego. And not for one moment does he risk himself under the strange snake-infested bushes of her extraordinary Paradise. He is afraid.

With "St. Mawr" we descend from the symbolic art that Lawrence maintained all true art was to an assault on the reader by plastering contrived symbolism over the tale with impatient crudeness in a bullying attempt to drive home his point. The story has been overvalued, notably by Leavis. Whole passages seem rhetorical, the dialogue frequently banal, and Lawrence resorts to stock figures who fail to convince. The heroine, Lou Witt, her name derived from Lee and Nina Witt in Taos, is a caricature of Mabel when young, whose solution to a thing was to buy it. Brenda Maddox amusingly equates the great sterile stallion with the author, and his name, "Mawr," the Welsh word for large or great, is not very far, she thinks, from "Lawr," as Frieda sometimes called Lawrence.

Lewis the Welsh groom is a forerunner of Mellors and a descendant of Annable. When asked why St. Mawr has no interest in the mares, the groom retorts, "Doesn't want to, I should think—same as me." The stallion's savage attack on a male rider is explained by the fact that St. Mawr feels "a great woe: the woe of human unworthiness." It is rare for Lawrence to give way to sentimentality. Only the dazzling scenes toward the end redeem this tale, when Mrs. Witt's daughter deserts her husband and goes to live on a ranch in New Mexico that is obviously Kiowa. There she tries to cope with the hordes of pack rats and live a chaste life, announcing that "I don't hate men *because* they're men, as nuns do. I dislike them because they're not men enough: babies and playboys. . . ."

Lawrence had nearly finished "St. Mawr" when he was struck down by a show of blood. He took to his bed in a paroxysm of rage when Frieda asked him to see a doctor she had called. He threw at her the iron ring he used for an eggcup and said he would go out and hide in the sage brush when the man came. How dare she send for a doctor behind his back? He was now committed to the "dying game" of denying the very use of the word tuberculosis, passing off attacks on his lungs as colds, bronchial trouble, even asthma. When the doctor arrived with plenty of blankets and took him down to Taos, he allowed himself to be examined meekly without complaint. Back again, he told Frieda what she was to say and what he himself strove to believe: "Nothing wrong: the lungs are strong. It is just a touch of bronchial trouble—the tubes are sore."

On September 14, 1924, only a few weeks before going south to Mexico to escape the Rockies winter he now feared, he was shocked to hear from Emily King of the death of his father. He had not expected to be so upset. Nevertheless "It is better to be gone than lingering on half helpless and half alive." A fortnight before the news he had sent his sister Ada ten pounds for him. He sent another ten pounds now, toward the funeral expenses.

His father had died on the day before Lawrence's birthday. He wrote to Murry, "The country is very lovely here at the moment, aspens high on the mountains like a fleece of gold. The scrub oak is dark red, and the wild birds are coming down to the desert. It is time to go south . . . where the cold doesn't crouch over one like a snow-leopard about to pounce."

Instead of heeding the doctor's advice to lie still, he got Frieda to prepare a poultice of mustard plaster for him, of the sort his mother had applied, and then was up making bread and getting ready to accompany Mabel and Tony Luhan for a two-week stay in Albuquerque to attend the annual Hopi snake dances in Arizona.

Frieda went too. Mabel made sure that Brett was left behind to look after the ranch. She had transferred her resentment of Frieda to this odd creature with "long thin shanks" who infuriated her more and more with her arrogant Englishness. In *Lorenzo in Taos* she owned up to feeling threatened by Brett's brass ear-trumpet "that seemed to suck into itself all it could from the air . . . inhibiting all one's spontaneity . . . it was an eavesdropper, a spy on any influence near Lorenzo. Do you think I like it when I saw that brass dipper swallowing Lorenzo's talk to me? It was worse than Frieda's restraining influence." The trumpet had turned into a person and a rival. No one would have been more delighted than Brett if she had known. Her apparent youthfulness, another source of annoyance to Mabel, was probably due to her upbringing, being treated as a child by her father until well into her twenties. In fact she was only four years younger than Frieda.

IN ARIZONA for the Hopi dances, Lawrence's chest and throat remained sore, and this hastened his need to leave. Intending to return to Kiowa the following spring, they looked in vain for an

Indian couple to live there as caretakers. Finally they dismantled and packed what they could and left their goods with the Hawks to store for them. In mid-October they were on the way, with Frieda reluctant and Brett eager for the adventure.

At El Paso they waited to have their passports signed at the Mexican consulate before boarding the train for Mexico. A young Mexican with nicotine-stained fingers shuffled through their documents. With a gesture toward Brett he asked Lawrence if she was his wife. He said no. "Your sister, then?" Lawrence said impatiently that she was a friend. Pointing at Frieda, who had put on a good deal of weight over the years, the pert young official asked if she was his mother. Brett recorded the encounter in gleeful detail in her memoir.

Revolution in Mexico was brewing yet again. On their train were soldiers sitting on the roofs of carriages, with an armored truck full of soldiers behind the engine. Brett, excited, devoured the landscape with her painter's eye. "You have got your wish at last," Frieda told her. "You are in old Mexico."

Mexico City, when they arrived, was somewhere to get out again as soon as possible for the Lawrences, who were both unwell with colds. Brett was keen to visit the museum, so Lawrence dutifully accompanied her. She should not walk about alone, he advised. When the attendant asked him to take off his hat he flew into a rage and marched out. Out in the street he said angrily, "They want to show their powers over strangers . . . they want to show they have the authority to make a white man take off his hat!" Brett, not wanting a repeat of the scene inside a drapery shop, where Lawrence and Frieda shouted at each other while the assistants grinned, said nothing. In the old church a calmer Lawrence said, "Perhaps the Virgin of Guadalupe will cure your deafness." Alas, it wasn't to be, but the many paintings of miracles fascinated her.

Lawrence had been invited to an evening with the P.E.N. Club and later lunched with Somerset Maugham. It would have been remarkable if they had hit it off. "He hates it here," Lawrence reported, so at least they had that in common. "He's going to Yucatan. He'll hate it there. I didn't like him. A bit rancid."

They were staying again at the Italian hotel they had liked before, the old Monte Carlo, which had no private bathrooms, but that was scarcely a hardship after the ranch. There was a touch of comedy when the bellboy refused to go into Brett's room alone with the water jug. Frieda wouldn't get up, so it was left to Lawrence to accompany him. "How old do you have to be, Brett," he asked furiously, "before he can come in by himself? Anyway, I'm not doing it again."

It was chilly in the city, the last thing they had expected: people coughing and sneezing, the snow low down on Popocatepetl. In Taos, Mabel, still bereft after her hero's departure, was told by Bynner that she was being foolish. "I suppose it is because you persist with the herd in taking him as an important mind. He always seems to me a strange, sick, precocious child, to be considered accordingly. Somebody else's child, thank God!"

A rescue plan for the Lawrences was provided by the British vice consul, whose brother, a man called Richards, was the Catholic priest at Oaxaca, 250 miles south of Mexico City. Richards generously offered them the use of part of his large house. Lawrence wrote to his sister Emily (sometimes called "Peg") to say that it had taken two days to get there, on yet another train bristling with soldiers. In this country there were always bandits "and so-called rebels—always attacking somebody or other." But the town, he added optimistically, was safe. More important, the climate was just like midsummer, a bright sun and a cloudless sky every day, with all the roses and hibiscus flowers out. "For a penny or two," he wrote, with Eastwood prices in mind, "one buys big bunches of really handsome roses." The Indians, Zaptecas, were small and upright and rather fierce-looking. They came in to the market like wild men with their woven blankets and "very jolly pottery," and he promised to send her a blanket for Christmas. The picture he painted for Murry on the same day was less pretty: the market a babel of unwashed wild people, and "awful things to eat—including squashed fried locust-beetles."

In the long low house belonging to the priest on the Avenida Pino Suarez they were very comfortable, in big rooms with a wide veranda at the rear, looking out toward dark blue mountains. They had their own personal servant or *mozo*: this was Rosalino, shortly to figure in Lawrence's *Mornings in Mexico*. Brett boarded at the Spanish Hotel Francia, her typewriter at the ready for more manuscripts from Lawrence. Somehow she had lost her ear-trumpet, and an enterprising local tinsmith made her a replacement, helped by her drawing of the instrument she wanted. The natives stood around in wonderment when she brandished it.

Most satisfying for Lawrence was the altitude, only five thousand feet. As soon as he was settled he hoped to finish his Mexican novel that a defeated Mabel had thought would have a New Mexico setting. "It was what I had called him here to do." The ingratitude caused her much grief. Lawrence wrote to thank the Hawks for riding round and looking after Kiowa. When he thought of it, he wished he was there. "Frieda of course pines for her ranch, and the freedom. So really do I."

Comfortable though he was, the chaos of the place alarmed him. To Murry he said that "The Indians are queer little savages, and awful agitators pump bits of socialism over them and make everything just a mess. . . . The Spanish-Mexican population just rots on top of the black savage mass."

The world was gruesome—by which he meant as always the world of people: such a contrast to the lovely countryside. The sugarcane was being cut, hauled in by old ox-wagons. He expected to stay until early spring, that is if Mexico stayed quiet. On their journey to Oaxaca they had changed first at Esperanza, crossing the line and climbing aboard the little primitive train for Tehuacan and on to Oaxaca. Their squad of soldiers was now more ragged than before, and heavily armed. Dropping down into the tropical belt, the stifling heat sent Frieda to sleep. Brett went looking for Lawrence, who had disappeared. Here in her memoir is a unique glimpse of the world-famous writer sitting quietly at the other end of the carriage, mending his socks. "Your bag is open beside you, with your little case of threads and needles and scissors laid out on the seat." They went past stations pockmarked with bullets, ruined villages on all sides.

Rosalino, their *mozo* at Oaxaca, had a story to tell, which he told after some time, feeling his way. There was something different about him, "a certain sensitiveness and aloneness, as if he were a mother's boy," dropping his head and looking sideways apprehensively. He had been badly beaten during an uprising for refusing to volunteer, saying *No quiero*, and his back was injured. He "is one of those, like myself, who have a horror of serving in a mass of men." He showed Lawrence where he slept, on a wooden bench near the double doors opening onto the street. One evening Lawrence found him on his bench, bent over a copybook. "What is it?" Lawrence asked. Rosalino attended a night school giving lessons in literacy. Sometimes, coming in from her hotel in the morning, Brett would come on Lawrence and his *mozo* sitting together on the hard bench, "Rosalino with a face of agonized concentration." Lawrence could never resist helping someone with a desire to learn.

The Plumed Serpent lay on his mind, waiting to be completed but for the moment he was unsure. He thought he might have to rewrite it all. Chapala, where it was located, he now saw as too tame, too touristy. Perhaps he had made a false start. He put it aside and plunged into the essays that comprise *Mornings in Mexico*. The chapters begin as delicious lighthearted asides, written for fun, then become steadily more serious. The opening chapter, "Corasmin and the Parrots," light as a soufflé, was written a week before Christmas, 1924. Let no one say that Lawrence lacked a sense of humor. We can hear him laughing all through the writing of it.

In the gardens behind the house the parrots imitated everything and everyone, such as Rosalino's whistle as he swept the patio with his twig broom. They caught his whistle exactly, "only a little more so. And this little-more-so is extremely, sardonically funny. With their sad old long-jowled faces and their flat disillusioned eyes they reproduce Rosalino and a little-more-so without moving a muscle." Then they switched to imitating someone calling the dog, Corasmin. "Perro! Oh Perro! Perr-rro!" *Perro* meaning dog. Corasmin was a little fat curly white dog who either lay in the sun or sought the veranda shade. "Perro!" called the parrots. "But that any creature should be able to pour such a suave, prussic-acid sarcasm over the voice of a human calling a dog, is incredible. . . . And one thinks: *Is it possible?* Is it possible that we are so absolutely, so innocently ridiculous?" The parrots even yapped like Corasmin, which was even funnier. They were able to make their voices "so devilishly small and futile," exactly like Corasmin—only more so.

The essays on Indian dances in *Mornings in Mexico* belong with his most profound, insightful, and beautiful prose. But something ugly was happening to his fiction. The world that he said gave him "the gruesomes" now, the enemy that sent him traveling the earth in a search for something else, had somehow got into his writing. The jeering he felt directed at him with a malignancy he loathed, that could be called homophobic, feeling it in the crowds and public places especially, when he was defenseless and out of touch with a sustaining nature, was now a jeering malice in some of the later satirical stories. Held in check to some extent in the retaliatory anti-Murry stories, it infected "St. Mawr" with a didactic and vengeful note as this indictment of human "unworthiness" unfolded. At its nastiest it produced "The Princess," a brutal story with a Brett-like central figure called "My Princess" by her slightly mad father. From him she has learned absolute reticence and the impossibility of intimacy, and seems like a changeling, looking out at the world with "cold, elfin detachment." In the American Southwest on a visit she rides off with her Mexican guide Romero, who quickly resents her superior manner, mistaking her for one of those American women "who always want to do a man down." She allows herself to be taken by this man who pants like an animal with desire, then is maddened by her control of herself. He tosses her clothes and boots into a half-frozen pool in the night, then rapes her repeatedly. After the Mexican is shot and the Princess regains civilization, she is in effect still virginal, though "her eyes were a little mad."

Critics since Murry have pointed to the evidence in Lawrence's work of misogyny, sadism, class hatred, racism, anti-Semitism, even a latent fascism. None of these labels gets us very far. Ever since *The Rainbow* prosecution and the hounding from Cornwall, he had felt himself to be in some sense hunted, a desperado, saying more than once that his so-called friends in England would like to see him dead. Books, stories, and later his paintings can be seen as acts of provocation, like his verses in *Nettles* and his final novel. As far back as *Women in Love*, a novel so disintegrative in its themes, Lawrence was out in the open as a lone figure, frightened of the consequences of his stance. "The book frightens me," he wrote to Catherine Carswell, "it is so end-of-the-world. But it is, it must be the beginning of a new world." Not since Shelley has anyone made such claims for literature. This new world he had envisaged then he was now struggling to flesh out in *The Plumed Serpent*.

In Oaxaca he went about with Brett a good deal, very aware of his guardian role. In the streets to the market the hill men, on foot and on burros, with small pointed hats, stared at him fixedly and made him angry, and so did the call "Cristo! Cristo!" he heard softly behind him. Because of the slow advance of his disease a look of dignified suffering had changed his face into something masklike. This is the face we are familiar with from one of the late photographs.

He thought it would be good to go out a little way into the desert in the mornings to write, and Brett to paint. Surely it would be safe enough, he said, with two of them. Frieda, he added, could join them later, with Rosalino carrying the basket of lunch.

Brett came along from her hotel, armed with her painting materials, Lawrence with his notebook. He told her he was glad to escape the confinement of the patio and garden, pleasant as it was. They came to two bushes, set far apart, and Lawrence made the decision to sit there. Over his bush he draped his coat to provide him with shade and sat there in his shirtsleeves, writing swiftly. Suddenly Brett, absorbed in her picture, was disturbed by his shadow falling over her canvas. If she was pleased with what she had done, the master was not. He delivered a lecture on how to execute a painting. "Do look at the mountain," he said irritably. "It has great bare toes, where it joins the desert. Here, let me have a try." He took over the picture, gave the mountain its toes and roughened the fir trees on the mountainside, then gave his pupil a final reprimand. "You are dumb, Brett; you don't look at things; you have no eyes." Instead of being demoralized, Brett, who now knew her Lawrence, said innocently that she would add the figures next day—knowing that he wasn't good at figures. He laughed, then looked anxiously at his watch. "Frieda can't be coming after all," he said, and got ready to go. Her snatched time of intimacy was over.

A few days later, with Frieda sick in bed with a cold, Brett came to the house and helped Lawrence cut up oranges to make marmalade. "There is trouble; the air heavy and disturbed," she notes in her memoir. The truth was that Frieda had had enough of Brett and Lawrence's morning jaunts in the desert, and of Brett's slavish devotion to her husband. She had found Brett's docile loyalty difficult to confront without making a fool of herself. Now, in front of them both, her accumulated wrath boiled over and exploded. How could he put up with such "an asparagus stick"? Clashes between the two women had always been one-sided, leaving Frieda gibbering with frustration before the blithe immunity of Brett's deafness. This time she delivered an ultimatum, which must have said in effect: either she goes or I do.

Lawrence bowed to the inevitable. On January 9 he gave Brett, on behalf of them both, her written marching orders: "You, Frieda and I don't make a happy combination now. The best is that we should prepare to separate: that you should go your own way. I am not angry: except that I hate 'situations,' and feel humiliated by them. We can all remain decent and friendly, and go the simplest, quietest way about parting. . . . Stirred-up emotions lead to hate. . . ." He made an effort, in the midst of this embarrassment, to sound gracious. "I am grateful for the things you have done for me. But we must stand apart." Certainly he would miss his valuable typist.

But he would never lose touch with the woman he regarded oddly as a sort of ward—not even with an ocean between them. Though they were about the same age, he had assumed responsibility for her when she joined them, and he was not one to take his responsibilities lightly. Brett, on her way back to the Kiowa ranch, had got as far as Mexico City when she received a guilty, censorious letter from him. She had mentioned a captain she had met, perhaps at her hotel. Frieda had already written hotly to tell her that her friendship with Lawrence was like that between a spinster and a curate. In Lawrence's diatribe one can hear Frieda's belligerent voice coming through. Asserting what he could hardly have known, though surely he knew Murry, he wrote, "Your friendship with Murry was spiritual—you dragged sex in—and he hated you. . . . You like the excitation of sex in the eye, sex in the head. It is an evil and destructive thing. Know from your captain that a bit of warm flame of life is worth all the spiritualness and delicacy and Christ-likeness on this miserable globe. . . ."

PERHAPS HE WAS already becoming ill when he wrote this mean-spirited letter. The year 1925 began horrifically, when the Mexican pantheon of ancient gods with unpronounceable names, Itzpapalotl, Huitzlopcochtl, and Quetzalcoatl, rose up and smote him in February. He had been courting them assiduously, reading their history with his usual thoroughness in Díaz's *Discovery and Conquest of Mexico* and gathering research from other authorities. Pushing on with his most difficult novel he was nearly there, now that Brett had gone, taking with her the reason for Frieda's "states," that Frieda knew herself to be jealousy without cause. She was talking longingly of seeing her mother again, and he himself, when he admitted it, had a hankering to go to England and see his sisters. He had been so long away from those roots that he abused but still needed in a secret part of himself.

Oaxaca was malarial, but Lawrence spurned the use of mosquito nets draped around his bed. He preferred to pull the sheet up over his face at night. One morning he saw mosquito bites on his nose: he went down with malaria "as if he had been shot in the intestines," followed by an attack of dysentery. Of course his tubercular lungs reacted with a horrible gush of blood from a near fatal hemorrhage. Doubled up with stomach cramps, shaking violently, he did not expect to live. The native doctor blamed a combination of malaria and typhoid. Frieda, who has been condemned for her incompetence in caring for Lawrence, was at least without fear. She prepared bags of hot sand to ease the pain in his chest. When he talked of being buried in a local cemetery she told him he was delirious and pretended to laugh at him. The place was too ugly, she said. One awful night that seemed to go on forever he said feebly, "If I die, nothing has mattered but you."

In the midst of this calamity a storm broke that seemed the forerunner of an earthquake. Dogs howled, horses stamped, the whole town shuddered on its foundations. The room plunged into darkness and the ceiling beams groaned and shook in their sockets as the walls trembled. Frieda, if she had no fear of catching her husband's disease, was terrified by this. She crawled under her bed and begged him to do the same. He was too weak to move.

Now more than ever, if he survived this, he wanted to go home, back to England. In the story "The Flying Fish" that would appear posthumously, he wrote of his hero, "He was ill, and he felt as if at the very middle of him, beneath his navel, some membrane were torn, some membrane which had connected him with the world and its day. Something in the hard, fierce, finite sun of Mexico, in the dry terrible land, and in the black staring eyes of the suspicious natives, had made the ordinary day lose its reality for him. It had cracked like some great bubble, and to his uneasiness and terror he had seemed to see through the fissures the deeper blue of that other Greater Day, where moved the other sun shaking its dark blue wings." He felt stranded, lost between the fatal greater day of the Indians and "the fussy, busy lesser day of the white people." The doctor, an educated Indian, injected him with quinine and dosed him with calomel.

It would be weeks before Lawrence was able to get up and crawl out into the plaza. So it was for his hero, Gethin. The square was like

> a great low fountain of green and dark shade, now it was autumn and the rains were over. . . . The low, baroque Spanish buildings stood back with a heavy, sick look, as if they too felt the endless malaria in their bowels. The yellow cathedral leaned its squat, earthquake-shaken towers; the bells sounded hollow. . . . Gethin sat half lying on one of the broken benches, while tropical birds flew and twittered in the great trees, and natives twittered or flitted in silence, and he knew that here the European day was annulled again. His body was sick with the poison that lurks in all tropical air, his soul was sick with that other day, that rather awful greater day which permeates the little days of the old races. He wanted to get out, to get out of this ghastly tropical void into which he had fallen.

8

No Sign of Bud Anywhere

(1925–1926)

Letters ceased to flow from Lawrence's invariably tireless pen, that kept him always in touch, so we can only guess at the date of their departure for Mexico City. It was probably February before he was well enough to travel even this far. They had moved from the house to the Oaxaca hotel so that the sick man could benefit from the better service. When they attempted the tortuous railway journey of 240 miles they had to break their traveling midway and spend the night in a primitive wayside inn. The heat was unremitting. All night long, wrote Frieda in her memoirs, she cried and said over and over to herself in her misery, "He is ill, he is doomed. All my love, all my strength, will never make him whole again."

Like a sick, frightened child he wanted to go "home," by which he meant his native ground and the ghosts there, as well as to be among his close relatives, especially Ada, whom he perhaps loved more than Frieda herself. He no longer cared that England was "small and tight and over-furnished": Ada was there, whom he felt understood him and was most like him in spirit. As for love, he felt that it had deceived him, sometimes denying its very existence. The sexual infighting he and Frieda had been engaged in for more than a decade had done its damage: that and the process of attrition that many long-term marriages know. Ada always blamed Frieda for neglecting her brother, and when quarrels broke out he thought his sister was right.

But he had left everyone for Frieda, and in the midst of this despair the old tenderness they had known at the beginning was rekindled. Lying in bed in Oaxaca trying to recover, by the big window that opened on to the parched street and was heavily barred, he had stared back at children who came to clutch the bars and gaze in with their huge shining eyes, through the fringes of their straight blue-black hair. "He lay in the nausea of the tropics, and let the days pass over him."

He had even allowed himself to be carried onto the train by stretcher when they left Oaxaca for good. In Mexico City he collapsed into the luxury of the Imperial Hotel for another three weeks. Though he detested being examined by doctors, he was seen by Dr. Sidney Ulfeder, head of surgery at the American Hospital, who announced in front of Frieda that her husband had tuberculosis. Lawrence sat saying nothing, only looking at her with "unforgettable eyes."

It was explained to Frieda alone that Lawrence was in stage three, with probably no more than three years to live. She wrote with an attempt at levity to Brett in New Mexico that "L has *Malaria* really and I have a scrap too, my nose is *too* thin, I don't like it. I had better stay fat!" To her mother she wrote a version of the truth: "Oh, Anna, a time of purgatory lies behind me—Now *forwards* once again—L is asleep—the worst was the emotional depression and the *nerves*, it drove one to despair—It was as if he couldn't or wouldn't live on."

The doctors had vetoed any thought of risking the long sea voyage to England and the cold northern spring. They advised returning to the ranch as the only real option. When Lawrence ventured into the city street he looked like a walking corpse. Furious at being stared at, he submitted to having his cheeks colored with some rouge that Frieda had bought. Now he had "such a lovely, healthy complexion that no one ever turned to stare at me again." In his wrecked state he set out with Frieda by Pullman for the frontier. After four nightmarish days on the train he endured an ordeal that he might have foreseen, and perhaps did. At El Paso the immigration authorities "nearly killed me a second time," he told Amy Lowell. He was given a taste of what he called the bolshevist method at its worst, ordered off the train to be stripped and detained while officials decided what to do about this deplorable specimen. It was a day and a half before he knew he had been granted a visitor's visa by this service he described as "insulting, filthy with insolence and of the bottom-doggy order." He had crossed over to the United States by the skin of his teeth, with friends at the American Embassy in Mexico City intervening on his behalf.

At Sante Fe they were met by Bynner, who was shocked by this frail, tottery shadow of a man he had seen less than a year before. Old Mexico had finished his nomadic life. Henceforth he went on as courageously and perversely as before, with concealment of his condition more of a necessity than ever.

The Plumed Serpent has been called his most desperately written book, an effort that left him dangerously weak. He fell ill as soon as he had finished it. Miraculously, there is no sign of strain in this major novel.

Murry, needless to say, would not have agreed. Seeing doom and disintegration throughout, he refers back first of all to "The Spirit of Place," the first chapter of *Studies in Classic American Literature*, where Lawrence says, "The curious thing about art-speech is that it prevaricates so terribly, I mean it tells such lies. I suppose because we always all the time tell ourselves lies. Truly art is a sort of subterfuge. But thank God for it, we can see through the subterfuge if we choose."

Murry chose, on the artist's behalf, since in his view the artist was by now incapable of telling lies from truth. And *The Plumed Serpent* was indisputably a work of art, crafted with immense care. For Murry the most obviously significant thing is that the Lawrence who had been present in *The White Peacock, Sons and Lovers, The Rainbow, Women in Love, Aaron's Rod,* and *Kangaroo,* does not appear in it. "The Man disappears, the Woman remains," he says grimly. Lawrence, in other words, has given up the ghost.

Murry is at his most subtle and deadly in his analysis of *The Plumed Serpent.* Whatever the premise being put forward in a novel by Lawrence, there is always some resistance to it, and it is nearly always female. Thus in *The Plumed Serpent* the Irishwoman Kate Leslie, who becomes involved in the imaginary regeneration of Mexico, "is to the end reluctant and rebellious," not to say deeply skeptical. And it is she who occupies the stage; she is the protagonist. "On the realistic level everything depends upon whether she is convinced, not in the matter of sexuality simply, but in the great religious issues which the book propounds." And as so often in a novel by Lawrence, there is doubt on the very last page. Kate feels a fraud for going along with it all, and is accused of not committing herself. She should "Listen to your own best desire."

Ramon, the leader, is asked by Kate in her role of the Nemesis of doubting man, as Harriet was in *Kangaroo,* why in his moment of triumph he has no confidence in his victory. He replies, "I feel as if my soul were coming undone." Kate can only pity him and say to herself, "He was a man—and therefore not quite real. Not true to life." For it is Lawrence, says Murry, split as it were into Ramon and the little Zapotec general, Cipriano, Kate's lover, whose soul has "come undone." And Murry finds unerringly the words of Ramon that he can apply to Lawrence: "My manhood is a demon howling inside me."

A subtle critic, he praises *The Plumed Serpent* as an imaginative achievement as well as, in his terms, an absorbing document. Lawrence, whom he has described truly as not being concerned with art but with prophecy, has here discarded prophecy for art.

"But the triumph of the artist is the defeat of the prophet," and this, for Murry, can only mean the defeat of Lawrence the man. "Instead of bread, he gives a stone," he ends with biblical solemnity; "instead of a fish, a serpent." Ramon is seen by Kate as someone calling out to be soothed, "like a great helpless wounded thing." Kate remains stubbornly herself, "with her expostulation and her opposition."

BRETT HAD HEARD the joyful news that Lawrence was coming back to the ranch, but she did not know exactly when. She hurried, down to Taos on her horse Prince to find that he had already arrived. There was no sign of him. Instead a beaming Frieda greeted her supposed enemy heartily. "He is here, Brett," she cried, "he is safe upstairs." Lawrence came down slowly and warily like someone old. He gripped her hand warmly, and she was shocked, as Bynner had been, by "how frail and thin and collapsed " he looked.

After staying a few days in Mabel's big house the Lawrences moved up to Kiowa. After assuring Brett in February that the three of them could live together amicably again he now said, shame-facedly, that it would be better if she lived elsewhere. She told him there was no problem, she was renting a cabin at Del Monte, two miles below them. Even so, he had to write to her on April 11 to clarify the position and pacify Frieda. He began awkwardly, "I don't believe Frieda would ever feel friendly towards you again—ever. And that means friction and nothing else. . . . You are, you know, a born separator. Even without knowing it you do it, you set people against one another. It is instinctive with you." It was the sort of thing he had said in 1924 to Mabel. Guilty and unhappy with the situation, he thanked her for helping them so willingly, then tried to blame himself. "Myself I have lost all desire for intense or intimate friendship. Acquaintance is enough. . . . A life in common is an illusion, when the instinct is always to divide, to separate individuals and set them one against the other. . . ." The dream of Rananim had been a mistake.

But Brett was still Lawrence's typist. If she *had* to visit Kiowa it would have to be on Frieda's terms, that is on Monday, Wednesday, and Saturday. Incapable of restraint, she told Brett flatly in a note that she was not to come whenever she felt like it because "you bully me here on my own ground. . . . I wish you no ill, but don't want you in my life." It was difficult to imagine a shy, deaf Englishwoman of breeding capable of bullying someone as strong as Frieda, but Brett had strengths of her own, despite appearances. She hung a box on a tall pine tree in the wood so that Lawrence could stay in touch with her by mail.

He was creating a sort of health routine for himself. He lay out on the small porch in the clear cold April air, drinking milk and eating eggs and buying bottles of Pantanberge Solution for his chest. Soon he was impatient to be active again. His powers of recovery had always been extraordinary and must have been at least partly due to a strong constitution. The irrigation ditch had to be cleared again, and he was helped by the young Indian, Trinidad, his wife Rufina taking on some of the chores.

Lawrence never enjoyed life more than when he was active physically, watering the patch of garden in bare feet, liking the feel of the cold mountain water running over his toes. He chopped wood for the stove and built a shelter for Susan the black cow. He resumed his favorite occupation, kneading bread and baking it in the outdoor oven. To Ada, who adored him, he wrote on April 30 to say nostalgically that the flowers in her garden sounded wonderful, especially the auriculas and the polyanthus. "I like them so much." These domestic letters, studded with the names of things familiar to him from his childhood, are always touching. Ada had moved to a new house, and he hoped the blanket he had sent her had arrived.

As for Kiowa, he was battling to make things grow in the terrible dryness. Only the scarlet and yellow wild columbines flourished. His garden seeds, nasturtium and sweet pea, were only an inch high: he spoke as if they represented his lost England. He hoped one summer, he wrote sadly, that Ada would come and see it all, "and learn to ride a horse." But he knew that could not happen—in September their visas expired.

He wrote more cheerfully of the young Indians "dobeying" the cabins, "plastering them outside with a sort of golden-brown mud—they look pretty. It is done every spring." And of the livestock, the white and brown hens, the black cow, the four horses—even a wild rabbit caught by Trinidad, who had seen a deer last week behind the cabins. "But I don't want him to shoot it." He was proud of the simple way he lived, pleased that he felt almost himself again. Frieda's nephew, Friedal Jaffe, a quiet boy, nice, had come to stay with them.

Tony Luhan came up one day and shot a porcupine. It made Lawrence angry, but out of the incident came his magnificent essay, "Reflections on the Death of a Porcupine." He began with mundane facts: the Indians, Mexicans, and Americans all said that the porcupine damaged trees and should be killed. A month earlier he had gone down in the brilliant moonlight and seen a big porcupine waddling off in the direction of the trees and the darkness. It was harmless, but he disliked its "beetle's squalid motion" and its attempt to climb "scrapily" up a pine trunk. "It was very like a great aureoled tick, a bug, struggling up." He found it repugnant, somehow brutal, and felt it was his duty to kill it, but his dislike of killing it was greater than the dislike of the creature.

Why was that? The effort to understand his reluctance to kill leads him to examine the whole question of man established on the earth, forced to fight for his place.

> Food, the basis of existence, has to be fought for even by the most idyllic of farmers. . . . Food, food, how strangely it relates man with the animal and vegetable world. . . . And how fierce is the fight that goes on around it. And when one watches the horses in the big field, their noses to the ground, bite-bite-biting at the grass, cropping off the grass, the young shoots of alfalfa, the dandelions, with a blind, relentless, unwearied persistence, one's whole life pauses. One sud-

denly realizes again how all creatures devour, and *must* devour the lower forms of life. It is an essential part of all existence and of all being. . . . The Buddhist who refuses to take life is really ridiculous, since if he eats only two grains of rice per day, it is two grains of life. We did not make creation, *we* are not the authors of the universe.

The writing ranges out, wider and wider, from this meditation on death and survival to the passionate eloquence of what is essentially the gospel he has preached in book after book. Man must blossom or he will die out. So far he is no more than leaves and roots. "No sign of bud anywhere." The artist has not killed off the prophet, as Murry predicted. In a passage anticipating the noble utterance of his last book, *Apocalypse*, he warns: "To men, the sun is becoming stale, and the earth sterile. But the sun itself will never become stale, nor the earth barren. It is only that the *clue* is missing inside men. . . . Vitality depends upon the clue of the Holy Ghost inside a creature, a man, a nation, a race. . . . Blossoming means the establishing of a pure, new relationship with all the cosmos. This is the state of heaven. And it is the state of a flower, a cobra, a jenny-wren in spring, a man when he knows himself royal and crowned with the sun, with his feet gripping the core of the earth. . . . Every revelation is a torch held out, to kindle new revelations. As the dandelion holds out the sun to me, saying, 'Can you take it?' "

AS WELL AS "Reflections," one of his most important essays, he wrote four more on the novel and why it mattered, calling it "the book of life." But as he moved into early summer he was acutely aware that their days in this little outpost of tumbledown cabins called Kiowa were numbered, though he would always hope to come back there one day. The place had deeply affected him, more so than any other. It would grieve him to leave the stupendous light, and his horses, his black cow, Moses the white cock, and his cat

Timsy, so pretty, so fine with "her bloom of aliveness," such a combination of "soft, snow-flaky lightness and lean ferocity."

Meanwhile the comical searching for black-eyed Susan the cow continued morning and evening as he went to milk her. He searched for her on foot and on horseback, using the opera glasses that had belonged to Frieda's mother, cursing her, and then being totally disarmed by her meek black gaze, her total innocence, and the twitching of her large ears.

One night Brett dreamed, and kept to herself, a dream of Frieda, Lawrence, and herself being met by a young man. The young man was Lawrence himself when young and beardless. "You had met your youth and fallen in love with it and gone off with it," which left the dream-Frieda bereft. As for Brett, she did not like this dream. Years later she was led to believe that it foretold death.

His childlessness still saddened him. He hated to talk of dreams but did mention a recurring dream of his nephew William as a boy who came toward him with open arms, stopped by a gulf between them. Rachel Hawk's little boy Walton fascinated him. A photograph of Brett's shows Lawrence giving the child a ride on his horse Azul, sitting astride it with his arms holding the little boy pressed to him safely.

The petty warfare between Frieda and Brett went on sporadically, dictated by Frieda's moods. Friedal Jaffe was sometimes the go-between, riding down with his aunt's letters alleging that Brett was a mischief-maker and she would not have her life messed up by her. Suddenly the worm turned: Brett said angrily to Lawrence one day: "If Frieda starts her spinster and asparagus nonsense again I will rope her to a tree and hit her on the nose until she really has something to yell about."

For once Lawrence was utterly at a loss for words. More letters were fired to and fro, including a fierce one from Lawrence, until Brett, according to her memoir, sat down and wrote a satire on the whole silly business and Frieda's notion of her as the breaker-up of happy homes. She gave it to Lawrence to deliver, who shook his head and said that unlike him, Frieda never knew when she was being intimate. "Have you not found that a bit inconvenient at times?" Brett remarked. She had struck a chord, and he smilingly admitted as much. Next morning he was delighted by her letter to Frieda, by its irony and the subtle dig at himself. And when the two women met again Frieda was at her nicest, simple and fresh as only she could be. Another time Brett found Lawrence dressed formally because there had been guests. Susan the cow was scared of him, so much so that he was unable to milk her. Not until he had changed back into his old corduroys and blue shirt did Susan, after sniffing at him carefully, allow him to approach with the pail.

In his new essays he had made significant claims for the novel as a "thought adventure" exploring "the relation between man and his circumambient universe." He expressed his philosophy in more personal terms to Mollie Skinner in Australia. "One can live so intensely with one's characters and the experience one creates or records, it is a life in itself, far better than the vulgar thing that people *call* life. . . ." Mollie Skinner's brother Jack had died, on whose life *The Boy in the Bush* was based. "Death's not sad, when one has lived," he said in his letter of condolence. Mulling over what he knew of her brother's life revealed aspects of himself he had never owned up to so plainly before. One could see in her brother's face, he told her, that he never really wanted to be a success: he preferred to drift. "I think if I had to choose, myself, between being a Duke of Portland or having a million sterling and forced to live up to it, I'd rather, far, far rather be a penniless tramp. . . . I believe that was what ailed your brother: he couldn't bear the social fixture of everything. It's what ails me too."

Not long before they left they were visited by Kyle Crichton, American journalist, who came with his wife on a kind of pilgrimage. Like Lawrence he was the son of a coalminer, and was trying to write a novel about a young man from the mines who had worked in steel mills (like himself) and was relieved to be back in the mines again. The two couples hit it off, with Crichton and his wife doubled up with laughter at Lawrence's impersonation of Ford Madox Ford, fixing an imaginary monocle in his eye and mimicking the "humph-humph almost unintelligible way that Ford's friends remember so well." The man was a bit of a fool, said Lawrence, but genuinely kind, and "gave me the first push."

After he had read through Crichton's draft he said with his usual directness that it was too journalistic, too much concerned with facts. One had to delve into the *human inside* more, below the workingman's consciousness. "Give the mystery, the cruelty, the deathliness of steel, as against the comparative softness, silkiness, naturalness of coal." Crichton should be aware of symbols. Coal was a symbol of something in the soul, "old and dark and silky and natural, and matrix of fire. . . . You've got to allow yourself to be the mystic your real self is, under all the American efficiency and smartness of the ego. . . ." When Crichton had asked him what made a man a writer, Frieda butted in to say, "Egotism . . . he wants to show the world what a great fellow he is." Lawrence shook his head. "It isn't that . . . a man writes rather from a deep moral sense—for the race, as it were. You want to see it published, but you don't care what's said about it."

Crichton noticed that they had no more than ten books in the house: they relied on people to send them things. In a second letter, written on board ship, Lawrence said he had been thinking of what Crichton said about not having the courage to be a creative writer. He understood why: "America, of all countries, kills that courage, simply because it sees no value in it: whereas it esteems, more highly than any other country, the journalistic effort: it loves a thrill or a sensation, but loathes to be in any way inwardly affected, so that a new adjustment is necessary. . . ."

He left Kiowa on September 10, 1925, after giving a last, long look from his perch in the Rockies over to the canyon of the Rio Grande. His essay "New Mexico" is a rehearsed farewell for that day in his heart, as he saw "the little brown adobe houses and the puckered folds of mesa-sides" and remembered the sun setting each dusk "above the shallow cauldron of simmering darkness," the round mountain of Colorado to the north. "It was beauty, beauty absolute." He would carry away with him the unforgettable dances of the Indian young men, running naked, smeared with white earth and stuck with "bits of eagle stuff for the swiftness of the heavens," brushed with eagle feathers by the old men to give them power. He would never forget their strange hurling run forward, "to come, by sheer cumulative, hurling effort of the bodies of men into contact with the great cosmic source of vitality which gives strength, power, energy to the men who can grasp it, energy for the zeal of attainment."

ON HIS WAY through New York to join the *SS Resolute* he managed to collect three thousand dollars in royalties from a Seltzer tottering on the brink of bankruptcy, who still vainly hoped to hang on to his author. The firm closed down in 1927, and Lawrence had seen the signs. He and Frieda were photographed on the deck by news reporters. Brenda Maddox's description is a haunting one: "he gaunt and wrung out, with the dazed staring eyes of one come out of the tomb: Frieda fashionable for once, beautiful, defiant and sad." Rumor had it that they were destined for Egypt, but in fact they were going to England and then Europe, and he would not leave Europe again. Anne Conway, a Scottish friend in Mexico City, had sent Frieda a sprig of white heather for luck. Lawrence in his thankyou note said wryly that "Whatever else married people share and don't share, their luck is one."

To his friends the Brewsters he wrote, three days out of Southampton, that the vague plan was to stay in England a month or so and then begin to move south, to escape that old enemy the northern winter. He said the same to the Hawks, and he was clearly bored. Unlike his other sea trips, this one was a disappointment. "I had one awful day, blind with a headache."

They landed in an England which had a million and a quarter

unemployed and on the dole, living on a bare subsistence. In London they stayed at Garland's Hotel in Suffolk Street, then were lent a flat in Gower Street, Bloomsbury. He wrote to tell Brett how damp and dreary it was, and how unreal. "I feel queer and foreign here but look on with wonder instead of exasperation, this time. It's like being inside an aquarium, the people all fishes swimming on end. No doubt about it, England is the most fantastic Alice-in-Wonderland country."

Old friends in London came and went, including friends from his time in Capri. He called on Compton Mackenzie one morning, found him still undressed and said, "I hate those damned silk pyjamas." "Not as much," answered an amused Mackenzie, "as I hate that godawful grey flannel shirt you wear every other day."

A new acquaintance was the young novelist William Gerhardie, met recently at a literary party. Lawrence's contradictory behavior fascinated Gerhardie, as did his turbulent marriage. When Frieda's husband attacked Lord Beaverbrook, owner of the *Daily Express*, for his anti-German bias, Frieda joined in fiercely. "Not so much intensity, Frieda." She retorted angrily in front of Gerhardie, "If I want to be intense I'll be intense, and you can go to hell!"

That autumn Murry came up from Dorset to see them. He had married Violet de Maistre, his assistant on the *Adelphi*, and they were expecting another child. Frieda had made herself scarce, and the two men met quietly, Murry at his nicest, but for Lawrence there was now nothing between them. He met Frieda's children for the first time; Barbara, the young one, "engaged to an absolute nothingness of a fellow, 35, would-be artist, born failure, sponge on a woman's emotions." She was about to break off the engagement, and her stepfather fully approved. Elsa, the elder, had a job and was "quite bouncy. Privately, I can't stand Frieda's children. They have a sort of suburban bounce and *suffisance* which puts me off." The son, Monty, declined to appear, which Lawrence took for a snub. He worked in the Victoria and Albert Museum "and soon, very probably, will sit in one of the glass cases, as a specimen of the perfect young Englishman."

In October they went up to visit Lawrence's two sisters. Emily was now in Nottingham, rather stolid and matronly; her marriage since the war had not gone well. They stayed with Ada at her new house in Ripley, Derbyshire. He thought Ada resembled him in looks. The visit must have been uncomfortable, because Ada blamed Frieda for taking her adored brother away. Not well, he was dosed like a child with Regesan Catarrh Jelly, but kept coughing. He grumbled to Secker, "Of course I'm in bed with a cold the moment I come here."

Barbara Weekley visited them in Ripley, and she saw at once how her mother was unable to fit in with Ada's regime in her spick and span villa. There was an angry outburst from Lawrence when Barbara, pressed to stay overnight, came back from a phone call to the friend of her father where she was staying to say that she did not have permission. Lawrence, white faced, cursed the "mean, dirty little insults" Frieda was being made to endure again because of him.

Brett was on her way to England, advised by Lawrence to try Capri: he had friends there who would look after her. Gertler maintained in a letter to Koteliansky that Lawrence hung on to Brett because she "intrigued" him for some reason. She was certainly as infatuated with him as ever, but the fact was that he simply felt responsible for her welfare, in spite of all the harsh words he had leveled at her. She hoped she would arrive in time to see him in London, but when she got there the Lawrences were already traveling to Baden-Baden. Writing from there, he kept watch over her with his usual protectiveness. She should see his friend Dr. Eder in Harley Place, he suggested: he might be able to cure her deafness by hypnosis. "He's poor, pay him a little fee."

He thought he and Frieda might perhaps end up in Capri themselves, but Frieda had other ideas. At Baden-Baden she went to a hairdresser and came back with her hair "bobbed, permanently waved, fluffed," her husband wrote disgustedly. It is difficult to imagine this transformation, and it must have soon grown out, but she was pleased: it made her look like Jane Austen, she said. She put her foot down when it came to going south. Northern Italy was her choice, so that she could stay within reach of her children and her mother. Martin Secker knew of a small villa, the Bernada, on the Italian Riviera at Spotorno, and there they settled for the winter.

THIS HOUSE on a hill overlooking the Mediterranean belonged to Angelo Ravagli, a lieutenant of the Bersaglieri in Savona. He showed Lawrence the house on the Italian queen's birthday and looked rather splendid, though small, in full dress uniform. Lawrence was taken with his plumed helmet and blue sash, and fetched Frieda to admire him. This man, married with three children, was twelve years younger than the effusive German and would live with her in America after Lawrence's death.

He impressed the Englishman at the outset by coming in over-alls to mend the stove, then climbing up on the roof with him to re-pair the chimney. The house was on three floors, Lawrence reported to William Hawk. They lived on the top floor in the Italian country style, with a bedroom below and the bottom floor stored with their belongings. But he missed the ranch. Alas, there were no horses to ride, no spring from which to fetch the water, no black-eyed cow to milk.

Frieda refused to have a maid: instead an old man, Giovanni, the gardener, who lived down below somewhere, did all their fetching and carrying, went shopping every morning at 7:30, pumped the water, and was always available. They were soon going for walks in the hills, braving the cold winds. "Yesterday we got oranges from the trees and made marmalade, which I burnt a bit. But it's good." The pine trees were not like at Kiowa; they were puffs of umbrella pines, in separate clumps on the stony slopes dropping down to the sea. He thanked the Hawks for taking care of their things—even the beds had been stored—and enclosed twenty-five dollars toward the horses. It was mid-December. He pictured their "jolly wood fires"—and probably bright crackly days.

Invitations were soon being dispatched to friends, urging them to visit. One actually went to Murry, who said he would come but for his wife's pregnancy. Lawrence suspected it was because he was unable to tear himself away from his precious *Adelphi*, and jeered, "Bah, that one should be a mountain of mere words!" Frieda, in a postscript to a letter from Lawrence to Brett, said that she felt happy for no reason, and why not: "Just feel like it and basta." But another postscript hinted at a reason. "We have a nice little Bersaglieri officer to whom the villa belongs. I am thrilled by his cock feathers, he is almost as nice as the feathers!" Brenda Maddox wittily comments, "A plumed serpent had glided into their lives."

Christmas was drawing near. Lawrence wrote on December 19 to Ada's son, John, enclosing a pound, "but it's only ten shillings to you. I want you to buy something for your Auntie Gertie with the other ten bob." Gertrude Cooper was not really an aunt—she had been a friend of the Lawrence children, together with her sister Frances. Their father Thomas Cooper had owned the property at Lynn Croft, the house with the bay window to which the Lawrence family moved in Eastwood when they went "up in the world." As a responsible uncle he instructed his nephew to write on Gertie's present, "From Bert and Frieda." He signed off, "Love from your Auntie Frieda and your ever estimable Uncle Bert."

He was now fond of Barbara Weekley, and she came for Christmas. Because of her father's veto she was forced to stay in Alassio and be chaperoned. All the same, much of her time was spent at the Villa Bernarda. Her stepfather taught her Italian and did his best to win her over to his side when hostilities broke out between him and her mother. He listened to her condemnation of Grandma Weekley, and a venomous monster of an old grandmother duly appeared in "The Virgin and the Gipsy." He wrote the novella at a furious pace in January 1926 and sent it off handwritten to Secker. Before

Christmas he had been writing short stories, a little lost because he had no novel to work on. "Sun" was on the theme of sun worship. It came out in a limited edition in September 1926 and with the Black Sun Press in an expanded version in 1928. "Glad Ghosts," another of his supernatural stories, was meant for Lady Cynthia Asquith's *Ghost Book*, though in the event she preferred "The Rocking Horse Winner." In general he was trying to care less about whether he wrote or not, lecturing Murry on the futility of taking things seriously. "To kill yourself like Keats for what you've got to say is to mix the eggshell with the omelette. . . . I'll contrive, if I can, to get enough money to live on," but that was all. "No, no! I'm forty, and I want, in a good sense, to enjoy my life."

These good intentions did nothing to prevent fights between him and Frieda, often when Barbara was present. She may have been unwittingly a cause, since the bond between her and her mother was close, and Lawrence was jealous. One evening in an ugly scene he accused Frieda in front of Barbara of not loving him and being incapable of loving anyone. "Look at her false face," he cried, flinging his red wine at her. His tall stepdaughter shouted, "My mother is too good for you . . . it's like pearls before swine."

IN FEBRUARY 1926, with Barbara still there, Frieda's other daughter Elsa came to stay. These two confident young women, "daughters who are by no means mine," talking volubly with their mother, made him feel isolated and "absolutely swamped out," he wrote angrily in his letter to William Hawk. To complicate matters in this situation of mounting tension, Lawrence's sister Ada arrived with a friend. All these intimate conversations were pushing him out, he complained to Ada. He fell ill with what he called his annual flu, and Ada, not slow to see the interest Frieda was showing in Ravagli's regular weekend visits, nursed her brother in his room and then locked the door against his wife, in Ada's eyes an immoral woman. "I hate you from the bottom of my heart," she told Frieda, who promptly retaliated by moving out with her daughters to a hotel. It was after this, most probably, that the affair with Ravagli really began.

Lawrence had boxed himself into a corner. As soon as he was well enough he accompanied Ada and her friend to Monte Carlo, before they returned home to England. His sister was not tempted to gamble, and he thought the place vulgar and boring. After she had gone he mooned about on his own, completely directionless. He might go to Nice, he wrote to one friend, or perhaps Spain. Sitting alone on the beach at Nice, he went into the Hotel Brice for a cup of tea and wrote miserably to his departed sister: "It *does* feel a bit lonely now, when I can't walk round and find you in your room. And I was awfully sorry we had all this upset: I was so looking forward to your coming and having a good time." He thought her friend Lizzie "awfully nice, so peaceful to have with one."

Because he had friends in Capri, as well as Brett, he decided to make for there. He would have loved to turn for home, but he and Frieda were in entrenched positions and he was the last person to admit he was in the wrong. He reached Capri on February 27. The Brewsters were there, about to travel to India in ten days. Brett, with Lawrence to herself at last, could hardly believe her luck. But one glance told her how down he was. He had come by launch from the mainland. She hurried to greet this figure dressed in a new gray suit, brown Homburg, brown shoes, and beneath the clothes "how delicate and collapsed you look." Achsah Brewster would put him up, and in the carriage ascending the hill, the bells jingling on the harness, the horse's plumes and ribbons fluttering in the wind, he talked longingly of their horses in the Rockies. "Think of Prince and Azul and Aaron with plumes on their heads," he said, "how surprised they would be."

Next day, on a walk with Brett, white and tired, he talked with such hopelessness of his situation that she began to think he had actually left Frieda. He spoke wildly of leasing a sailing ship to sail among the Greek islands and be free, but his words had no conviction. He saw Faith Mackenzie who was there alone, and took her out to dinner. Over the wine she referred to her open marriage.

Some months later she would serve as a model for the woman in his short story "Two Blue Birds," and no doubt regretted her indiscretion. Another story, "The Man Who Loved Islands," angered Compton Mackenzie enough for him to consider a libel action. Lawrence wrote to Ada that Faith Mackenzie was "another woman who loves her husband but can't live with him."

With the Brewsters busy packing he wandered down to Brett's hotel to see her "primrose Christ," a picture she had just finished. If she thought he would be pleased, she had miscalculated. "It's too like me," he said flatly. "You'll have to change it." He asked her in some astonishment how she had come by the idea. She said in defense that he had in effect inspired it. Not only Christ in the crucifixion scene but the head of Pan below him were both Lawrence. "It is you," she said again, to which he replied grimly, "Perhaps."

They crossed over one day to Ravello on the mainland, now that the Brewsters had gone, to visit two painters he had known in Sicily, Miss Beveridge and Miss Harrison. "We are the only two left," he said gloomily to Brett. "Only you and I. Everyone else has gone over to the enemy." Brett, appalled at the despair in his voice, could only say that she thought it would all come right for him in a little while. "If not," she ventured, "why not break free?" He still spoke nostalgically about New Mexico, and she tried to encourage him to return with her. But a newly established quota system for immigrants meant that though the way was clear for her, he, as he well knew, was not healthy enough. When they attempted to find hotel rooms in Ravello there were none available. Finally they heard of a cottage that had rooms they could use. That night they climbed a tortuous path to the old wooden door in a stone archway. Lawrence brandished the huge rusty key he had been given. They clambered up to their rooms and said goodnight. Brett blew out her candle and jumped into the "hard, relentless bed."

In her nineties in Taos she had a different story to tell. Lawrence, she claimed, joined her in bed. Elaine Feinstein thinks her account could well be an invention, and for the puritan Lawrence to have abandoned his principles at a time when, according to Frieda, he was virtually impotent because of the advanced state of his disease, would have meant risking yet more humiliation. In any case he had never found Brett sexually attractive. Brett's feeling of inadequacy, inflicted by her father and again by Murry, could perhaps have helped to create this wish fulfillment dream toward the end of her life.

Lawrence, wondering when his "chapter of dismalnesses" would end, said goodbye to a disappointed Brett after helping her to pack for her return to the United States. He had uttered the words she had not wanted to hear: "I may go back to Frieda soon; she is quieter now, more friendly. I can't tell. Her last letter was so much better." But when he wrote to say he might be coming back she was noncommittal. A drawing he had sent her with his last letter showed Jonah about to be swallowed by the whale, over the inscription, "Who is going to swallow whom?" She did not find it funny.

Not sure of his ground, he took his time about returning, traveling slowly north in the company of the two maiden lady painters, staying in Rome, Perugia, Assisi, Florence, and Ravenna. Frieda as it happened had begun to enjoy the separation, now that she was back in the villa with her two daughters, walking under the almond trees and flirting with Ravagli. Her daughters too were loving it, she wrote to Koteliansky, "and the Italian youths hang around like bees! And I feel like the proud old hen. . . . The spring is here pink and white!" And so it was. April had come, and back came a chastened Lawrence to be welcomed at the station by three females "all dressed up festively" in their nicest clothes. Later, when he felt established again, he swore that Frieda's girls had made the reconciliation possible because the time alone with their mother had turned their sympathy to him. What they had apparently said to her was, "Be reasonable, you've married him, now you must stick to him." Lawrence painted a somewhat different picture in his letter to Ada, saying that "her children are very fierce with her, and fall on her tooth and nail. They simply won't stand for her egotism for a minute: she is furious, then becomes almost humble with us all. I think they've taught her a lesson."

9

Return of the Native
(1926–1927)

The lease was about to expire on the villa, and Lawrence had a long-held desire to write a travel book about the Etruscans. Why not find a house on the outskirts of Florence? Some extensive reading around the subject had suddenly inspired him. He wanted to visit the painted tombs in Tuscany and Umbria and then pay homage to this lost culture.

Weakened more than he knew by his insidious illness, he was in a mood to sit down under a tree and simply come to himself. He wrote to Earl Brewster in India that "The more I go around, the nearer I do come, in a certain way, to your position." The passivity of Brewster's religion had begun to appeal to him. "I am convinced that every man needs a bho tree of some sort in his life. What ails us, we have cut down all our bho trees. . . . Still, here and there in the world a solitary bho tree must be standing, 'where two or three of ye have met together.'"

The bho tree, where the Buddha sat to achieve enlightenment, was still on his mind when he exclaimed to Mabel Sterne, "Lord, what a life! It's pouring with rain and I'm feeling weary to death of struggling with Frieda. I feel like turning to Buddha and crying basta!" This was hardly what she wanted to hear. Why didn't he turn to her, a more suitable partner in every way? He had finished her book, "Memoirs of a Born American," and could not believe she had naively failed to change the names. "Remember, other people can be utterly remorseless if they think you've given them away." Her book was not art, because "art always gilds the pill, and this is hemlock in a cup."

At last he was on the move again with his party, "for where I don't quite know." First stop was Florence, where they arrived on April 20 and booked in to the Pensione Lucchesi, where Lawrence had stayed before. Frieda's daughters would have liked to have seen more of Italy, but time was running out for them, and they returned to England on April 28. Mussolini had taken over Italy, with bands playing martial music in the streets. Detractors of Lawrence who allege fascist tendencies have chosen to ignore his contempt for the local *fascisti* when in Sicily, and his response to the news of the attempted assassination of Mussolini on April 7. The dictator escaped with an injured nose, and Lawrence's reaction was, "Put a ring through it."

While in Florence they met two English brothers, the Wilkinsons. Arthur Wilkinson lived with his family in a villa seven miles out of Florence. He was acquainted with Raul Miranda, who owned the farm-villa next to his. The property had a top floor that was vacant. The Lawrences looked it over on April 29. It looked grand from the outside but inside was rather basic, virtually empty on its top floor, the lower floors cluttered with equipment for the making and storing of wine. Upstairs, where they proposed to live, there was a sequence of rooms, all linked in the old Italian manner, with superb views all the way down to Florence and its famous Duomo. For a whole year they could live for four thousand lire—they had paid the same amount for four months at Spotorno. They were at Scandicci, which was the tram terminus from Florence. From the terminus you walked for half an hour up through the hills, until the Villa Miranda appeared in the midst of vineyards, olive trees, and woods.

Pleased with their find, Lawrence wrote a cheerful letter to his niece Margaret King on May 3, a day before the Trades Union Congress in England called a general strike. There was already a coal strike in Eastwood, but he hoped it wouldn't spread. As it was he felt "a bit sickish about it." The villa they had taken had only about five sticks of furniture in its brick-floored upper rooms. It was old and lovely, with two gardens below, the vines and olives sloping away, and three families of peasants close by to work the place. He was delighted to find himself with congenial if eccentric neighbors who, like them, favored the simple life.

Arthur Wilkinson was an English artist, his wife Scottish, and they had with them a daughter and son, all fitted out with sandals and knapsacks. Wilkinson "has the wildest red beard sticking out all round," but they were jolly and intelligent, "paint and play guitar and things." Arthur and his family had toured with a puppet show in England with puppets made by themselves, traveling everywhere by caravan. Lawrence told his niece that if they brought the show here to Italy he would go with them "and bang the drum in the Italian villages." The Lawrences and Wilkinsons were soon visiting each other for tea and finding they liked the same things, charades and singsongs. He urged his niece to hurry up and get a good job with her shorthand and save her money so that she could come out and see them. Not in the mood for literary work, he was supposed to be reading up about "my precious Etruschi."

With his growing aversion to fascist ideology and its mimicry of the Roman Empire, he felt instinctively attracted to the Etruscan world "whom the Romans, in their usual neighborly fashion, wiped out entirely in order to make room for Rome with a big R." He had already read George Dennis's standard English work, *Cities and Cemeteries of Etruria*, probably supplied in the Everyman edition by Koteliansky. The textbook he had written for schools to earn money, *Movements in European History*, had probably obliged him to read Mommsen's *History of Rome*. Millicent Beveridge, now back in England, supplied him with R.A.L. Fell's *Etruria and Rome*. These authorities were all dusty and dull but spurred him on to "take the imaginative line" when he was ready to do so. This would not be for some time. He asked his sister-in-law Else Jaffe on May 26 to look at Weege's *Etruskische Malerei* and tell him whether the reproductions were good. His book would, he thought, be a counterblast to ancient Rome, not to apes of the caesars like Mussolini who were a joke.

For once he was in no hurry. There were lovely things in the Etruscan Museum in Florence that he would like Else to look at with him. Thanking Millicent for Fell's book, he considered him very thorough in "washing out the few rags of information we have concerning the Etruscans," but that was all. In the end he would delay visiting the sites and tombs until he had a companion, who would be Earl Brewster.

CONTENTMENT is not a word one associates with Lawrence, but his period at the Villa Miranda must surely count as among his happiest. Frieda was at her most indolent, reluctant to move, even to see her mother, though the old lady's seventy-fifth birthday on July 14 would make it imperative. As the weather warmed up, Lawrence was content for once to live quietly, wearing only shirt and trousers and sandals and going on picnics out to the stream. Publishers were asking for another novel, but "Let the public read the old novels," he retorted. He was still raw inside at the thought of *The Plumed Serpent* and how it had laid waste to him.

To a friend he wrote blithely, "The cicadas rattle away all day in the trees, the girls sing, cutting the corn with the sickles, the sheaves of wheat lie all the afternoon like people dead asleep in the heat. I don't work, except for an occasional scrap of an article. . . . Why do any more books? There are so many, and such a small demand for what there are. So why add to the burden. . . . Because it costs one a lot of blood." The scene of the corn harvest would have taken him back to his youth, to hot days helping with the hay harvest at Haggs

Farm in an atmosphere like a picnic, the stack rising "disheveled and radiant among the steady, golden-green glare of the field," the farmer bringing out dinner and tea in the milk-float, everything still as a trance in the heat. How far off those days must have seemed, how passionate the friendships in the intense sunlight, how carefree and healthy he had been.

WRITING to his niece again toward the end of June he described one of his typical summer days. Everyone got up at 4:30, and then from 1:00 till about 3:30 in the afternoon the whole countryside went to sleep, not a peasant anywhere in the corn or among the vines, "all deep asleep. We take a siesta too. Then the evening comes cooler, and the nightingales start singing again. . . . The wheat is very fine, and just turning yellow under the olive trees."

"Flowery Tuscany" sprang from his pen here at Scandicci, an essay as famous as it is entrancing. He loved Tuscany for its secrecy and for not drawing attention to itself, "so many hills popping up, and they take no notice of one another." In a region so intensively cultivated as Tuscany, he marveled that there was yet so much room for the wild flowers and the nightingale. "Talk of hanging gardens of Babylon, all Italy, apart from the plains, is a hanging garden." For centuries

> man has been patiently modeling the surface of the Mediterranean countries, gently rounding the hills, and graduating the big slopes and the little slopes into the almost invisible levels of terraces. Thousands of square miles of Italy have been lifted in human hands, piled and laid back in tiny flats, held up by the drystone walls, whose stones came from the lifted earth. . . . It is the gentle sensitive sculpture of all the landscape. And it is the achieving of the peculiar Italian beauty which is so exquisitely natural, because man, feeling his way sensitively to the fruitfulness of the earth, has molded the earth to his necessity without violating it.

No one has written more eloquently of the sun and the sunshine, and this essay ends with his tribute to it. "We can think of death, if we like, as of something permanently intervening between us and the sun: and this is at the root of the southern, under-world idea of death. But this doesn't alter the sun at all. As far as experience goes, the one thing that is always there is the shining sun. In the sunshine, even death is sunny." That is why for him the Tuscan landscape was free of any sense of tragedy.

Van Gogh in the south felt exactly the same. In the north his apprehension of death emerged as grim indeed. Yet *The Reaper* he painted in Provence draws close almost invisibly in a guise of yellow, the green glint of his scythe the only clue, the sun flooding everything in broad daylight. This is an "almost smiling" southern death.

Happy though they were to do very little as the Italian sun strengthened, the Lawrences, always keen to stay in contact with expatriates, would have regular expeditions to Florence, walking down through the hills and getting on the tram at the terminus. Reggie Turner, a fey, kindly novelist with a private income, was someone to visit if one wanted to be amused, and it was through him probably that Lawrence now got to know the plump antiquarian bookseller Giuseppe Orioli, who had a shop on the Lungarno Corsini. Lawrence would be a constant visitor here during the birth of *Lady Chatterley's Lover*.

It may have been Reggie Turner who arranged a meeting between the Lawrences and Sir George and Lady Ida Sitwell, "parents of the writing trio" as Lawrence described them to Millicent Beveridge. Their castle, fourteen miles out of Florence, was enormous and seemed to be stuffed full of antique beds, of which Sir George was a collector: "those four-poster golden Venetian monsters that look like Mexican high altars. Room after room, and nothing but bed after bed." When Lawrence asked slyly whether guests were put in them, the eccentric Sir George cried, "They're not to sleep in— they're museum pieces." Also everywhere were "gilt and wiggly-carved chairs." A weary Lawrence ventured to sit down on one and shot up in alarm when his host barked, "Those chairs are not for sitting in." In his letter Lawrence remarked without enthusiasm that "the trio" would be out there in September from England, so they supposed they would meet them.

The senior Sitwells were not impressed with their red-bearded visiting writer and his wife. Lady Ida, writing to her son Osbert, wrote acidly to say that "A Mr. D. H. Lawrence came over the other day, a funny little petit-maître of a man with flat features and a beard. He says he is a writer, and seems to know all of you. His wife is a large German. She went round the house with your father, and when he showed her anything, would look at him, lean against one of the gilded beds and breathe heavily."

In July they were heading north to Baden-Baden to mark the occasion of his mother-in-law's seventy-fifth birthday. Because he felt well he was not keen, yet he did think he might like to visit London, if only to ginger up the theatrical society that seemed about to commit itself to a staging of his play *David*. Also there was Ada to consider. She had taken a bungalow in Mabelthorpe for August and wanted her brother to come—but not his wife.

He had become acquainted in correspondence, but not yet in the flesh, with Rolf Gardiner, a young farmer and Cambridge graduate who looked to Lawrence as a potential leader and prophet. With characteristic ambivalence, Lawrence was as much alarmed as gratified by Gardiner's approach, though he had in fact brought it about by the ideas of leadership explored in *The Plumed Serpent*. In the realm of ideas Gardiner was undoubtedly a disciple, for whom Lawrence was a torchbearer. He had been following the novelist's books closely while setting up Land Service camps for youth in Germany and England. Fired by the older man's interest and by Lawrence's evident dislike of democracy, he wrote to him at Baden-Baden suggesting a meeting.

The reply to Gardiner on July 22 was far from discouraging. The young man's letter had been "like a bluster in the weather":

Lawrence was holding his hat on. But he was prepared to fit Gardiner into his arrangements on coming to London on July 30. He and Frieda would be in a small flat at 25 Rossetti Gardens, Chelsea, from which he would roam off to see his sisters in the Midlands and go to Scotland. "I believe we are mutually a bit scared, I of weird movements and you of me, I don't know why."

Gardiner had proposed a visit to one of his camps in Yorkshire. Lawrence thought he would like to come. "I should like even to try to dance a sword-dance with iron-stone miners above Whitby." Was he serious? His confession immediately following this was more than serious: a genuine cry from the heart. "I should love to be connected with something, some few people, in something. As far as anything *matters*, I have always been very much alone, and regretted it. But I can't belong to clubs, or societies, or freemasons, or any other damn thing. So if there is, with you, an activity I *can* belong to, I shall thank my stars."

Long before this he had mourned, talking to Dr. Eder and others, the loss of the societal instinct in his fellow countrymen. Here he was admitting how deprived he felt now as a person, hugging his "rather meaningless isolation" to himself. He had sufficient humility to consider himself a beginner who was willing to try an activity he had not known since his youth, but he must have realized it was too late. "If only," he said wistfully, "in the dirty solution of this world, some new crystal will begin to form." And then he added the inevitable proviso: he would be wary beyond words of making any commitment.

Later he warned his disciple not to take himself too seriously, to the extent of overburdening himself with a mission. For Lawrence, missions were about to be consigned to the past. He would announce his new stance through his resurrected savior in *The Man Who Died*, an extraordinarily tremulous novella in which the man who had died "looked nakedly on to life" and repudiated his passion for saving the world.

IN LONDON he met Frieda's son Monty for the first time. The young man had been persuaded by his sisters to meet his stepfather. They were near in their rented flat to the Victoria and Albert Museum, where Monty worked. Frieda was gratified beyond measure to see the two men getting on. Monty, to his surprise, heard Lawrence saying in a Midlands accent, "Sargent, sooch a bad peynter."

Before joining his sisters at Nottingham and then going on to the bungalow at Mabelthorpe that Ada had rented, he took Millicent Beveridge up on her invitation to visit Scotland. On August 9 he caught the train to Edinburgh. This was his first trip to Scotland, and he was determined to enjoy it. The grouse season was about to open—"an event for those that shoot, and a still bigger one for those that get shot"—but he was more interested in the heather out on the moors. On an excursion to Fort William and Mallaig in the West he sailed with his friend to the Isle of Skye. He liked it so much, in spite of the rain and the white wet clouds obscuring the mountains. On one cloudless blue day he was moved almost mystically by the sight of the bare northern hills "sloping green and sad and velvety to the silky blue sea." It was like the twilight beginning of the world, like the beginning of Europe itself, in this almost uninhabited land.

On August 21 he got out at Nottingham, the station he knew so well, and spent the night at Emily's house. Then, joined by Ada and her husband, Eddie Clarke, they went off as a family to Lincolnshire for a short holiday by the sea. The nation was at war with itself, split by the strike. He feared the class hatred, "the quiet volcano over which the English life is built." Yet now, up on his native ground, he found an attachment for England again that he had not realized was still there. He was more deeply rooted than he knew, as his last novel would show. The English people touched him with their "funny sort of purity and gentleness and at the same time, unbreakableness." After Mabelthorpe, he moved into a bungalow named

Duneville at Sutton-on-Sea so that Frieda could be with them. His sisters left on the day that Frieda appeared. As for Sutton, it was blowy and blustery in the way of North Sea resorts, always described on the railway posters as "bracing." Lawrence liked that too. He was sure it must be good for him. He watched Frieda paddling in the surf, fearing to join her because of his bronchials, a word that had replaced lungs in his vocabulary.

It was perhaps during the time with Ada that he became extremely concerned about his sister's lodger, Gertrude Cooper, who was now consumptive. In 1918 he had been at the bedside of Gertie's sister, Frances, like Gertie a contemporary of his from his youth. Tuberculosis was rife in the Cooper family, and she was dying. Frances was a favorite of the Lawrences. Declaring war on the family curse was a real irony for this man already under sentence because of this disease. He told Koteliansky in a letter that was all urgency, "I want to get Gertie away as soon as possible to some cure, she's delayed too long." His sights were set on Mundesley Sanatorium, where Gertler had been a patient. At first he thought of taking Gertie there directly if she could be persuaded, then settled for an examination first in Nottingham, asking Ada to find the best doctor available. "Tell him her case—ask for an examination as soon as possible, and tell him you would like an X-ray photograph . . . and *don't tell* Gertie . . . let her imagine she is only being looked at." This, if he had but known it, was his last visit home, and before he left England he managed to get Gertie into the sanatorium. Back again at the Villa Miranda he kept in close touch with Gertie, mixing affectionate concern with advice he should have been heeding for himself.

How he felt about his homecoming went into an article, "Return to Bestwood," which would be published posthumously. Riven by his usual ambivalence, he tried to fathom why he should be depressed by his native district. Why was it that he felt more alien now in Eastwood than in any of the places he had visited as a world wanderer, whether it was Mexico City, George Street, Sydney, or even

London? "I feel at once a devouring nostalgia and an infinite repulsion." Was it because he longed for his boyhood, when he waited to be served at the Co-op? "I remember our Co-op number, 1553A.L better than the date of my birth—and when I came out hugging a string net of groceries." It was not much changed, yet everything in him had changed. Butcher Bob, huge and fat, at the corner of Queen Street, was long dead, and the placc was all built up.

The coal strikes, still going on, dominated everything. In his boyhood the police sergeant was a quiet, patient, respected man. Now there were policemen everywhere, big and strange, that the local people called "blue-bottles" and "meat-flies." Ada and Eddie Clarke's drapery shop was prospering, and it was clear from their neat modern house (called "Torestin," a borrowing from *Kangaroo*) with its glazed doors and tiled hall that his sister had "got on," to use his mother's phrase. How would his mother regard him now if she were alive, the snotty-nosed little collier's lad who had always been weak in health? Had he "got on"? Now that he was over forty, not owning a motor car, his "getting on" was surely not as concrete as his sister's. After *The White Peacock* was published, the editor of the *English Review* had predicted that Mrs. Lawrence's son would be riding in his own carriage by the time he was forty. His mother is supposed to have sighed and said, "Ay, if he lives to be forty!" Well, he was forty-one and still alive, "so there's one in the eye for that sighing remark."

Home and yet not home, alien and yet caught up in a remembrance of how it had once been, he watched the "lurching, almost slinking walk of colliers" as they swung their heavy feet and thought he was among phantoms. They went to the local football match in silence like ghosts, drinking in the welfare clubs with a dumb hopelessness. These men of his own generation moved him strangely. It was almost a pain to be among them.

> They are changed, and I supposed I am changed. I find it so much easier to live in Italy. And they have got a new kind of shallow con-

sciousness, all newspaper and cinema, which I am not in touch with. At the same time they have, I think, an underneath ache and heaviness very much like my own. . . . They are the only people who move me strongly, and with whom I feel myself connected in deeper destiny. It is they who are, in some peculiar way, "home" to me. I shrink away from them, and I have an acute nostalgia for them.

Out of these aching feelings, true to his roots in spite of all his exile, he tried at the end of his piece to thrash out a vision of hope that would match the reality with which he was faced. He knew that England was on the brink of a class war. And for all his distrust of democracy and what it would mean in terms of shoddiness, he called for the establishment of a society that these people with whom he felt deeply connected, living, many of them in misery, "families living on bread and margarine and potatoes," could accept as something true and just. "I know that we could, if we would, establish little by little a true democracy in England: we could nationalize the land and industries and means of transport, and make the whole thing work infinitely better than at present, *if we would*. It all depends on the spirit in which the thing is done."

He meant of course a religious spirit. And that was nowhere to be seen. It meant a system of education based on something other than "the fact that twice two are four." Above all it meant belief, vision. And who wanted such a system, where was the vision? "What we need is some glimmer of a vision of the world that shall be, beyond the change. Otherwise we shall be in for a great débâcle."

AT THE VILLA MIRANDA in October he sat down to reflect on how English he truly was, for all his traveling. Several people in London had noticed how he had physically changed, commenting especially on his habit of sitting with his knees pressed together, his hands out of sight under them. He thought their top floor rather austere even for him, as well as shabby, and arranged for the walls to be whitewashed, purchased a stove, and had rush matting laid over the old brick floor: after all, the winter was approaching.

Before he could concentrate on any work he had to reply to a letter from Gertie Cooper and find out how she was faring at the sanatorium. He would have no peace of mind until he knew she was comfortable. And he strove to give her a picture of life in Italy to lift her spirits, that would be like a window on a world she could look out on, to escape her incarceration. It must be sickening, he told her, to be stuck there in that place, but he was thankful she *was* there just now, being cared for.

It was like summer still where they were, he went on. Peasants were bringing in the grapes, in big wagons drawn by white oxen. The grapes were very sweet this year, little and round and clear. To amuse her he told her about Willie Hopkin's daughter Enid who had come to visit them in London. Her husband was very nice but ordinary, "too ordinary for Miss Enid." Lawrence never understood why she was so discontented, the unrest working away in her "like Brewer's yeast." What he failed to tell her was that on a walk with Willie Hopkin, the mentor of his youth, they had walked out into the countryside near Haggs Farm where Jessie used to live, and Willie had asked why Lawrence had never married Jessie. "I would have had too easy a life, nearly everything my own way," he had answered, and sounded almost angry.

Their first visitors that autumn were Richard Aldington and Arabella Yorke. Aldington was surprised to find Lawrence so cheerful, his illness apparently in remission. Left alone one day, the women off shopping in Florence, they sat under the trees as peasant urchins in bare feet came up with offerings of grapes. In return Lawrence would go into the villa to bring chocolate or some sugar, great luxuries for the children, as he explained to Aldington.

Toward the end of October Frieda went over to their neighbors the Wilkinsons at the Villa Poggi to tell them they were back. She was happy to see them again, so to complete the reunion Mrs.

Wilkinson sent her husband to fetch Lawrence. At first he failed to hear Arthur Wilkinson's knock, whistling away as he peeled chestnuts for their evening meal. In fact he was now a little deaf.

Then on October 22 the Lawrences took the tram into Florence to join Aldous and Maria Huxley for lunch. The Huxleys were staying in Cortina but had come to the city to see a dentist. The two couples barely knew each other but were soon friendly. Initially it was Huxley's dry, somewhat abstract turn of mind that put Lawrence off, but he was to value Huxley's friendship to the end of his life because of the other's immediate recognition of "something different" that Lawrence possessed. Shortly after their meeting, Maria, a young Belgian woman, brought over some canvases belonging to her brother and left them at the Miranda with Lawrence. He must have mentioned his interest in painting, which went back to his early days when he did careful copies of paintings for himself and his mother. He had done nothing original, though he made Paul Morel in *Sons and Lovers* an aspiring painter. He liked to copy classical work as a way of "getting inside" the picture in order to grasp its essence. Now he was about to give this intuitive approach full rein by giving himself up to the post-Romantic embrace of art he had always employed when composing books. Pictures, like fiction and poetry, needed to be in the service of instinct and intuition and allowed to *happen*.

But before he could make a bold splash on these inviting bare canvases with some leftover decorating paint and housepainter's brushes, Lawrence began writing again, after telling his agent that he would do only "short stories and smaller things," since it was so nice and peaceful in the big empty rooms of the Miranda. To his publisher Secker he said the same: not wanting to become embroiled in "a long effort" and just thinking of a "shortish story." By October 26 he had written forty-one pages of the first version of *Lady Chatterley*. He thought it would be a novella, no longer than *The Virgin and the Gipsy*, and like that story would have a Sleeping Beauty theme. Walks with his old friend Willie Hopkin had revived memories of a youth that now seemed golden and romantic, as did the woods he passed through, with their magical atmosphere. Beginning his novel he sat every morning against a pine tree in the wood below the Miranda. Nearby was a small cave where he could shelter from any rain.

From the outset it was a collaboration, in that Frieda would listen to him reading his morning's work after lunch. Her input has not been recorded, but he would have attended keenly to her reactions, as he always did to women whom he had involved in his writing in the past. She has put down a picture of him setting out along the path by the olive trees, heading for his umbrella pine, past thyme and mint tufts, purple anemones, wild gladioli and carpets of violets. "White, calm oxen were plowing. There he would sit, almost motionless except for his swift writing. He would be so still that the lizards would run over him and the birds hop close around him. An occasional hunter would start at this silent figure." At a loss to describe the story except to say that he was as always "breaking new ground," she wrote to her son Monty that it had the "curious class feeling this time or rather the soul against the body, no I don't explain it well, the animal part. . . ." The first version of the novel would have confused her in its opening pages, dealing as much with the sense of imminent class war that Lawrence had brought back from England as it did with sex. Parkin the gamekeeper in the first and second versions was loyally working-class and belonged to a world in which Frieda had no bearings. Possibly her influence was at work in the elevation of the hero to Mellors, the ex-officer, in the final version.

Brenda Maddox in her biography says ingeniously that the story is like an adult version of Frances Hodgson Burnett's *The Secret Garden*. In Burnett's great house lives a cosseted upper-class invalid, unable to walk, whom the heroine, aided by one of the estate workers, reintroduces to the healing power of the earth. But to say that the model for Sir Clifford Chatterley with his "bright, haunted blue eyes" is the author himself is to rule out the parallels with Parkin, as well as the history of Lawrence's own sexual experience. It is true that Lawrence was almost certainly impotent, like Clifford, during the writing of this novel, and was being betrayed by his wife's affair with Angelo Ravagli. There are also references to Clifford's ambitions as a writer and to Connie's part as a helper who saw her role as a proud and necessary one. "It was as if all her soul and body and sex had to pass into these stories of his." These were inferences missed due to ignorance when the book was published.

He began with a desire to restore the "phallic tenderness" to sex, though underlying it was the degradation of the "country of my heart" that he had recoiled from during his visit home. By the beginning of December 1926 *The First Lady Chatterley* was done. He saw at once that the ending left one of his main themes unresolved. The class difference between Parkin and Connie remained a gulf between the lovers, as Parkin reminds her when she returns from a trip abroad. For her part, "Her two men were two halves. And she did not want to forfeit either half, to forgo either man."

Lawrence was too honest to fudge the issue, and by insisting on realism he realized that a commercial publisher would never accept unabridged the explicit language taboos he had breached. Norman Douglas had brought out books of his own privately through Giuseppe Orioli in Florence, and Lawrence thought he might do the same. It would mean risking his own money. With the prospect of this new freedom in mind he put his first version aside and began scrupulously to write a second, the longer and more elaborate *John Thomas and Lady Jane*. It seems more useful to look closely at this novel, which some critics prefer, than to add to the enormous amount of the discussion and analysis surrounding the final *Lady Chatterley's Lover*, an angrier, sometimes hectoring work.

BETWEEN BURSTS of writing he turned his attention to Maria Huxley's stretched canvases and in a spirit of pure joy began to paint free visual "stories" for the newly whitewashed walls of his *salotto*.

Making pictures, he soon found, was a more enjoyable activity than writing. His paintings have been either derided as ugly and ludicrous daubs or treated with false deference because of his stature as a great writer. No one can deny that his pictures are clumsy, and the figurative painting he most wanted to do exposed his draftsmanship at its weakest. He had not studied anatomy and was too impatient to start now. But Lawrence was not in any sense a naive painter, and it would be patronizing to view him in this light. One remembers Cézanne and his long struggle with the nude bathers that obsessed him.

For his first effort he launched into a group of three figures he called "Unholy Family," unholy because the rounded blond woman with the Frieda-like look is being embraced profanely by a swarthy young man who cups her left breast, watched by a curious child. The Wilkinsons, asked over to see Lawrence's handiwork hung up in his freshly decorated living space, must have been easily shocked. They heard their friend explain that it was a modern picture as he gave them tea, and smiled politely. In private they thought it "a revolting blot on the wall," reminding them of "Uncle Roger and an imbecile fat woman with most of her clothes missing." Quick to notice their disapproval, he asked Secker, "Why do vegetarians always behave as if the world was vegetably propagated?"

He went on to paint "Boccaccio Story," a horror the Wilkinsons would have loathed on sight. This was a Lawrence they knew nothing about. It illustrated a sly Boccaccio story about the deaf and dumb peasant lad who becomes a gardener at a nunnery. Because of his disability he is seen as safe, sleeping with each of the eight nuns in turn, as well as the abbess. Lawrence shows the exhausted young man at rest under a tree, his genitals exposed by a breeze while he is asleep, observed by a passing group of nuns. The color gives a warm glow to the earth and the umbrella pines, and there is something essentially innocent in the humor. Frieda, watching her busy husband at work, absorbed and joyful, using his fingers, rag, his palm, brushes, advised him, "Try your toes next." Lawrence told his painter friend Brett in faraway New Mexico that it was rather fun, "discovering one can paint one's own ideas and one's feelings."

Soon he was bridging the distance between them by challenging Brett to what he called a pictorial combat. "I'm just finishing a nice big canvas, Eve dodging back into Paradise, between Adam and the Angel at the gate, who are having a fight about it."

Children of the *contadini* were still stealing up shyly now and then through the bushes with bunches of grapes. "Look, there's another. Pretend not to see," he would say to his visitor, trying to make out the child's name and going in for bits of chocolate or sugar, for he believed the sugar was good for the children's health.

For all the distraction of his new pastime he had not forgotten Gertie Cooper, thankful she was being cared for in a sanatorium but identifying with the misery of her confinement. Searching for positive words, he told her it must be cheering to look into the mirror and see her face looking plump again "as it used to be in Lynn Croft when I was going to college." Also, the fact that she was putting on weight was, he said, an excellent sign, showing that "the germ is making no headway at all." Before long her temperature would start to drop, he predicted, like a doctor at her bedside. He took care to praise her for being a good patient and gave her his prescription for most conditions in life. "It's a fight, and as a fight we've got to look on it." His solidarity with her struggle was absolute.

Then after months of hoping for the best he heard that the doctors had operated. Cast down terribly, he wrote to Ada that "one really has to refuse to think about it. But it leaves a little thorn stuck in one's mind, which makes one jump when it is touched." Thoughts of his own state of health would have been reactivated, though compared with the previous year he was having a good spell. He went back again and again to Gertie and to the fight against self-pity he was always waging inside himself and urging on others. Nothing took away his distress over Gertie. Memories of her dying sister Frances came back, and that whole wretched time in the past. Sunday evenings were bad, and the fight would be on once again "to keep oneself on top of things. . . . It starts Lynn Croft all over again."

He stopped painting and writing over Christmas to provide the *contadini* and their children with the kind of festive season that was a novelty in Latin parts. The three families, twenty of them, brought along ten children, to luxuriate in the comparative splendor of the Lawrences' *salotto* with its centerpiece, a Christmas tree. When Frieda had suggested to their friend Pietro that they could buy one in the market in Florence he shook his head. It was no problem, he said, to get one for the signora in the priest's pine wood. With his help they dressed it with gold and silver streamers and hung colored wooden toys and candles on the branches. Their guests' pleasure was a joy to behold. They were treated to sweet wine and biscuits, and the men got a cigar apiece. None of them had seen a decorated tree before. The half-wild children handled their cheap presents like jewels.

His painting was resumed. *Fight with an Amazon* was crudely vigorous and combative, depicting a thin, dark, bearded man with narrow shoulders who looked suspiciously like the artist wrestling fiercely with a large blond nude resembling Frieda in her heyday.

He picked up the second draft of the novel and attacked it in "sudden intense whacks," then was knocked off balance by the news of the operation to remove Gertie's left lung. Thrown back into the past, he overcame its power to haunt him by running it into his novel. "Sometimes it seems so far off. And sometimes it is like yesterday." His book, he would say later, was in effect the epilogue to his life's travels. His visit home had rekindled his hatred of industrialism with its mechanizing of the common people in his own regions. Like an angrier, more personally identified Ruskin, he railed against the inevitable, imagining a Samson-like strength for his spirit that would bring down around his ears the world of squalor that made him sick, seeing it everywhere in the Midlands, "the utter negation of natural beauty, the utter negation of the gladness of life, the utter absence of the instinct for shapely beauty which every bird and beast has. . . ."

> See if your skies aren't falling!
> And my head, at least, is thick enough to stand it, the smash.
> See if I don't move under a dark and nude, vast heaven
> When your world is in ruins, under your fallen skies.
> Caryatids, pale-faces.
> See if I am not Lord of the dark and moving hosts
> Before I die.

He had told Rolf Gardiner on December 3 that he would not be coming to England after all for the staging of *The Widowing of Mrs. Holroyd*. He had done with journeying. It was always liable to put his health at risk. In August in England he had gone down with a devil-ish cold. He listed yet again, as if to convince himself, the ailments that were different from Gertie's tuberculosis: his were "chest-bronchial troubles and pneumonia after-effects." Gardiner, touring the Midlands, should go to Newstead, where Byron's heart was buried, and look for Robin Hood's Well, that he had seen himself with Will Hopkin when they skirted Haggs Farm and Lamb Close House, home of the Barber family who owned the mines. In a wood he had seen the cottage of a man who lived there in seclusion when he was a child, who it was said beat his wife. The dream of Rananim rose again in his letter of encouragement to Gardiner. Didn't he think that what was needed was some place with a big barn and a bit of land, where the young could gather and run a small farm, and hike, and "learn wordless music like the Indians have. And try— keep on trying."

Settling down in earnest after Christmas to write his second draft, steeped in his memories of his visit and of the past, his child-hood and youth, he read daily again to Frieda from his work. And perhaps she realized as never before how utterly English he was. The political preoccupations of the first draft are left behind and we go deeper into the character of Parkin, and his conviction that public involvement in society is useless. Only individuals matter, only what they can salvage in love and trust between them can give hope for the future.

John Thomas and Lady Jane begins exactly like its successor, hitting the same note of irony with the very same sentence: "Ours is essentially a tragic age, so we refuse to take it tragically. The cataclysm has fallen. . . ." But by the end of the first chapter of this second draft things accelerate to a state of desperation. Connie has set her strong will on seeing things through, with her shattered husband back from the war "more or less in bits." Instead she has begun to see the whole world as a madhouse, with Wragby its lunatic center. She goes through the days with a monotony that is sheer lunacy, and this "tick-tock of mechanistic monotony became an insanity to her."

Parkin the gamekeeper has no appeal for her at first. She dislikes his harsh tenor voice, as she does the furtiveness of his movements, "as if he were hiding himself." Yet before long she appreciates his solitary quality: it is an instinct she feels in herself, to keep away from mankind.

One of the guests at Christmas is Tommy Dukes, a friend of Clifford. In the course of the general conversation he broaches the idea of a civilization based on the inspiration of touch. He believes it is coming, this next civilization, and it could be Lawrence writing passionately to Rolf Gardiner. Connie says rudely, "But you never want to touch anybody," and one hears Frieda goading Lawrence for his puritanical fastidiousness. Tommy Dukes laughs, but keeps expounding. This new civilization, he insists, will be a democracy— "the democracy of touch . . . the mystery of touch and all that means: a field of consciousness which hasn't yet opened into existence. We paw things—but probably we've never truly touched anybody in all our lives, nor any living thing. . . . We're only an experiment in mechanization, that will be properly used in the next phase." It is an extraordinary prophecy for a brigadier general, and reminds us that for Lawrence a novel that is worth anything exists primarily in the realm of ideas. And the sex, when it comes, is part of the same thought-adventure.

Mrs. Bolton, now no longer elderly, becomes vital in this second draft, both in ministering to Clifford and acting as a go-between, in contact as she is with local gossip and able to tell Connie what she knows about Parkin's failed marriage to Bertha Coutts. At the age of eleven he was frightened by Bertha's act of exposing her pubic hair: she was five years older than himself. Initially he was unable to consummate their marriage until Bertha had shaved off this hair. We are back to Ruskin. Rid of Bertha, he is still the maimed person who falters before Connie and wants her to go away, to leave him be. The tender touch of "true sex" has passed him by. Mrs. Bolton, in her role of half-nurse, half-mother to Clifford, recalls her dead husband with a memory of sex tenderness: "The touch of him. I've never got over it to this day, and I never shall. And if there's a heaven above he'll be there, and will lie up against me so I can sleep."

Because Parkin is uneducated and inarticulate, the story is told through the sensibility of Connie. The fact that Frieda was so pleased with it tells us a good deal about her contribution, and the information she would have provided about what it might have been like to be Connie must surely have been influenced by her experience with Lawrence and his frailty. Lawrence's preoccupation with his childlessness enters just as surely when Connie reveals that Parkin, for all her desire for him, did not touch her heart. "That, as usual, remained free. Nobody touched her heart, except, perhaps, children. Yes, her heart belonged to children. Clifford, she was attached to him personally. The other man held her with passion. Nothing and nobody held her altogether, and she did not want it." We can recognize Lawrence's grudging admission of Frieda's bond with her children, and perhaps his hope that Ravagli's passion would fare no better.

Tenderness and the lack of it crops up throughout the essentially straightforward tale. How rapturous, always, in Lawrence is the spring: how poignant are its lessons in tenderness. "The oak-buds had opened soft little brown hands. Everything was so tender and full of life. Why oh why need man be so tough, always tough and insentient, hard as iron gripping the wrong things, and missing everything! Why could human life never be soft and tenderly coming unfolded into leaf and blossom? If men were leaves of grass, why was it never tender young green grass, new and soft with spring!" "Leaves of grass" is a direct reference to Whitman, the great poet who meant so much to him.

Toward the story's end, confronted by the meanness of class hatred, Connie understands that "There was no longer any such thing as class. The world was one vast proletariat . . . ," no more than a division between the haves and have-nots, owners and wage earners, capitalists and workers. "It was all Robot. And it was the suicide of the human race." To hang back from Parkin because he is lower class is, she sees, nonsense. In his solitary self he is the same as her. "Class is an anachronism. It finished in 1914. Nothing remains but a vast proletariat . . . and then a few individuals who have not been proletarianized."

When the scandal of their association drives Parkin from the wood and he goes away to lodge in Sheffield with a friend, working at the steel mills, she manages to convince her lover that he should let her get him a little farm. He struggles with his pride, then says that perhaps it is better to be beholden to a woman than live a life of misery. Finally he makes a confession that is so telling for our insight into Lawrence. His mother had said he was only half a man. "If I've got too much of a woman in me, I have, an' I'd better abide by it." His intense bitterness moves her almost to tears. She cries, "You ought to be proud that you are sensitive, and have that much of a woman's good qualities. It's very good for a man to have a touch of woman's sensitiveness. I hate your stupid hard-headed clowns, who think they are so very *manly*."

The work in Sheffield is too hard for a man of Parkin's slender physique. Connie remembers his white, slender arms "and the delicate white shoulders," and sees how he is being dulled and dragged down by the heavy labor. In an encounter with his friends the Tewsons in Sheffield she offers to send five pounds so that Tewson can bribe the foreman into giving Parkin lighter work. The scene between the assertive, righteous Tewsons and "her ladyship" is wonderfully perceptive and right, one that only Lawrence at that time could have pulled off. At tea in Blagby Street, with Mrs. Tewson saying jealously that "You must eat, or we s'll think it's not good enough for yer," Connie accepts a bit of currant loaf, marveling at the spread. Parkin at her elbow, "inwardly squirming," spoons up his tinned peaches and thickened cream. He would have writhed again to hear Mrs. Tewson say, on parting, that "I mother 'im all I can, an' I think 'e feels at 'ome with us." He says nothing, and it is left to Connie to reply with heavy irony, "I'm sure he does!"

They walk side by side down the steeply sloping dreary street. "He looked a poor little working man," and she knew he felt it, "how he had been brought down." In the tram Connie looked around at the poorish working-class passengers, "without grace, color, or form: or even warmth of life. It was too gruesome." Parkin is indeed a little man, given back his spark of life by Connie, but with none of the glamour of the gamekeeper Mellors in his next incarnation. Lawrence had not forgotten his sight of the slinking, half-crushed colliers around Eastwood, the pickets with bleached faces in silent groups, with a remoteness upon them. At the football matches all he heard was a poor, ragged, spiritless shouting. "And I," he wrote in "Return to Bestwood," "who remembers the homeward-trooping of the colliers when I was a boy, the ringing of the feet, the red mouths and the quick whites of the eyes . . . and the strange voices of men from the underworld calling back and forth, strong . . . with the queer, absolved gaiety of miners—I shiver, and feel I turn into a ghost myself." These workingmen, once so noisy and lively, had their pride in their pockets, "and the pocket has a hole in it."

They stay in touch by letter and gropingly make plans. Parkin is not quite able to let her set him up in a small farm, at least not yet, but he tells her he is leaving the steel mill and will try to get farm laboring work: the corn harvest is coming on. Meanwhile he is waiting for his divorce from Bertha to come through. Their letters cross, and hers tell him that she has made up her mind: she is leaving Clifford. Her false situation is now unbearable.

He replies to her news with real understanding. Where would she go? "I think sometimes a dry ditch is better than a bed in people's houses." He suggests a meeting in Hucknall, before they part temporarily to await developments. She would go to her sister's, and he would wander and take any farm work he could. As for the world they are defying, "I shouldn't care," he writes, "if the bolshevists blew up one half of the world and the capitalists blew up the other half . . . so long as they left me and you a rabbit hole apiece to creep in. . . ."

After seeing him in Sheffield as a rather pinched, insignificant little working man, she goes to meet him almost in dread. He emerges from a squalid street and she sees that his face has recovered its courage again. They go for sanctuary into the dark empty church. She looks at the slab "behind which rests the pinch of dust which was Byron's heart." She is with child and sits miserably, not knowing what Parkin is thinking. Then he puts his hand on her belly "and it was like the sudden warmth of the sun, after a bitter winter." Below his hand the child to come lay invisibly "like a pinch of life."

These closing pages are unsurpassed in the whole of Lawrence for their delicacy and truth of feeling. Everything is perfectly judged and right. The tenderness he has preached comes to fruition, in the novel at least. Leaving the church they take a footpath toward Felley Mill, find a little hollow, and sit under the trees, hidden from the world by brambles and dog rose bushes. Starved for the touch of each other, they embrace under their clothes. "And once more her womb was soft with peace and that queer, sap-like happiness over which one has no control, save to kill it." They are disturbed by a gamekeeper who lets them stay, with a warning that they should not stop long or the old squire might come by with his friends: irony of ironies, in a novel rich in irony, to be warned of a squire who "hates couples," as the woman lies with her face hidden against the man, arms round his body. Connie and Parkin return slowly to the path "where long ago Byron must have limped in his unhappy inability to feel sure in his love." In a book as intensely personal as this, one is bound to speculate. How sure was Lawrence now in his love for Frieda?

On the last page the pretence of a fictional location is cast aside and the actual place names flood in: Haggs Farm, Underwood, Eastwood, Felley Mill. We are made to feel Lawrence's grief at this countryside, the walks so lovely in his youth and still close to his heart, lying abandoned "like everything that is not coal or iron."

10

The Journey Out of Life

(1927–1928)

John Thomas and Lady Jane was finished by mid-February 1927. He told Brett that he liked it but that it was improper and could not be printed conventionally. "And I will *not* cut it. Even my pictures, which seem to me absolutely innocent, I find people *can't even look* at them. They glance, and look quickly away. I wish I could paint a picture that would just *kill* every cowardly and ill-minded person that looked at it." Painting away still, he had done an "Eve Regaining Paradise," begun a "Resurrection," and then been felled by "this cursed flu."

Clearly he was girding himself for a fight, the same "Onward Christian Soldiers" fight he urged on Gertie Cooper, whose operation had not yet taken place. "Eh, one wishes things were different. But there's no help for it. One can only do one's best, and then stay brave. Don't weaken or fret. While we live we must be game. And when we come to die, we'll die game too."

Always seeking for ways to cheer her, he said the narcissus flowers were out in the garden already, and lots of wild Christmas roses. It was sunny, a Sunday, and they had been for a walk over the hills and ate in a dark little inn, like a dark hole, where the food was good: on Sundays you were always sure of beef-tea and macaroni, and boiled beef. The Appennines in the distance were shrouded in deep snow and looked beautiful, "glimmering faint and pinkish in the far, far distance." Close at hand the country lay in the sun, open and rolling. If it was sunny like today you could see a butterfly flapping, out, and even a bee. "I even saw the tail of a lizard go whisking down a hole in the wall."

Given the writing of this home-based novel it is not surprising that his thoughts kept returning to Eastwood and Lynn Croft. He asked Gertie if she remembered the autograph albums they used to have then, writing verses in them. With his phenomenal memory he could recall one that Frances Cooper wrote for someone:

> But human bodies are such fools
> For all their colleges and schools
> That when no *real* ills perplex 'em
> They make enough themselves to vex 'em.

He had told Gertie in his last letter about three friends who came to lunch, one a young Russian woman of twenty-five or so. Her Eton crop, black jacket, and narrow skirt deceived Guilia their servant into calling her the *signorino*, thinking she was a gentleman. Outraged as only Lawrence could be, he found her appearance repulsive. "Why can't women be women—and a bit charming!"

Out of the blue on February 10 came a letter from an old colleague from his teaching days in Croydon, Arthur McLeod. He was now forty-three, Lawrence estimated, clearly delighted to hear from him. Philip Smith, their headmaster at Davidson Road School, was retiring, and Lawrence enclosed two pounds toward his retirement present. He had a fond memory of Philip Smith bringing him a winter aconite and laying it before him on the table in Standard VI. And he mentioned a dream he still had which troubled him to this day, of forgetting to mark the register and finding the class gone home. "Why should I feel so worried about not having marked the register? But I do."

Lawrence, who by now did not need to have his suspicions confirmed about Ravagli, was irritated by the obvious visits of their previous landlord. He had called in on November 15, and suddenly arrived to surprise them around the end of February. His excuse was that he had been ordered to Florence to attend a court-martial. Lawrence asked Ravagli to show him his official papers before he could put on a show of civility.

After completing *John Thomas and Lady Jane* and being still dissatisfied with the novel, he put it aside to write a number of reviews and then a story for Cynthia Asquith, who had asked for a murder story. "The Lovely Lady" concerns an elderly woman of some refinement, Pauline Attenborough, who has defied the ravages of aging and lives outside London with her son and a niece. More an occult tale than a murder mystery, it presents the mother as a woman who has forced her son Henry to die because he was made to choose between her and the girl he wanted to marry. One is reminded of the death of William Morel in *Sons and Lovers*, and the swing away from sympathy for his own mother in Lawrence's references to her in "Return to Bestwood."

By the beginning of March Lawrence and Frieda had finalized their separate travel plans. Frieda would leave on March 17 for one of her trips to Germany. No doubt Lawrence guessed that she would call on Ravagli, now a captain and posted to Gradisca, near Trieste. The Brewsters, back from India and now living at Ravello, had called at the Villa Miranda in January, and Lawrence must have discussed with his amiable Buddhist friend Earl the idea of looking at some of the Etruscan tombs together. Now he invited himself to stay with this hospitable couple for a week or so, before he and Earl traveled to Rome and then nearby to a site at Cerveteri. Hinting darkly at changes inside himself he told Earl, also in his forties, "You and I are at the *âge dangereuse* for men: when the whole rhythm of the psyche changes: when one no longer has an easy flow outwards: and when one rebels at a good many things." This could well have been a reference to Frieda's latest dalliance. "It is well to know," he went on, "the thing is psychological: though that doesn't nullify the psychological reality." He felt in his friend, he said, "a terrible exasperation," something that hardly fits with what we know of Brewster, who never seemed to be anything other than the soul of patience.

In Ravello these two men at the dangerous age had an enjoyable time, with Lawrence painting his *Fauns and Nymphs* and Achsah Brewster making use of him as model for a picture of her own. The Brewsters' daughter, Harwood, remembered the visit with pleasure, "Uncle David" joining in with their folksinging. Before setting out on their exploration of the tombs, Lawrence with his usual thoroughness took Earl to the Rome museum to look over the collection of Etruscan tools, weapons, cooking utensils, and small figures retrieved from the various sites.

Etruscan Places, not published in book form until after Lawrence's death, though the essays appeared in *Travel* and *World Today* over a period of two years, is as fine as any of his travel books, which is saying a great deal. Written like *Sea and Sardinia* as a kind of diary, it combines material in the form of studies with spontaneous day-by-day impressions of people he encounters, from the young German archaeologist to the spurred shepherd in goatskin trousers they see in a dark cavern where mule drivers sit drinking blackish wine. Nothing escapes his attention; his curiosity never flags.

His preconceptions are set out frankly on the first page for us to accept or reject. He could have called the book "Shadowy Etruscans," for these lost peoples of antiquity remain a mystery, settling first on the coast of Italy about 800 B.C., and slowly moving to occupy much of the peninsula. Probably originating in Asia Minor, these half-Asian tribes were wiped out entirely by the Romans, dubbed by Aldington "those Prussians of the ancient world." What were they like, these Etruscans whose society was a religious oligarchy, who were essentially peaceable and therefore defenseless, and whose tombs gave evidence of an attitude to death which was far from gloomy in the Christian or Greek sense? All the signs indicated, so Lawrence believed, a way of life in harmony with nature rather than one that sought to exploit it. Hence, even before seeing the tomb paintings, looking at Etruscan things in the museums "I was instinctively attracted to them."

With the gentle Brewster, one of whose virtues for Lawrence is that he never argues or opposes his English friend's assertions, no matter how wild, Lawrence sets out from Rome over the Campagna in the direction of Pisa. He has just recovered from yet another bout of his flu but is risen again and eager for this new "thought-adventure." His railway guidebook tells him that the nearest station to Cerveteri, their first site, is Palo, five miles away. But there is mention of a bus.

Of course at Palo there is no sign of a bus, and no one has heard of one. They decide to walk, leaving their two bags at the little buffet. They tramp along a flat white road; beside it "the tall asphodel is letting off its spasmodic pink sparks" this sunny April morning. Ahead is all that is left of Caaere, the Etruscan city now called Cerveteri, and no more than an old Italian village with a few crooked gray streets. Hungry, they make for *Vini e Cucina*, Wines and Kitchens, the deep cavern where they see the faun-faced, shaggy-legged shy shepherd, grinning and ducking his head.

The tombs are something of a disappointment because everything has been taken away, mostly deposited in the Gregorian Museum in the Vatican. So they go on to the next site, Tarquinia. But how? There is a bus after all, to take them back to Palo, and after a struggle by train to Città Vecchia. The train to Tarquinia leaves at eight o'clock next morning, so they find a hotel for the night. Next morning, over the flat Maremma land, by the sea and green wheat and spiky asphodels, they come to Tarquinia. They find an inn in advance and meet a little lad who seems no more than twelve, sticking his chest out proudly. This is Albertino, one of the shining little characters in the book, a diminutive, fatherly hotel manager who is really fourteen and runs the whole establishment; "from five in the morning till ten at night he was on the go." Albertino does everything. "How Dickens would have loved him! . . . He was absolutely unsuspicious of us strangers." He takes them to two small rooms. Lawrence is touched by the boy's solicitous attention, as he demonstrates by tapping their flimsy dividing wall that they should not feel lonely or frightened in the night since they can talk to each other if they wish.

These painted tombs of Tarquinia are for Lawrence the high point of their expedition, cursory though it is because his stamina is not up to visiting other sites on his list, such as Arezzo, Cortona, Chiusi, Orvieto, Norta, Bieda. Even if he had managed to visit these there would have been another forty to see according to authorities such as George Dennis and others. The miracle is that he accomplishes what he does. Weeks before leaving the Miranda he was woefully short of breath.

Before plunging underground he heads for the museum at Tarquinia. He gives credit to the Florence museum for its splendor, but essentially museums for him are wrong. At least the things here are all Tarquinian, so that there is some sort of organic sense about them.

On the way there they pause to drink coffee at a tin table by the gate. Lawrence gazes around, his imaginative sympathy already prepared to run free. How lovely it is to think of the small wooden temples of the early Greeks and the Etruscans, "small, dainty, fragile, and evanescent as flowers. We have reached the stage where we are weary of huge stone erections, and we begin to realize that it is better to keep life fluid and changing than to try to hold it fast down in heavy monuments." He gives us the benefit of instincts we show little sign of having: it is Lawrence who realizes for us.

One is tempted to quote endlessly from this marvelous book of life. He lets his imagination leap about on this unsullied April morning, as alert to the shapes of the hills and the swing of a valley as to anything he might be shown below. If the living Tarquinians trod these hills, as they must have done, then this is where they had their bright wooden houses, "that is the hill where the dead lie buried and quick, as seeds," in their painted houses of the dead underground. The hill where they lived and worked and the burial hill beside it "are as inseparable as life and death, even now, on the sunny green-filled April morning with the breeze blowing in from the sea. And the land beyond seems as mysterious and fresh as if it were still the morning of Time."

Eager though he is to be true to his instant sympathy for Etruscan culture, he has no intention of idealizing away the reality. His aim from the beginning is to uncover the intriguing puzzle of the race. As long ago as 1921 he wrote to Catherine Carswell, "Will you tell me *what* was the secret of the Etruscans?"

In his effort to penetrate and grasp their elusive spirit he goes back to the dim beginnings. The book is rich with poetic images as he writes of those Homeric days when a restlessness seems to have seized the whole Mediterranean "and ancient races began shaking ships like seeds over the sea." He has learned that there was never an Etruscan nation, only a group of tribes comprising aboriginals and newcomers from these peoples on the move. The Etruscan nobles had slaves, that was certain, and their remains are there below stored in jars and laid in a sacred place. There was nothing comparable "to the vast dead-pits which lay outside Rome . . . in which the bodies of slaves were promiscuously flung."

One has heard of his superlative skill as a teacher in schools, and in this book the scholarship he has acquired sits lightly on every page, yet is so invigorating and quick with his excitement. We share the experience of those friends and visitors who found a walk with him so memorable.

They arrange for a guide to take them to the painted tombs, "the real fame of Tarquinia." All this hill in front of them, says the guide, is tombs, all tombs. "The city of the dead." They are led to a little flight of steps, almost hidden, and as the guide kneels to light his acetylene lamp his old terrier lies down resignedly in the sun. Nothing is too negligible for Lawrence's eye. He regrets the unfairness of his first impression, thinking that this fat, good-natured fellow has no interest in tombs. In fact appearances are deceptive. The guide is knowledgeable and sensitive, yet never intruding himself, and turns out to be an extremely pleasant companion.

The first chamber is quite small, not like the spacious tombs at Cerveteri. It is the Tomb of Hunting and Fishing, badly damaged, probably dating from the sixth century B.C. Yet as they grow accustomed to the light they are rewarded with wonders. The frescoes around the walls are composed of birds and fishes flying and leaping in the haze of sky and sea, and small figures of men hunting, fishing, rowing. A blue-green sea bathes the lower part of the wall in a rippling motion. Entranced by the felicity of all he sees, Lawrence matches it in his descriptions with the felicity of a poet. A naked, shadowy but distinct man "is beautifully and cleanly diving into the sea," while behind a boat a great dolphin leaps up. Colors in the bands of color that border the walls in horizontal ribands all round the room are red and black and dull gold and blue and primrose, and from these bands are suspended loops of garlands, flowers and leaves and buds and berries, representing "the flowery circle of female life and sex." The surface is badly damaged, bits of the wall have fallen off, damp has bitten into the colors, "yet in the dimness we perceive flights of birds flying through the haze, with the draught of life still in their wings." Taking heart they look closer. "Men are nearly always painted a darkish red, which is the color of many Italians when they go naked in the sun, as the Etruscans went. Women are colored paler, because they did not go naked in the sun." Nothing is impressive or grand. "But if you are content with just a sense of the quick ripple of life, then here it is."

The careless sensuality of it all enchants him, on page after page. There is the boat that has a beautifully painted eye on its prow "so that the vessel shall see where it is going." All through the tombs are frequent Etruscan banqueting scenes, yet these are banquets of the dead. "While the living feasted out of doors, at the tomb of the dead

the dead man himself feasted in like manner, with a lady to offer
him garlands and slaves to bring him wine, away in the underworld.
For the life on earth was so good, the life below could not fail to be
a continuance of it."

There is the lovely Tomb of the Lionesses, and then the Tomb
of the Painted Vases, which has amphorae, two of them, with scenes
painted on that are still distinct.

> On the end wall is a gentle little banquet scene, the bearded man
> softly touching the woman with him under the chin, a slave-boy
> standing childishly behind, and an alert dog under the couch. . . .
> Rather gentle and lovely is the way he touches the woman under the
> chin, with a delicate caress.

And this is what appeals to him profoundly, this perfectly illustrated, utterly delicious sense of touch that is for him one of the
main charms of the Etruscan paintings. This is what he strove to
evoke with such ability as he could muster in his own paintings, and
we are returned to the tenderness proclaimed in *John Thomas and
Lady Jane* as a field of consciousness based on the mystery of touch,
which would need to happen in "the next phase of civilization" if
man were to become really alive. Now here in the dim tombs of
Tarquinia he could see the inspiration of touch brought alive before
his eyes.

How this vivid and glamorous people lost their vitality is a puzzle over which he ponders repeatedly. The cosmos was alive for
them, a vast breathing and stirring creature. Out of the "wandering
huge vitalities of the world" they drew life into themselves. *The
Tomb of the Leopards* is a little room which charms him utterly, ruined
by vandals to some extent but still fresh and alive. Dancers on the
right wall

> move with a strange powerful alertness onwards. The men are
> dressed only in a loose colored scarf, or in the gay handsome
> chlamys draped as a mantle. The *subulo* plays the double flute the

Etruscans loved so much, touching the stops with big exaggerated hands, the man behind him touches the seven-stringed lyre, the man in front turns round and signals with his left hand, holding a big wine-bowl in his right. And so they move on, on their long, sandaled feet, past the little berried olive trees, swiftly going with their limbs full of life, full of life to the tips.

We are being given a foretaste of his final little book, *Apocalypse*. Drawing close to death himself he is fascinated by the "one radical thing the Etruscan people never forgot, because it was in their blood as well as in the blood of their masters: and that was the mystery of the journey out of life, and into death; the death journey, and the sojourn in the after life. The wonder of their soul continued to play round the mystery of this journey and this sojourn. . . . Man moves naked and glowing through the universe. Then comes death: he departs into the underworld." How simply and subtly he expresses it. What a priest he would have made! And perhaps essentially that was what he was.

IT IS EASTER, with Jesus and the Resurrection never far from his thoughts. Always in these tombs are depictions of water and the sea. "The fish is the *anima*, the very clue to the vast sea. . . . For this reason Jesus was represented in the first Christian centuries as a fish, in Italy especially, where the people still thought in Etruscan symbols."

There are passages as extraordinary as those in his shamanlike early essay "The Crown," written in England, which was pure vision from start to finish. "The treasure of treasures is the soul," he writes now, "which, in every creature, in every tree or pool, means that mysterious conscious point of balance or equilibrium between the two halves of duality, the fiery and the watery. This mysterious point clothes itself in vividness from the right hand, and vividness after vividness from the left. . . . But the soul itself, the conscious spark of every creature, is not dual: and being the immortal, it is also

the altar on which our mortality and our duality is at last sacrificed."
And when death comes it does not vanish but is stored in the egg,
"or in the jar, or even in the tree which brings forth again." Often in
these painted scenes a man holds up an egg, the symbolic egg of resurrection "within which the germ sleeps as the soul sleeps in the
tomb, before it breaks the shell and emerges again."

Everywhere he sees symbols, a multiplicity of symbols, that he
interprets with his astonishing capacity for entering the pagan world
as if he truly belonged there. And such a beauty of interpretation,
with his teacher's gift of bringing details to symbolic life. Garlands
offered by maidens and placed over the men's heads and laid on
their shoulders are symbols of the maidens' mystery and different
strengths, "For whatever is laid over the shoulders is a sign of power
added." Priests or augurs with their bird-headed staffs watched the
flights of birds across the sky, "reading the signs and portents. . . .
To us it may seem foolish. To them, hot-blooded birds flew through
the living universe as feelings and premonitions fly through the
breast of a man, or as thoughts fly through the mind. . . . And since
all things corresponded in the ancient world, and man's bosom mir-
rored itself in the bosom of the sky, the birds were flying to a por-
tentous goal in the man's breast who watched, as well as flying their
own way in the bosom of the sky."

Out again in the drab twentieth-century world, seeing the drab
peasants muffled in their ugly modern clothing, he is glad to be back
in the dark little hotel to be revived by the bustling boy manager Albertino, amusing and vivacious as ever, who calls the three Japanese
guests Chinese, and when Lawrence corrects him he dashes off for a
school atlas to be instructed. Lawrence would have clearly loved to
tutor this intelligent lad, who should have been at school instead of
being run off his feet at fourteen in a hotel.

A dozen miles to the north lies another site, Vulci (now called
Volci). They take a train the short distance to Montalto, then have
the problem again of the five miles to Volci. Where can they get a
carriage to take them there? They go into a café and ask. "Difficult"

is the inevitable reply. They are faced with the slow smile of the peasants and the lethargy, the glint of ridicule in the black eyes. There was a carriage but it had gone off somewhere. When would it be back? Nobody knew. Lawrence insists—he is good at insisting. Somebody mentions a *carretto*, a two-wheeled gig, and after more delay this is produced, driven by a youth, Luigi, whom they had met while buying bread. Luigi is the baker's assistant, with a dirty face, and to begin with "in an agony of shyness, stupefied." They trot along, pulled by the mulberry mare, making a good pace, and Luigi is coaxed to tell them about himself. Lawrence is as attentive to these details as he is to the details of the tombs—the novelist has taken over. The boy's father is dead, his brother has married and gone, and Luigi helps the baker but much prefers to be out here in the open Maremma country, a wide flat plain now largely water-logged, abandoned, and wild. Not under the Etruscans, it seems: they were clever drainage engineers, and in their day it was a great waving bed of wheat. Then the Romans came and the complex system of canals and levels fell into decay. Mosquitoes bred "like fiends" and with them came malaria, the marshes deadly and gradually abandoned. All the same Luigi loves its moorland; the space is precious to him in his loneliness "as it is to a moorland bird." Nearing the ruined castle he asks an urchin how to get through a wire fence, and instantly sees, "intelligent as a wild thing, out here in his own spaces."

They inspect the tumuli, Coccumella and Coccumelletta, but getting into the tombs means crawling over mounds of rubble and going into holes like rats, with bats fluttering around their faces blindly. Inside there is nothing, all excavated, plundered, passages and nothing but passages, like scrambling inside a pyramid. Out again through the bramble-covered entrance they are thankful to be out in the open, even if the air is heavy with "isolation, suspicion, guardedness . . . like being in the Middle Ages."

They give up and go on to Volterra, the most northerly of the sites, not easy to reach. It is located thirty miles from the sea on a huge outcrop of rock exposed to all the winds there are and oversees the world, "looking out down the valley of the Cecina to the sea, south over vale and high land to the tips of Elba," north to Carrara, inland to the heart of Tuscany. Volterra, they will find, is in a sense an island, isolated and grim.

From Cecina the small forlorn train reaches the famous old salt works, now state-owned. Passengers such as themselves are transferred to a one-coach train and at long last this coach "starts to creep like a beetle up the slope, up a cog-and-rachet line, shoved by a small engine behind." Almost at a walking pace they toil up through vineyards and olives, rising slowly to the bluff of rock with its towers ahead. Then some shuffling and clanking, till "the fragment of a train eases up at a bit of cold wayside station." They are there. Below them, the world. They transfer to a little ancient bus and are lifted up to the last level, a cold and gloomy square where the hotel awaits. Lawrence, vulnerable in his dangerous thinness and fatigue, finds the April afternoon icy. But marvel of marvels, there is central heating in the rough, simple hotel, and it is working. Volterra is not high, only eighteen hundred feet above sea level, but is "cold as any alp."

It is Sunday. When they go out to explore they find a cold gray afternoon, winds cutting round "the hard dark corners of the hard, narrow medieval town," with crowds of black dressed squat men and dressy young women jostling in the streets. It is some sort of political occasion they have stumbled on: a new *podestà* has come from Florence to govern the city under the new regime. "Anyhow, the cheeky girls salute one with the 'Roman' salute out of sheer effrontery: a salute which has nothing to do with me, so I don't return it. Politics of all sorts are anathema. But in an Etruscan city which held out so long against Rome I consider the Roman salute unbecoming, and the Roman *imperium* unmentionable."

He is amused to see chalked up on the walls *Morte a Lenin!* "And more amusing still is the legend permanently painted: *Mussolini ha sempre ragione*! Some are born infallible, some achieve infallibility, and some have it thrust upon them."

Most of the tombs have had their contents emptied and been filled in again, so next morning they hurry down the bleak street as an icy-cold rain starts to fall. They retreat to the museum, wanting to see the old alabaster jars, a peculiarity of Volterra, which are really sarcophagi, and the ash-chests. A rather old and vague uniformed man arrives, asking them almost scared what they want. "Why, to see the museum." "*Ah! Ah! Ah si-si!*" As if he just realizes what the museum is there for.

George Dennis, who for Lawrence is more aware than Ducati of that which is alive, nevertheless doesn't find much art in Etruscan things. This rouses Lawrence to scorn: he has never had much patience for "perfect art." "Even Dennis said that the Etruscans never approached the pure, the sublime, the perfect beauty which Flaxman reached. Today this makes me laugh: the Greekified illustrator of Pope's *Homer*! But the same instinct lies at the back of our idea of 'art' still. Art is still to us something which has been well cooked—like a plate of spaghetti. An ear of wheat is not yet 'art.' . . . One wearies of the aesthetic quality—a quality which takes the edge off everything, and makes it seem 'boiled down.'"

He remembers that at Tarquinia they had been dogged during their viewing by a young German in velveteen knee-breeches and thick boots, who turned out to be a graduate who intended to be an archaeologist. He had been studying ruins in Sicily and Tunis, was "a fretful and peevish" young man who looked as if he had swallowed vinegar, so Lawrence thought. Nevertheless he felt sorry for him, for his aimless modernity, and his phrase for anything he looked on was *Nicht viel wert!* (not worth much). He had no time for the Englishman's intuitions; what he saw was mere decoration. Ach, nothing, not worth much, he said doggedly when confronted by scenes that Lawrence and Brewster found beautiful, with their enigmatic, archaic innocence. It is a measure of the quieter, more tolerant Lawrence that he felt challenged to some extent by the disbelief of the young German, who was going on to Greece, though he didn't expect to think much of that either. Yet he did have his usefulness, pointing out details with his flashlight that Lawrence might have missed.

There is no nay-sayer at Volterra, just an old man who knows nothing. They wander round alone and untroubled, with Lawrence wondering if there is a definite connection between the scene on an ash-chest and the dead whose ashes it contains. For instance,

> When the fish-tailed sea-god entangles a man to bear him off, does it mean drowning at sea? . . . And the soul carried off by a winged centaur: is it a man dead of some passion that carried him away?
>
> Fascinating are the scenes of departures, journeyings in covered wagons. . . . This is surely the journey of the soul. It is said to represent even the funeral procession, the ash-chest being borne away to the cemetery, to be laid in the tomb. . . . But more interesting even than the symbolic scenes are those scenes from actual life, such as boar-hunts, circus-games, processions, ships sailing away, city gates being stormed; then so many really tender farewell scenes, the dead man saying goodbye to his wife, as he goes on the journey; then the soul alone, with death-dealing spirits standing by with their hammers that gave the blow. It is as Dennis says, the breeze of Nature stirs one's soul. I asked the gentle old man if he knew anything about the urns. But no! no. He knew nothing at all. He had only just come. He counted for nothing. He was one of those gentle, shy Italians too diffident even to look at the chests he was guarding. But when I told him what I thought some of the scenes meant he was fascinated like a child, full of wonder, almost breathless. And I thought again, how much more Etruscan than Roman the Italian of today is: sensitive, diffident, craving really for symbols and mysteries. . . . The will-to-power is a secondary thing in an Italian, reflected on to him from the Germanic races that have almost engulfed him.

Etruscan Places ends somewhat abruptly with the Volterra essay, for Lawrence meant to go on to inspect many other sites but lacked the strength to continue. He ends with a little story triggered by the massive medieval castle which serves now as a state prison. There is an old man inside those walls whose passion was the piano. Whenever he played his wife nagged him, and one day in a violent spasm he suddenly killed her. "So, the nagging of thirty years silenced, he got thirty years of prison, and *still* is not allowed to play the piano. It is curious."

LAWRENCE GOT BACK to Frieda and the Villa Miranda on April 11, after enduring five hours of having his backbone jolted on a bus. On April 15, Good Friday, with the tombs of the Etruscans in mind, he wrote to Mabel Sterne, "This is the day they put Jesus in the tomb, and really, those three days in the tomb begin to have a terrible significance and reality to me." He and Brewster had gone past a little shop in Volterra, seeing in the window a plaster model of a white rooster escaping from an egg. Intended no doubt as an Easter toy for children it prompted Brewster to suggest a title: "The Escaped Cock—A Story of the Resurrection." He had meant it as a joke, but this was the seed, dropped into his friend, that soon became Lawrence's novella *The Man Who Died*. When the short novel came to be published in London he was talked out of the title "The Escaped Cock" by Secker, who thought it too suggestive.

He reported to Brewster on May 3 that he had written the first part of a story, explaining laconically that "Jesus gets up and feels very sick about everything, and can't stand the old crowd any more—so cuts out—and as he heals up, he begins to find what an astonishing place the phenomenal world is, far more marvelous than any salvation or heaven—and thanks his stars he needn't have a 'mission' any more." In a parallel effort three weeks later he had finished painting his "Resurrection" picture in a style imitating that of Giotto and the Italian primitives he admired. In a slangy description to Brewster he told him, "It's Jesus stepping up, rather grey in the face from the tomb, with his old ma helping him from behind, and Mary Magdalen easing him up towards her bosom in front." When he came to finish writing his delicate wincing tale he set in motion a resurrected Jesus figure with nowhere to go, sheltered at first fearfully by a peasant in a yard near Jerusalem who has a young cock tethered by its leg to a post. The peasant's wife sweeps the yard and lays a mat, and the half-dead stranger lies down in the morning sun. He lies inert with his thin legs and his thin colorless arms, listening to the clucking hens and looking at the tethered cock which had escaped, and which he had helped to catch with his white shroud. He dozes, opens his eyes

> and saw the world again bright as glass. It was life, in which he had no share any more. But it shone outside him, blue sky, and a bare fig-tree with little jets of green leaf. Bright as glass, and he was not of it, for desire had failed.

This reads so poignantly, when one thinks of Lawrence's failing desire, his slow sinking toward death. But always with this man there is the call for more life, the challenge of renewal.

> The man who had died looked nakedly on life, and saw a vast resoluteness everywhere flinging itself up in stormy or subtle wave crests, foam-tips emerging out of the blue invisible, a black and orange cock or the green flame-tongues out of the extremes of the fig-tree. They came forth, these things and creatures of spring, glowing with desire and with assertion. . . . The man lay still, with eyes that had died now wide open and darkly still, seeing the everlasting resoluteness of life. And always the man who had died saw not the bird alone, but the short, sharp wave of life of which the bird was the crest. . . . And when the man threw a bit of bread to the cock, it called with an extraordinary cooing tenderness, tousling and saving the morsel for the hens. The hens ran up greedily, and carried the morsel away beyond the reach of the string.

One dawn, when he is better, the stranger, never named as Jesus, moves on slow, sore feet to the garden where he had been betrayed. A woman in blue and yellow hovers there, a former follower called Madeleine. He asks for refuge but then withdraws from her need to devote herself to the Messiah, who is no more. He is now only a man.

FACED WITH THE NEED to renew the lease on the villa in May or find somewhere else, the Lawrences took the Miranda for a second year. Troubled again about money, vexed at the small rent increase he would have to pay but more by the exchange rate that had gone against him and the news that Britain intended to deduct 20 percent tax from the royalties of British authors living abroad, he began to work up an income from journalism, writing small features and reviews for Curtis Brown to place for him in newspapers and periodicals. And he was soon writing more stories for them to submit. By the end of May he had completed "None of That," a story in which the heroine was modeled on Mabel Sterne, easily identified by her page-boy hairstyle, her round cheeks and bright eyes, and her dynamic American energy, like "a locomotive engine stoked up." Ethel Cane is enthralled by a bullfighter in Mexico City and sees in him a challenge to her will, which has always subdued the men she has encountered. This time the man is more than her equal. On a visit to his house she is dismissed with contempt, then handed over to his friends to treat her as they wish. The brutal tale may have been worked up from gossip Lawrence had heard. The power struggle he wanted to depict would have immediately brought Mabel Sterne to mind. After the implied rape, Ethel Cane still arranges to leave some of her wealth to the bullfighter before she commits suicide, as if in acknowledgment that she has met her match.

As the heavy heat of Tuscany began to weigh down on them that summer, he thought of escape but could no longer contemplate the trip to England to see his play *David*, about to go into production at the Regent Theatre, London. Instead he stuck to his regular routine, writing under a tree in the mornings and painting or picking fruit in the sultry afternoons when everyone around him slept.

In early June he went with Frieda to stay with the Huxleys at Forti dei Marmi on the coast near Viareggio. It should have refreshed him. He wrote to Gertie who was still ill in bed to tell her that he had bathed in the sea, and it was so warm, even a bit sticky. Back again, he was writing to her at eight in the morning with the sun already fierce, big grasshoppers singing so loudly in the trees that "you'd think a dozen little people were working sewing machines outside." He gave her a vivid picture of the peasants cutting the wheat, the whole family setting out at four in the morning, working behind one another with the sickles and "laying the armfuls by: just as Ruth did in the Bible." He was looking forward to being rejuvenated by a visit to Germany in about a month, where he hoped the mountain air might freshen him up.

One of his most spirited reviews at this time was of *Solitaria* by V. V. Rozanov. The wrapper of the book told him that Rozanov was considered by Prince Mirsky to be one of the greatest Russians of modern times. Superlatives like this made him "diffident," not to say suspicious. The review was undertaken as a favor to his friend Koteliansky, who had translated the book. Nevertheless he did not pull his punches. Murry thought Dostoevsky a great revelation, which was enough to make Lawrence spit, and here in Rozanov "one fears one has got a pup out of the Dostoevskian kennel . . . a so called nihilist: in reality a Mary-Mary-quite-contrary." But for all that Rozanov "has a real man in him," and we meet him at his most integral and grave, insists Lawrence, in the twenty pages from *The Apocalypse of Our Time* that were included here.

He went on to review a batch of American fiction that included Hemingway's *In Our Time*, a collection of sketches that were "like striking a match." He applauded the honesty, but one was left with the limitations. Inside him he had a tramp who could feel real sympathy with the Hemingway character who is endlessly moving on. "He doesn't love anybody, and it nauseates him to have to pretend he does." If he doesn't want to go anywhere, why should he? If he doesn't care about anybody or anything, why shouldn't he be straight about it and say so? "Anyhow, he doesn't."

Wanting to write a book on the Etruscans that would have been twice as long as the one we have, he contemplated a visit to some of the burial chambers he had not yet seen, now he could appreciate fully that for the Etruscans a tomb was "a house, a home." At the end of June he wrote to Brewster that he hoped to go "etruscanizing" again in a week's time, in the company of Frieda. Then suddenly came a collapse as terrible as the one at Oaxaca. The veracity of Frieda's account has never been questioned. Lawrence had been gathering peaches in the garden. He came in with a basketful to show her, then went to his room. She heard him a few moments later calling "in a strange, gurgling voice. I ran and found him lying on his bed: he looked at me with shocked eyes while a slow stream of blood came from his mouth. 'Be quiet, be still,' I said. I held his head, but slowly and terribly the blood flowed from his mouth."

A frantic message went to their friend Orioli in Florence, who came at once, accompanied by a Florentine specialist he had secured, Dr. Giglioli. The heat now was particularly intense, enough to curdle iced milk. Giglioli thought the hemorrhage might have been brought on by bathing in the sea at Forti dei Marmi. To Lawrence's relief he said a sanatorium was unnecessary. The dreaded words "lungs" and "tuberculosis" were not used, words now strictly taboo in the sick man's letters and conversation. The patient could lie down at home. The doctor prescribed altitude, and something that Lawrence called Coagulin, to stop the bleeding. Lawrence's own explanation of the cause was, as David Ellis puts it, "characteristically psychosomatic." To Else Jaffe on July 18 he wrote, "My illnesses I know come from chagrin—chagrin that goes deep and comes out afterwards in *hemorrhage* or what not."

He lay like a corpse for days and allowed Frieda to nurse him "alone day and night for six weeks, till he was strong enough to take the night train to the 'Tyrol." One day his defiant spirit and inherent toughness got him up out of bed, and he walked shakily in the woods. The next morning "the hemorrhage came again. Frieda wept, and I felt like all the martyrs in one."

The Huxleys drove over in their big car from Forti dei Marmi to visit him, Aldous afterward telling his father that their novelist friend had long-standing tuberculosis which had suddenly "taken a turn for the worse." He thought "the poor wretch" did not have the strength at present to contemplate moving into the cool of the mountains. He noticed—and he was not the first—that Lawrence was now quieter and more mellow in character. Up to now "this extraordinary man, for whom I have a great admiration and liking," had been hard to get on with, so passionate and violent. "However, age is improving him and now his illness has cured him of his violences and left him touchingly gentle." This was too sanguine by half. Lawrence's ravaging of "the hen-roosts of the bourgeoisie" would soon be resumed. The russet-colored fox was still running.

WHILE STILL CONFINED to his bed and nursing his "bronchials," he responded with amazing liveliness to an article, "Speaking of Resistances," by the American analyst Trigant Burrow, calling him "the most amusing person that writes to me." He had read copies of other articles by Burrow and would shortly be grappling with his new book, *The Social Basis of Consciousness: A Study in Organic Psychology*, which he clearly thought seminal. Burrow's piece on resistances struck home to such an extent that he was given an uncomfortable picture of himself. "All bullies, all being bullied." Swallowing down the jargon for the sake of the importance of Burrow's thinking he even used the "beastly word, societal" to admit that "what ails me is the absolute frustration of my primeval societal instinct. The hero illusion starts with the individualist illusion, and all resistances ensue. I think societal instinct much deeper than sex instinct—and societal repression much more devastating. . . . I am weary even of my own individuality, and simply nauseated by other people's."

On August 3, three days after Burrow's book arrived, he went further in condemnation of himself. Trigant Burrow's findings tallied with his feelings exactly. It was being cut off from people that constituted our most serious ailment, "and out of this ailment everything bad arises." He went so far as to suggest himself as a member of one of Dr. Burrow's group-analysis sessions one day. He suffered badly, always had, from being so cut off—but what was the solution? "At times one is forced to be essentially a hermit. I don't want to be. . . . One has no real social relations—that is so devastating."

After being struck down so recently, "in bed for a bit, and furious," he was speaking for himself as well as for modern man when he wrote to Burrow, "Now is the time between Good Friday and Easter. We're absolutely in the tomb. If only one saw a chink of light in the tomb door.—But your book too is a chink."

In November 1927 he reviewed *The Social Basis of Consciousness* in New York's *The Bookman*. With his darting intelligence he disposes of some of our shibboleths or turns them on their heads. Burrow, a lapsed Freudian, might well have raised his eyebrows at Lawrence's idiosyncratic, if largely enthusiastic, interpretation. "Individuals rebel," he wrote in his review,

and these are the neurotics, who show some signs of health. The mass, the great mass, goes on worshipping the idol, and behaving according to the picture; and this is the normal.

By the idol and the picture he meant the picture man has made for himself.

Freud tried to force his patients back to the normal, and almost succeeded in shocking them into submission with the incest-bogey. But the bogey is nothing compared to the actual idol.

In this book, in which Lawrence found so much that was in accord with his own position, more than in anything he had read for a long time, he was most convinced by Burrow's analysis of the image problem that dominates our civilization. In Burrow's words, "It would appear that in his separateness man has inadvertently fallen a victim to the developmental exigencies of his own consciousness. Captivated by the phylogenetically new and unwonted spectacle of his own image, it would seem he has been irresistibly arrested before the mirror of his own likeness and that in the present self-conscious phase of his mental evolution he is still standing spellbound before it."

Lawrence cuts through impatiently to what most concerns him, spelling out the issue in personal terms. There is "the horror of his isolation, and the horror of the 'stoppage' of his real vital flow." Everything, it seemed to him, was contaminated by this image consciousness. Sex repression was not the evil: that was a false trail. "Men and women alike, when they are being sexual, are only acting up. They are living according to the picture." And in fact "Sex does not exist: there is only sexuality. And sexuality is merely a greedy, blind self-seeking." For man, in the little picture he also has of himself, "must look after his own self-interest. Every man, every woman, just seeks his own self, her own self, in the sexual experience." He concludes, with a certain impudence which he acknowledges, that the analyst must try to liberate his patient from his own image. But how liberate a whole civilization, how reverse what Lawrence despairingly calls the "death of spontaneity"? Not with a book, not by means of an analyst, one can hear him saying grimly to himself.

With the heat intensifying almost daily as August approached, the Arno shrinking to a stream and the bedclothes too hot for the sick man to bear, plans were made for the Lawrences to take the night train into Austria on August 4. Orioli was away but had provided the use of his flat as a resting place on the way to the station. The Wilkinsons helped too. Traveling overnight in a sleeping coach to an Austrian resort, Villach, Lawrence wrote to Ada from the Hotel Fischer after a pleasant three weeks, though now he was bored as ever with hotel life, looking forward to a move into Bavaria. His first thoughts were about Gertie, needing to be cared for and with her money dwindling away. Always conscious of the precariousness of his own finances, he still wanted to help provide for her until she was stronger. "I could tell the bank to pay her fifty pounds a year—and I'd never know, when it goes out that way. . . . So don't let her bother about money, but let me know if she still has enough. And don't tell anybody, I hate these money things talked about."

And inevitably, when felled by a desperate bout of illness, he turned against the place where it had occurred. He was thankful to be out of the "bossiness of Fascist Italy. I find that Italy has almost withered me."

At the end of August they moved to Irschenhausen in Bavaria, deep in the countryside, and to the same wooden summer house owned by Edgar Jaffe that he and Frieda had lived in before the war at the very beginning of their relationship. To be there again was moving, and Else Jaffe still retained Anna, the Jaffes' servant of fourteen years ago. Lawrence was glad to be remembered by her, and now to be mothered, feeding him venison and trout and telling him sternly to eat up.

A friend of Else's, Hans Carossa, who happened to be a literary man as well as a doctor, came to Irschenhausen in late September to examine Lawrence, who then told his sister-in-law Johanna that Carossa's verdict was cheering. "He listened to me—could hear nothing in the lungs, only the bronchials—and doctors aren't a bit interested in bronchials." But any thought of hot-air inhalations was vetoed because of the danger of bleeding starting up again. Carossa had a friend with him, Franz Schoenberner, another literary figure who wanted to meet the famous writer. Carossa's diagnosis to his friend as they made their way to the station bore little relation to the one Lawrence had been told, presumably to avoid letting the invalid know he was doomed. He said to Schoenberner, "An average man with those lungs would have died long ago. But with a real artist no normal prognosis is really sure. There are other forces involved." He thought the Englishman could live for another year or two. "But no medical treatment can really save him."

At the little Villa Jaffe in Irschenhausen, with the forest of dark fir trees behind and at the front the wide, open valley and blue mountains beyond, Johanna, Else, and Frieda came together, talking joyfully and nonstop. Lawrence had long ago found Johanna attractive, and she responded to him flirtatiously. It was perhaps this flattery that made him feel she was better than Frieda at reinforcing a man's manliness. Her second marriage was no more successful than her first, and she asked her brother-in-law, "But what is it about marriage that makes us hate it so?" She was teasing him and he knew it. Amused by the incessant talk, he marveled at the way the sisters "sit in the sun or in the shade and schwätzen, schwätzen all day long. Impossible that any three people should have so much to say to one another."

BY OCTOBER 19 he was back in Italy, albeit reluctantly. His mother-in-law and Frieda's sisters had spoiled him thoroughly— "they really cudgel their brains to think of any way to help"—and he was sad to leave. At Florence station the kindly Wilkinsons were waiting to take him to the Villa Miranda in a hired car. At the villa their servant Giulia Pini was there to welcome them. Lawrence noticed how pretty she was now: if they did move on she would be sorely missed. Her duties were far from onerous: for twenty lire a week she came up at seven in the morning to prepare the coffee, then cleaned and washed the dishes. She called in briefly at midday, and in the evening was often around for whatever needed to be done. Frieda valued her as a friend and companion.

Lawrence was restless now, his cough a permanent reminder that he was "in the straits of illness" and in no condition to move off anywhere. Not that his dreams of escape were curtailed. Casting around for destinations he even thought of Devonshire, the worst place for him in the damp and cold. Then he wondered if he could afford to splurge on an extended sea voyage: for instance, the Messageries Maritimes would take them round the world for 120 pounds. With the ranch never far from his mind he thought they might "drop off at San Francisco and see Taos again." These were pipe dreams. But surely, he persisted in believing, there was a place somewhere that would be good for him. The reality was hard to accent, and he would always fight it. Walking uphill left him gasping for breath. He blamed this on his "asthma."

Huxley came and went, and with his sharp observation and deep sympathy saw further into Lawrence than anyone except Frieda. The change in his friend to someone milder was welcome, but in the introduction to his selection of Lawrence's letters he would write: "The secret consciousness of his dissolution filled the last years of his life with an overpowering sadness. . . . It was, however, in terms of anger that he chose to express this sadness." And it was true that Lawrence preferred anger as a more honorable emotion than melancholy. All his life he had waged war on self-pity, in himself as well as in others. He hoped he would not lose the strength to "spit in the face of the narrow-gutted world and put its eye out."

With the spectacle of fascism in Italy before him he wrote to Rolf Gardiner in a mood to put behind him the whole business of leaders and followers that he had explored in novels. In *The Man Who Died*, his risen man has left his mission behind in the tomb. *Lady Chatterley's Lover*, in the second version especially, envisages a life "based on the reciprocity of tenderness. The reciprocity of power is obsolete."

His convalescence in Germany had at least slowed him down, and he always improved with rest. Now he got down to selecting and revising his *Collected Poems* for Secker, dividing them into two volumes, rhyming and unrhyming verse. The grave and sonorous poems at the end of his life were still to come.

At the beginning of November he ventured out with the Wilkinsons on a trip to San Gimignano. Later in the month he was in Florence to meet Orioli and Norman Douglas. On this day it seems he was persuaded by Douglas's example—he was publishing his new novel privately—to do the same thing himself. And by chance, walking by the river, he bumped into Michael Arlen, a writer he had known during the war whose real name was Dikran Kouyoumdjian, described by Lady Ottoline at Garsington as "a fat, dark-blooded tight-skinned Armenian Jew . . . coarse-grained and conceited." In 1924 Arlen published *The Green Hat*, a novel soon to become a runaway best-seller. A film made from it appeared the following year, starring Greta Garbo. Lawrence despised this meretricious tale, but it was of course just what the Jazz Age wanted. Yet he felt an odd affinity with Arlen, feeling sorry for his wifeless state and the fact that he was unwell. He needed "somebody to comfort him a bit, his fortune isn't enough." He had heard that Arlen had had a tubercular testicle removed—"so it only means more tuberculosis." Lawrence, worried about his finances, with his earnings from Knopf and Secker not amounting to a great deal, and dwindling, talked to Arlen of his anxieties. Next day he had a bitter reaction because he had lowered his guard, feeling he was no better than all those who made money their lives. "Definitely I hate the money-making world, Tom and Dick as well as en gros," he entered in his diary. "But I won't be done by either."

David Ellis in his book, which forms part of the composite biography of Lawrence published by Cambridge University Press, is insightful regarding the way Arlen was seen by Lawrence, as he is when he discusses the altered tone of the final version of *Lady Chatterley's Lover*, which made it strikingly different in a number of ways from the other two. Lawrence said approvingly of Arlen that the "Florentine snobs cut him dead." This wouldn't have been a new experience for the Armenian, who had suffered prejudice for years in his attempt to mingle with the English upper classes. Why he should have wanted to mingle is another question. Rebecca West wittily called him "every other inch a gentleman." For Lawrence he was on the margins like himself, an outlaw whom people hated, in Arlen's case because they were envious of his wealth.

In the final *Lady Chatterley* there is a noticeable coarsening of the characters and a harshness throughout, as the attacks on modern industrial society become more frequent and bitter. A new character, Michaelis, an Irish playwright clearly based on Michael Arlen, is introduced. We are told that Connie Chatterley has had a previous adultery before her affair with Mellors, hence the new character Michaelis, whose sexual encounters with her initiate a new theme, that of the child yearning for maternal love. When they first become lovers "the infant crying in the night was crying out of his breast to her, in a way that affected her very womb." She pitied his "stray-dog's soul," unable to resist the "awful appeal in his full, glowing eyes. . . . From her breast flowed the answering, immense yearning over him: she must give him anything, anything."

Clifford in his need for Mrs. Bolton also regresses to an infant state. After she sponges his blond helpless body she lightly kisses his flesh, "half in mockery. And he would gaze on her with wide, childish eyes, in a relaxation of Madonna-worship. It was sheer relaxation on his part, letting go all his manhood." Only an author aware and afraid of his own temptation to surrender himself to maternal love could have presented Clifford's scene of hysteria with such intensity, suggests Ellis.

Another significant change is that of the gamekeeper himself. In *John Thomas and Lady Jane*, Connie sees her husband and the very different Parkin as two men who are both, for some time, necessary to her and who complement each other. The latest keeper has risen from his working-class roots to the rank of officer during the war. He has the appearance of a gentleman, he reads books and is fluent when it comes to expressing ideas about society. Ellis points out that this articulate lover has obvious parallels with Lawrence, is physically more frail than his predecessors, and has a persistent cough. His first girlfriend, who nurtures his reading and a second who

242 : *Body of Truth*

"loved everything about love except the sex" recall for us Lawrence's youth and his relations with Jessie Chambers and Helen Corke. If we are now in autobiographical territory, where should we look for the real-life counterpart to Bertha Coutts? The savage accusation against Mellors' wife for her predatory, insatiable rapaciousness could only have come, suggests Ellis, from Lawrence's fear and hatred of Frieda's "liberated" sexuality. "Where else but from his relations with Frieda could he have accumulated such a reserve of intense sexual distaste?"

The novel is more complex than many have supposed. Even the charge of misogyny is hard to sustain. The scholar Lydia Blanchard points out that the title is possessive: Mellors belongs to Connie. He is uncertain, she knows what she wants and gets it: a new life and a baby. "That was why you wanted me then, to get a child?" Mellors asks, and she does not deny it. Women come first and men second throughout Lawrence's work, for all his belief that it should be otherwise.

It took him no longer than six weeks to write the 120,000 words of the new and final novel, an astonishing feat for someone so weakened by disease. Pausing briefly to spend another Christmas of celebrations, decorating another tree for the peasant children, he went on to finish his novel on January 9, 1928. Only the unfinished book prevented him from following the example of the Wilkinsons and retreating to the comfort of a centrally heated hotel for the festive season. With a touch of malice he told his mother-in-law that Frieda had got one of the Bandelli children into hospital for a hernia operation. "But thank the Lord the child is being difficult, and Saint Frieda begins to be bored and turn all-too-human again. The Wilkinsons had left for a holiday in Rome, leaving the Lawrences the present of a Christmas pudding.

The weather was damp and foggy, making his cough worse. To Gertie he wrote that it had become colder and drier suddenly, "enough to blow the skin off your face," but sunny. He sat hugging the warm stove because of his "bronchials." When he was out that very morning "the vapor froze in my beard: never been so cold here." On December 23 he was telling his gloomy friend Kot, "I do think this is the low-water mark of existence. I never felt so near the brink of the abyss." It was out of character for him to own up to such pessimism, though God knows he had every right to do so. The celebrations with the peasants on the 24th cheered him up, as did the Christmas Day dinner he and Frieda shared with the Huxleys in Florence.

It was probably during this visit that the idea of accompanying Huxley and his brother Julian (with their wives and children) on a skiing holiday in Switzerland originated. The intention was for the Lawrences to start out on January 16, 1928, but he went down with "flu." It was another four days before they were on their way to Les Diablerets. His cough went "raking on," but he was too restless to delay further and sick of being driven yet again back into bed.

11

O Galilee, Sweet Galilee

(1928–1929)

At Diablerets, a few miles from Lake Geneva, they were in the midst of a host of Huxleys: as well as Aldous, Maria, and their young son there was Julian the biologist, his wife Juliette and their two small sons, and Juliette's mother, all closeted in a chalet a few minutes away from the Lawrences in their Chalet Beau Site. Lawrence was in need of a tonic, he told Koteliansky, and thought of staying a month. The journey over the Simplon had been fine: they came "tinkling from the station in a sledge." The idea of Lawrence skiing in his condition sounds bizarre, but he was determined to act as normally as possible and hated to be left out of anything. But he was not up to winter sports "yet," he said to Secker and to Emily a few days later. He took delight instead in witnessing the struggles of Frieda as she ended up repeatedly on her bottom in the snow, "unable to rise because of those thundering long sticks on her feet." And the congenial company provided by the Huxleys was always enjoyable. They had tea together on most days, and when the Lawrences were hosts in their chalet, Juliette had memories later of Lawrence's "delicious lemon curd on crisp little pasties" that he had baked himself. He contented himself with watching Aldous, "thin and half blind," trudging uphill for more than half an hour in order to "slither down again in four minutes—it's a lot of hard work for a bit of fun." He and Frieda ventured out for short walks, wearing dark glasses against the glare, with Frieda amusing herself on a little toboggan.

Juliette Huxley was Swiss. Lawrence had met her once before, at Garsington when she was seventeen. On this holiday she found him lovable and Frieda hard to take. Apparently she had no idea he was consumptive. What she described as the "radiating creativeness of his presence" was dulled somewhat when she read his new novel. Shocked, she told him angrily that he ought to call it "John Thomas and Lady Jane," which appealed to him at once as a title. "Many a true word spoken in spite," he said, laughing uproariously. It was Aldous who talked him out of the idea, pointing out that it would be an easy target for customs with such a label. Juliette remembered that "he had a very special way of laughing, tilting his head and pointing his small red beard at one, his bright blue eyes twinkling."

A letter from Beatrice Campbell set him dreaming of a trip to Ireland, though with his "wretched chest—bronchials really" he wondered about the rain. If he painted his nudes there, he joked, would he be thrown into the dungeons? He asked about the color of her hair and said that Frieda was now a bit gray and he had found two white hairs in his beard.

Toward the end of February the party began to split up, Frieda to visit her mother in Baden-Baden and the two Huxley families to London. Juliette, in difficulties with her marriage, stayed a little longer, helping Lawrence down thoughtfully from the heights in case the descent proved too much for him. Her reference to Frieda departing for one of her "periodic prowls" seems an apt description of the detours she was making to see Ravagli. When one considers the honesty with which both she and her husband expressed their feelings it is strange that neither he nor Frieda chose to bring the situation into the open. Barbara Weekley had assumed that his comment, "Every heart has a right to its own secrets" meant that he was aware like others of the part Ravagli now played in Frieda's emotional life.

Whether or not he accepted the fact of her secret "other life" in his own heart, he waited as eagerly as ever for her return at Milan on March 6. His train and hers should have arrived at approximately the same time, and Achsah Brewster must have been at the station to meet them, as well as the Wilkinsons. According to Achsah's notes, Frieda's train came in at ten, without Frieda. Lawrence waited to meet the twelve o'clock express, with the same result. "He ate his lunch hurriedly and rushed back for the 2:20 local, but returned shortly looking disconsolate. 'She's probably lost her passport and been held up, or her purse.' We tried to cheer him up, but in vain."

At last she came, and the Wilkinsons were there again with a hired car to drive them out to San Paolo. Peasants were at the village to greet them with primroses, violets, and anemones. The weather was not good, rain fell continually, and the cold winds were unpleasant, so that he felt "like being in a knife box." He got down to the business of having his completed novel typed, running into the first of many problems. Nellie Morrison, who had undertaken the typing, was too outraged to continue. In the end it was Catherine Carswell and Maria Huxley who got the job done between them. Lawrence took the typescript into the same non-English-speaking printer that Orioli had recommended, with Orioli overseeing the operation.

By publishing his novel privately he knew he would avoid the tax now being levied on British writers living abroad, but his agent advised that securing copyright for a book branded obscene would be impossible, leaving his Florence edition wide open for pirating. He decided to do what he had sworn not to do: prepare an expurgated edition for Secker and Knopf while going ahead with a book in Florence aimed at collectors. The task of expurgating was such a headache that he soon gave up and handed over the fileting for Secker to do as best he could.

Grappling with the proofs was literally to be immersed in a comedy of errors. Errors appeared thick and fast on every page. The Florentine firm had set "dnd't, did'nt, dnid't, din'dt, didn't like a Bach fugue." He took on the publicity single-handedly, had fifteen hundred subscription leaflets printed, and wrote endless letters to friends and acquaintances to enlist their support in the battle ahead.

His lease on the Villa Miranda ended in April. After the disaster of the preceding year he had no wish to subject himself to another Tuscan summer. Proofs of the novel were still only half done on May 4 when he wrote to Else Jaffe, but he had another reason for eventually renewing the lease for a further six months. He had begun to pack, removing his pictures from the walls, relenting only when Frieda, who wished to stay, "became so gloomy." Despite paying for six months' rent, he still intended on leaving for a while, perhaps to Diablerets again where he had felt reasonably well.

To leave the villa empty offended Lawrence's thrifty nature. Would the Brewsters like to use it rent free? One day in early June they came to lunch, finding Lawrence dressed in his summer garb, a bright blue Bavarian jacket with white buttons. Both the Brewsters were painters, and Achsah put on record her unprejudiced and fascinated response to his pictures, admiring their "sensitive color, ease of technique, spontaneity and expressiveness."

Over the meal it was proposed that the Brewsters would come to Switzerland too. Achsah Brewster has said that they felt time was running out for them to enjoy their friend's company. He had one more task to accomplish. The Warren Gallery in London, run by Dorothy Warren, a friend of Barbara Weekley, were keen to exhibit his paintings. How did one pack pictures? He asked Mark Gertler, "Would you take the big pictures off their stretchers and roll them? Paint is a bit thick in places, it might crack off."

MONEY FOR HIS BOOK was coming in from all quarters across the world, from individuals and from specialist booksellers. He had also hit on an easy way of earning money by freelance journalism, spurred on by Nancy Pearn at Curtis Brown. When the first copy of *Lady Chatterley* reached him, looking very handsome and dignified with his phoenix design on the cover, he was at the Grand Hotel in Chexbres, polishing off two more articles for the London *Evening News*. He wrote to Orioli on July 28, 1928, to say how pleased and excited he was, and Frieda too, by this outwardly beautiful volume.

A few days earlier he had been subjected to an unpleasant experience after checking into the Hotel des Touristes at St. Nizier de Pariset in Savoie. Lawrence's incessant coughing had upset the manager, and he and Frieda were asked to leave. The Brewsters and Frieda tried to keep the truth from him, but he knew. To Orioli he wrote, "The insolent French people actually asked us to go away because I coughed." Now he hated France and liked Switzerland.

Near the village of Gsteig, only a few miles from Diablerets, they went in search of a chalet and found the Chalet Kesselmate, a steep climb up from the village. The Brewsters stayed below in the Hotel Viktoria in Gsteig. Almost at once he was felled by a hemorrhage. Writing to Aldous and Maria Huxley on July 31, he had recovered his sense of humor sufficiently to say he had been feeling perfectly wretched, and made a design for his tombstone with the inscription, "Departed this life, etc.etc—*He was fed up!*" Everywhere was steep, steep, "and I just can't climb." Thoughts about resurrection were turned on himself. "I wish the Lord would make a new man of me," he said grimly to Koteliansky, "for I'm not much to boast about now."

From his outpost just above the snowline he directed his publishing operation with the kind of business acumen he had long displayed in his literary dealings. All orders were to be sent to him, he directed Orioli, who afterward complained that he should have been paid more than 10 percent for his part in the enterprise. He wanted his partner to be tougher on booksellers: they should not be given copies before they had paid up. If the authorities moved in, shops might refuse to pay. There was exhilaration in feeling himself in charge of his own destiny for once, and Frieda felt it too, enjoying the intrigue of outwitting the enemy by shipping copies in bulk to willing collaborators.

He heard from a new admirer, Maria Chambers, a Mexican aspiring writer married to an American and living on Long Island. He liked the sound of her because she was eager to help with the distribution of his novel, but replied too warmly and personally, as Harriet had accused Somers of always doing in *Kangaroo*, and was soon having to fend off her effusions. She sent photographs and was threatening to come to Switzerland to meet him. Electing for the brutally frank reply, he warned: "But now listen—what do you expect to find? Here I am, forty two, with rather bad health, and a wife who is by no means the soul of patience." She was bound to be disappointed if she thought that by meeting him the heavens would open. "They will never open." What would they do except talk, have lunch, walk, talk again; and he was weary of talk. If she wanted to visit Europe, then good luck, but if her intention was to come for the thrill of meeting him she should forget it. "And then of course my wife doesn't look on me as a shrine, and objects to that attitude in other people: at which one can't wonder."

Frieda's supply of patience was indeed limited. The Brewsters labored up the hill devotedly to see them. No one was more devoted than Achsah. Good, considerate soul though she was, she exasperated Frieda with her spirituality; "Achsah always in white and her soul is white too, like white of egg, and they call Lawrence 'David,' and she paints him as a blue-eyed *Eunuch*!"

As well as directing operations and feeling God-like he wrote more pieces for the *Evening News*, a short story, "Blue Moccasins," and broke into *Vogue* with a batch of reviews. Because their chalet was roomy and he couldn't bear the thought of waste, he invited his sister Emily, who had never visited him, to come over and bring her daughter Peggy. Perhaps with his memories of childhood stirred up in anticipation of this visit, he sat up in bed after another bad day to write "Hymns in a Man's Life." Only four pages long, it is one of his most appealing essays. At the outset he confesses almost shamefully that the hymns he learned as a child had more value for him, finally, than the finest poetry. How could this be, when the words were so banal?

Each gentle dove
And sighing bough
That makes the eve
So fair to me
Has something far
Diviner now
To draw me back
To Galilee.
O Galilee, sweet Galilee
Where Jesus loved so much to be,
O Galilee, sweet Galilee,
Come sing thy songs again to me!

He had no desire to go to Palestine, or know where the Lake of Galilee was, yet the very word "Galilee" was somehow wonderful. "Galilee is one of those lovely, glamorous worlds, not places, that exist in the golden haze of a child's half-formed imagination. And in my man's imagination it is just the same. It has been left untouched."

Another hymn he loved had the words

Fair waved the golden corn.
In Canaan's pleasant land—

And the word "Canaan" "could never be localized."

At the core of his beliefs now were two elements, touch and wonder. And perhaps the most precious was wonder, which had filled his child's heart with sheer delight. What did it matter if the miracle of the loaves and fishes was historically a fact or not? "It is part of the genuine wonder."

He was grateful to have been brought up a Nonconformist and a

Congregationalist. He had escaped both the hierarchies of class in the Church of England and the emotionalism of the Primitive Methodists, "for I always had a horror of being saved." He had fond memories of their chapel, with its pale green and blue color-washed walls, its stillness and its light. A man, when he was a child, could still sing "Hold the fort, for I am coming," and believe it. These were the battle cries of stout souls.

> Stand up, stand up for Jesus,
> Ye soldiers of the Lord.

"Here is the clue to the ordinary Englishman—in the Nonconformist hymns."

In the event, Emily and Peggy's visit became for him just something to get through dutifully. Emily seemed unaware of his acute discomfort. She made him realize that he had never really been the "Bert" his relatives thought him, just part of the "eternal price list" of their lives. He hid his true feelings from them, and felt bound to hide *Lady C* out of sight in a cupboard. Photographs taken by Peggy Needham tell the story of his emaciated condition more shockingly than any words. His wretched mood is caught too by the camera's oblivious realism. Sitting beside his weighty relatives, he draws attention to his alarming thinness, as he does next to Frieda, tense and unsmiling in his baggy suit.

A little party was held on September 13 at the Hotel Viktoria to celebrate Frieda's forty-ninth birthday. Then the Lawrences left for Baden-Baden. The Brewsters stayed in Geneva, joining them briefly in Germany in the early autumn. It was a time of birthdays: Lawrence's on September 11, followed by Earl Brewster's a week later.

THE URGENT NEED was for Lawrence to go south in search of the sun. Frieda went off alone to retrieve their belongings from the Villa Miranda while her husband made his way by stages to join the

Aldingtons on the Ile de Port-Cros, off Hyères: Richard Aldington had the use of a converted Vigie or observation post there. Aldington's account, like much of his writing on Lawrence, is a mixture of admiration and veiled hostility. Lawrence would not, he says, come to the island without Frieda, and he found himself sending telegrams with prepaid answers to his friend, getting the same reply "Waiting for Frieda" each time.

Lawrence's delayed-action maneuvers took him to Strasbourg with the Brewsters. To keep warm he joined them in a movie theatre, finding himself subjected to a film called *Ben Hur*. After half an hour of being nauseated by "doves fluttering around baby-faced dolls, brutal Romans accursed with hearts of stone, galleys of inhuman slaves," he left, as sickened by the sight of the open-mouthed audience as by the film's idiocy.

At Port-Cros Lawrence immediately succumbed to his "flu," brought on by catching Frieda's cold that she had brought back from Italy. He had not expected to find Aldington, who was in the process of discarding his wife, with not one but two mistresses, Arabella Yorke and Brigit Patmore. Also with them in the fort was their Sicilian manservant, with whom Arabella had an affair during their stay. It took forty-five minutes to toil uphill from the port to the walled Vigie, so for much of the five weeks Lawrence was confined to the compound or his bed. Down below was his beloved blue Mediterranean to mock him, with others in the party gloriously healthy, "full of jape and jest and adultery," as Aldington put it. Lawrence's host, perhaps smarting from his appearance in a short story, or more likely simply envious, felt obliged to set down in his account that "the wife of the erotic genius was condemned to underclothes of an austerity combining the extreme decorum of a nun with the cheerlessness of a charlady."

It was while Lawrence was incarcerated at Port-Cros that he told Aldous Huxley he found his new novel *Point Counterpoint* "rather disgusting," no doubt with one eye on the scene around him. Here too at the end of October he read clippings of attacks on his novel in *John Bull* and the *Sunday Chronicle*. *John Bull* wanted British customs to halt the circulation of "the foulest book in English Literature" and wished its author could be clapped in prison. The *Sunday Chronicle* contented itself with the observation that *Lady Chatterley's Lover* "stank with obscenity and lewdness." Lawrence's sophisticated companions seemed to find these tabloid ravings laughable. Unable for the moment to share their amusement, he was hurt and disturbed enough to be heard saying, "Nobody likes to be called a cesspool."

Toward the end of his miserably bleak stay on Port-Cros, while others were running down to swim or to eat at the hotel, he was surprised by a letter that must have raised his spirits, even if his correspondent's name did fill him with emotional turmoil, flooding his heart with memories of the lost world of his youth. This voice from the past was that of David Chambers, Jessie's younger brother, now a professor of economics at Nottingham University. In his reply on November 14 Lawrence reveals how lonely he often was for his own people, exclaiming that

> I hardly recognized you as J.D.—and you must be a man now, instead of a thin little lad with very fair hair. Ugh, what a gap in time! it makes me feel scared.
>
> Whatever I forget, I shall never forget the Haggs—I loved it so. I loved to come to you all, it really was a new life begun in me there. The water-pippin by the door—those maiden-blush roses that Flower would lean over and eat—and Trip floundering round—and stewed figs for tea in winter, and in August stewed green apples. . . . Tell your mother I never forget, no matter where life carries us.— And does she still blush if somebody comes and finds her in a dirty white apron? Oh I'd love to be nineteen again, and coming up through the Warren and catching the first glimpse of the buildings. Then I'd sit on the sofa under the window, and we'd crowd round the little table to tea, in that tiny kitchen I was so at home in.

He had never written a more affectionate letter. If there was ever anything he could do for David, he wrote, he had only to say. "Because whatever else I am, I am somewhere still the same Bert who rushed with such joy to the Haggs."

Even when unhappily isolated by illness and distaste on Port-Cros, he had kept writing, turning out the pungent, quasi-journalistic pieces, at once gutsy, sardonic, and philosophical, that made such quick and welcome money. Nancy Pearn placed "The Real Trouble About Women" with the *Daily Express* and "Do Women Change?" with the *Sunday Dispatch*. These articles, between a thousand and two thousand words in length, he could knock off with ease in an hour and a half. He had also begun to write short verses by the dozen, which he wanted to be "fleeting as pansies," and which Frieda called real doggerel. Each scrap of verse, he explained later, was "just a thought put down," impromptu, not to be nailed down, simply "the breath of the moment." He was perhaps at work on them when Brigit Patmore shouted in through his window one day to say she had seen three rainbows in the valley. Bent over his writing he raised his head, said "There, there," and went on working.

Unsure of their next abode, the Lawrences made for the little French resort of Bandol, a tiny port on a sheltered bay between Toulon and Marseilles, intending to stay only for a fortnight while they considered their next move. It was so congenial, and such a contrast to Port-Cros, with no punishing hill to climb, that Lawrence stayed for nearly four months, cheered by the weather, warm and sunny even in November. It was good to be clear of Aldington, who he had sensed was treacherous. If he was a "friend," give him enemies, so that at least he knew where he stood. The man's good looks, broad shoulders, and charm only added to the sick writer's resentment. Unknown to him, Aldington was soon writing to his wife Hilda Doolittle of "demented scenes," from which "I emerged with the conviction that Lawrence is really malevolent and evil."

Frieda and he were now truly vagrants, their belongings in store in Florence. Lawrence listened to Frieda's familiar complaint about hotels and having nothing to do, placating her with the assurance that it was merely temporary. They were at the pleasant Hotel Beau Rivage, in two upstairs rooms with a connecting door. It was cheap, only forty francs a day, and Lawrence's money worries had diminished considerably with the knowledge that he was to clear a net profit of a thousand pounds from the sales of his novel. Huxley had suggested that either he or Orioli should go to Paris to arrange for the distribution of the two hundred paperback copies that were still available, and perhaps find a printer there who would bring out a new edition. The show of Lawrence's paintings had been postponed until next June, so that Paris and London were in his mind as future destinations. As well as these, he had begun to talk of Spain, somewhere he had never been, where he could be sure of the sun. With his illness apparently in remission, he was content for the moment to stay put. Not until the end of the year did he realize he was in the very hotel where Katherine Mansfield had once stayed in the winter of 1916 in her search for health. It wouldn't have seemed a good omen.

Nevertheless he settled down with a determination to enjoy the peaceful little resort. He attacked his money-spinning articles in the mornings and turned more and more to poetry to refresh his soul. Preparing his *Collected Poems* had rekindled his desire to write poems. In the next twelve months he wrote continuously in an extraordinary poetic flowering. His last prose work, *Apocalypse*, in itself a kind of poem, would be written here, and the magnificent *Last Poems*.

His routine could not have been more humdrum, but it suited him. After lunch he wandered off alone along the front, content to observe others exerting themselves with "life," watching the games of *boules* being played by the locals. He was cultivating a kind of solitariness that was surprisingly to his liking, in spite of the lonely acceptance he had written about in one of his pensées, called at first "Numbness":

> I cannot help but be alone
> for desire has died in me, silence has grown
> and nothing now reaches out to draw
> other flesh to my own.

Solitary or not, he was never one to turn away visitors, but to invite someone along sight unseen was something new. Charles Lahr, owner of the Progressive Bookshop in Red Lion Street in Holborn, knew the young Welsh writer Rhys Davies, and must have let Lawrence know that the Welshman was staying impecuniously in Nice, eking out an American advance for his second novel. Acting on impulse and evidently feeling he might have an affinity with Davies, who came from a mining village in South Wales and whose grandfather had been a miner, he wrote asking the young man to visit them for a few days. Knowing Davies was poor, he said he would foot all expenses.

DAVIES CAME OVER from Nice on November 29, not knowing what to expect but not wanting to miss the opportunity. Expecting from all accounts a gaunt biblical prophet, he was astonished to be met at the station by a man in a blue blazer and cotton trousers, who came smiling forward to say he had a hired car waiting.

He stayed three days, finding Frieda even easier to converse with than Lawrence. When he told her that the young in England looked to her husband for leadership, she implored him to tell Lawrence. "He feels *everybody* hates him." Davies thought that for someone so famous he was remarkably unpretentious, but Lawrence promptly told his guest that young writers needed to find some guts and break free for themselves, now that he had shown them the way. Modern society made him feel "like a monkey in a cage," he said angrily. "But if someone puts a finger in my cage, I bite—and I bite hard."

These memories appeared first in *Horizon* and then in Davies's autobiography, *Print of a Hare's Foot*. Meeting his hero for the first time on the station platform he thought he had "an elusive touch of delicate attentiveness in his manner. He gave a first impression of classless aristocracy." In his faded jacket, wispy trousers, and floppy black hat he did not look English somehow. "To be with him was to feel a different and swifter beat within oneself. The stupid behavior of ordinary life, the little falsehoods, attitudes, rituals and poses dropped away and one sat with him clear and truthful. But he could be irritating also, a smacking schoolmaster."

Davies recalled Lawrence squatting by the side of the road on his heels, "collier-fashion" like a bird, "his shut eyelids lifted to the sun, while he and Frieda left their horse-drawn carriage and walked up a hill behind Bandol that the invalid couldn't manage. Like Mabel Sterne and many others, he had his theory about the causes of quarrels between the couple that he witnessed. While Mabel suspected Frieda of arousing her husband's rage in order to keep him attached to her, Davies thought that by attacking his wife Lawrence "kept her simmering subtly; for a natural inclination to a stout German placidity threatened to swamp her fine lioness quality."

In the mornings Lawrence wrote letters, painted a bit, and composed his *Pansies* (not knowing its slang use, he enjoyed the joke when Davies told him) sitting up in bed, "a bead-fringed African skullcap on his head. 'It keeps my brain warm,' he said, and bought me one of these straw caps in a Bandol shop." When he began to cough, a steady, tormented wracking sound, he would excuse himself abruptly and disappear.

The very mention of money, and the miners made to accept charity to survive, was enough to make him rant. Why didn't the young rise up instead of letting the moneyed lot turn everything into a series of vulgar transactions? What was the good of an industrial system that piled up rubbish and everyone working instead of living? Damn it all, why couldn't we be like birds? Frieda would break in to tell Davies that *they* lived like that, on so little money. "Everybody could be like us," she cried naively.

The young Welshman found himself asked directly if his home life had been as screwed down as Lawrence's. "Didn't you ever want to spit in their eye and write your Lady Chatterley?" And didn't it nauseate him, with his background, to see all the rich English stuffing themselves down here on the Riviera? Nor could he abide these damned American women "with hammers in their voices."

But he was not done for yet. Davies could see he was far from well, but what kept a man potent was the spirit. Didn't he agree? "That's what endures." And suddenly he cried out an appeal that was half an order: "Whatever you do, don't desert your class! Don't run away from your class!" As his visit came to an end, and in spite of the Lawrences' "queer little bursts of fury with each other," the young Davies liked and esteemed them both.

The liking was mutual. He was soon back on a second visit, this time accompanied by an Australian, P. R. Stephensen, who had come to Nice to drum up custom for the deluxe editions of books published by the Franfolico Press. An associate, Jack Lindsay, meeting Frieda in Florence, had asked to see her husband's pictures and then broached the idea of a book of reproductions. Lawrence was enthusiastic, and when Stephensen detached himself from Lindsay and founded the Mandrake Press, the book headed his list of titles. Stephensen came to Bandol to discuss the matter, and out of their conversations arose the idea of a "good peppery foreword" to the volume.

Lawrence seized the opportunity to write a sustained essay, "Introduction to These Paintings," that he thought one of the best things he ever did. Considering the advanced stage of his tuberculosis, it is remarkable to find the vehemence and passion of his argument and analysis unimpaired. In what is in part an extended essay on Cézanne, with whom he identifies movingly as a solitary man engaged in a struggle to cope with his isolation and see truly, he provides at the same time an historical context for his new doctrine of touch and tenderness.

What, one wonders, is the twenty-first-century reader, overwhelmed, in Saul Bellow's words, by the sexual madness of the Western world, to make of Lawrence's assertion that what modern man has now is "a grinning travesty of sex" and a masturbatory culture that swindles and degrades us at every turn? He has confronted the swindle in his novel: now he turns to consider how it has come about by an examination of painting since the Renaissance. At the outset he advances the startling notion that a fear of the instincts and a horror of the living body took a grip on the Northern consciousness and came to haunt the Elizabethans. "The real 'mortal coil' in Hamlet is all sexual; the young man's horror of his mother's incest, sex carrying with it a wild and nameless terror which, it seems to me, it had never carried before. . . . Hamlet is overpowered by horrible revulsion from his physical connection with his mother, which makes him recoil in similar revulsion from Ophelia, and almost from his father, even as a ghost. He is horrified at the merest suggestion of physical connection, as if it were an unspeakable taint."

With characteristic force he goes on to argue that this horror and terror of the physical at the end of the sixteenth century came, "I believe, from the great shock of syphilis and the realization of the consequences of that disease." This terror-horror, lodged deeply in the human imagination, led to the rise of Puritanism and, says Lawrence, to the crippling of the consciousness of modern man. To illustrate this he focuses on the plight of Cézanne with his "heroic sincerity," seeing him as a prisoner of sex, caught by an overmastering dread of the body—the desired female body being the greatest dread—and wanting desperately through painting to regain his own flesh. This, Lawrence maintains, was his prime torture, and quotes him as saying, "I am so feeble in life." Unable to forget the Arcadia of his youth, living on the riverbanks with Baille and Zola like a happy savage, he wanted all his life to return, not out of nostalgia

but in order to begin truly. So his terrible craving to paint naked figures in the style of the great masters was born. No one else wanted
his male and female bathers, but he kept on.

Why Cézanne is a hero for Lawrence, in spite of his failure in
the eyes of his contemporaries, soon becomes clear. In his struggle
to paint the nude he came up against the cliché: the classical, the romantic, the optical. The slur put about by those who maintained
that his eyesight was defective is fatuous. He could turn out the
cliché with the best of them, but what he wanted was "true-to-life"
representation. Only he wanted it *more* true to life. And once you
have got photography, it is a very, very difficult thing to get representation *more* true to life: which it has to be." As Lawrence puts it
with his usual felicity, "The true imagination is for ever curving
round to the other side, to the back of the presented appearance."

How is this relevant to Lady Chatterley and the curious vacillations of Parkin and Mellors before the "torment" of sex? Cézanne,
suggests Lawrence, was unable to "prostitute one part of himself to
the other. He *could* not masturbate, in paint or words. And that is
saying a very great deal today." If he could even paint an apple truly,
all would be possible: his lost intuitions, instincts, the lost earth itself would be regained. Lawrence's concentration on the central
dilemma of our time is unswerving. "All we know is shadows, even
of apples. Shadows of everything, of the whole world, shadows even
of ourselves. We are inside the tomb. . . . Specters we are to one another."

A PRESENT came on Christmas Day from Rhys Davies to express
his thanks for their hospitality. The silk dressing gown took
Lawrence aback: he was troubled by the extravagance, since Davies
could not really afford it. He looked very resplendent, he said, as he
sat in bed having coffee, but forbade the sending of anything dearer
than two shillings sixpence in the future. "But thank you very much
and I shall swank my little swank in it." Frieda thanked him too,

adorning her letter with a drawing of "Lorenzo . . . looking not only like one prophet but all the prophets of all times and ages rolled into one," and she added some outlines of pansies to remind him of the poet's doggerel, flowering now in great abundance.

Aware now of the savaging of his novel in England, Lawrence vented his spleen in one pansy, the first of many on the same subject:

How beastly the bourgeois is
especially the male of the species—

Full of seething, wormy, hollow feelings
rather nasty—
How beastly the bourgeois is!

Standing in their thousands
in damp England
what a pity they can't all be kicked over
like sickening toadstools, and left to melt
back into the soil of England.

A pansy that could have been prompted by *Ben Hur* recorded an experience he would not repeat:

When I went to the film, and saw all the black-and-white
    feelings that nobody felt,
and heard the audience sighing and sobbing with the
    emotions that nobody felt. . . .
and caught them moaning from close-up kisses, black-
    and-white kisses that could not be felt,
it was like being in heaven, which I am sure has
    a white atmosphere
upon which shadows of people, pure personalities
    are cast in black and white, and love
in flat ecstasy, supremely unfelt and heavenly.

Rhys Davies must come again, Lawrence told him, "before we flit." It was perhaps a consolation to have a young protégé in attendance now and then, even if he did have doubts, after reading Davies's first novel, about the Welshman's sexuality. And something about the young man aroused Lawrence's protective feelings. Davies had occupied the large corner room that he thought afterward was the one Katherine Mansfield had once stayed in. One day, unwell in bed, he was surprised by a concerned host appearing with a spoon and some syrup for Davies to swallow.

When he told Lawrence of the moving account he had read of Murry's visit to the Gurdjieff Institute to be with his dying wife, Lawrence squirmed and cried out, "Wrong! This is what really happened. When Murry turned up at that crank's institute a friend staying there went to Katherine's room to tell her of his arrival. She said, 'Keep that bugger away from me,' and then had her last hemorrhage."

A letter came from Ottoline Morrell, who had made her peace with him after a fashion. He replied after Christmas, full of hope as ever, to say that he was getting better all the time, and to hastily clarify his motives regarding *Lady Chatterley*. She musn't think he advocated perpetual sex. "Far from it. Nothing nauseates me more than promiscuous sex in and out of season. But I want, with Lady C., to make an adjustment of consciousness to the basic physical realities."

He was indeed feeling better, ever since coming to Bandol. Even his appetite recovered, cruelly illusory though these signs were. More upset than he would admit by his sister Ada accusing him of hiding some part of himself from her, he invited her to Bandol for a holiday. Her antagonism toward Frieda had subsided, but when she came her very presence, fond though he always was of her, depressed him horribly because of the feeling of hopelessness that now oppressed her. The day she left he wrote to say how unhappy he felt because of her misery, urging her to see her present state as temporary. As for him hiding from her, it wasn't true. "I am always the same. But there is something you just refuse to see and refuse to accept in me."

Now that it had turned colder he was afflicted once more by a restless need to seek the sun. He favored either Spain or Corsica. Frieda was reluctant to go anywhere that took her farther away from Ravagli, but could hardly say so. Lawrence, ordering a new suit, confessed to Huxley that "I want a metamorphosis or metempsychosis or both—a reincarnation into a dashing body that doesn't cough."

It was an impossible dream, and in his heart of hearts he knew it. The decision about a new destination was postponed when a Parisian bookseller expressed an interest in bringing out a new edition of his novel. This would head off the risk of a pirated edition being sold in Paris. He would need to go there himself. When Davies volunteered to accompany Lawrence to the French capital, Frieda said it would suit her to go again to Baden-Baden. On March 11, 1929, they set off in their different directions.

12

The Last Green Leaf

(1929–1930)

Frieda had gone speeding away in an express from Marseilles. Lawrence, not wanting to tackle the journey to Paris "at one go," took a stopping train, spending a night with his Welsh acolyte in a dreary provincial hotel on the way. There was one room available and one bed in it, which he and Davies shared. It is remarkable that, as with the Huxleys and their children at Diablerets, no one seemed alarmed at being in close proximity with someone so ill with tuberculosis. In the curtained alcove Lawrence bathed himself. Davies caught a glimpse of his companion's "frail, wasted body, so vulnerable-looking." The sight filled him with foreboding.

The account of their time together in Paris is given verbatim by Davies in his *Print of a Hare's Foot*. It makes harrowing reading. On their way by taxi to the Hotel Grand Versailles—which had nothing grand about it—Lawrence lost his temper with the driver's ineptitude, then changed his tune abruptly when the man told him he was a Russian exile. "Did you see his face?" Lawrence asked Davies later. "A human being at last. That man lives in his blood, solidly in his blood. These slippery French, they're all mind, cold little minds."

Once installed at the hotel they went on what proved a fruitless meeting with Frank Groves, who ran a bookshop in the Palais Royal district. He had misunderstood Groves's intention, which was to sell pirated copies of *Lady Chatterley* that he had acquired. All Lawrence had to do was "authorise" the edition by allowing a printed slip to be inserted in each copy. Unable to decide, he approached Sylvia Beach at her shop at 12 Rue de l'Odéon. She was prepared to sell original copies but not to bring out a new edition under her own imprint. Though not liking the novel, she was charmed by the man, directing him to Edward Titus, a fellow American.

Back at the hotel, Lawrence had had more than enough for one day. Davies, alarmed by his friend's exhausted state, asked if he was all right. No, said Lawrence grimly. Shouldn't he lie down? "I'm sick to death of lying down!" When the young man mumbled his apologies, Lawrence asked him in a whisper to be patient with him.

In the night Davies lay listening to the sounds of horrible distress in the next room. Finally his anxiety drove him to investigate. "The dark tormented face and haggard body was like some stormy El Greco figure writhing on the bed." Alarmed, Davies suggested a doctor and made for the telephone. The harshly coughing Lawrence sat up and ordered him away from the phone. "Do as I say, damn you," he raged, spluttering and coughing.

Davies asked what he could do to help. "Stay in the room with me," said Lawrence, almost pleading. "I feel so hopeless, that's all." When asked if he would like a drink, he just said, "There's an evil spirit in my body. It leaves one part and goes to another. That's why doctors are no use."

Should he get a message to Mrs. Lawrence? Again the answer was no: she would arrive in a day or two, in her own good time. As if to himself he murmured that he used to believe it was crucial, not to be betrayed. But it wasn't that important. Only to the ego. Frieda was Frieda. She did everything too much: ate too many cakes, smoked too many cigarettes. "I shall take it out of her hide, one way or another." In a changed voice he said he spoke in confidence because they were of the same class, they understood one another. He wouldn't confide in the Huxleys, nice though they were: their kind were always mixed up in some adulterous stew or other. It was the subject of all their little novels.

It helped to have some human presence nearby who thought kindly about him. Having seen Davies making notes assiduously, he said he had something for the other's notebook. When he wrote *Lady C*, he wrote what amounted to the epilogue of his travels. That was why it was sad. He had come to the end of his journeying: he was knocked up.

Davies said loyally that for all that, he always recovered. That sounded like Frieda, Lawrence said, with a grim laugh. At two in the morning he asked for a glass of water. As Davies moved obediently to the door he heard the invalid say softly, as if to himself, "I wish there were miracles, Davies."

In Sylvia Beach's bookshop he had been approached by Edward Dahlberg, a young American writer who wanted to thank Lawrence for his generosity in consenting to write an introduction to his first novel, *Bottom Dogs*. After all, they had never met. Later, hearing that Dahlberg was living in a room on one meal a day, the Englishman sent him five pounds and urged him to stick to his guns: "that bony stoicism is the thing." Dahlberg had taken in "the goatish jaw with beard, russet, earthed hair, and a potato nose . . . and squashed seeds for teeth." Meeting him by chance another time on the Boulevard Raspail he realized, he said later, "that the man was dying in his clothes," and took him back to his hotel.

In his lengthy introduction to *Bottom Dogs*, Lawrence declares it to be a genuine book, "as far as it goes," and takes the opportunity to have his final say on America:

> When we think of America, and of her huge success, we never realize how many failures have gone, and still go, to build up that success. It is not till you live in America, and go a little under the surface, that you begin to see how terrible and brutal is the mass of failure that nourishes the roots of the gigantic tree of dollars. . . . An

English novel like *Point Counterpoint* has gone beyond tragedy into exacerbation. This novel goes one further. Man just *smells*, offensively and unbearably, not to be borne. The human stink! It reveals a condition that not many of us have reached, but towards which the trend of consciousness is taking us, all of us, especially the young. It is, let us hope, a *ne plus ultra*. The next step is legal insanity, or just crime. The book is perfectly sane: yet two more strides and it is criminal insanity. It is sheer bottom-dog style, the bottom-dog mind expressing itself direct, almost as if it barked. That directness, that unsentimental and non-dramatized thoroughness of setting down the under-dog mind surpasses anything I know. I don't want to read any more books like this.

Unwilling to give up on Paris until he had accomplished something, he contacted Edward Titus at his premises close to the Hotel Grand Versailles. A deal was struck to issue three thousand copies of a photographically reproduced new edition.

Satisfied that his efforts had finally borne fruit, he went off to stay with the Huxleys at Forti dei Marmi for a few days. Aldous Huxley was dismayed by his friend's wretched state, writing to the poet Robert Nichols, "How horrible this gradually approaching dissolution is—and in this case specially horrible, because so unnecessary, the result simply of the man's strange obstinacy against professional medicine." He did manage to persuade him to see a French doctor for an Xray. Lawrence backed out from the appointment the moment Frieda arrived, infuriating Huxley, who afterward blamed Frieda for her inadequate nursing. "We've told her that she's a fool and a criminal but it has no more effect than telling an elephant." Rhys Davies on the contrary saw her influence as restorative. On her arrival he went out for the afternoon. Returning to the hotel he knocked on Lawrence's door and Frieda's voice sang out, telling him to come in. She had joined her husband in bed. "The couple lay in bed under a tumbled counterpane of crimson velvet, Lawrence's bearded head nestling contentedly on a hearty bosom." Davies had brought her a bar of nougat and Frieda sat up at once to devour it, laughing at the young man's embarrassment. "I retreated in confusion, making some excuse. Never have I seen such a picture of married bliss. Was this the person, I asked myself, who insisted that connubial love entailed the virtual sacrifice, for her own good, of the woman to the man?"

ABOUT TO LEAVE for Spain, Lawrence blamed Paris for his "bit of grippe" in an irritable letter to Secker, who was dithering over a forthcoming edition of *Pansies*: "I want you to put in *all* the poems that won't expose you to Jix." The home secretary, Sir William Joynson Hicks ("Jix") was about to intensify his campaign against obscenity.

The Lawrences spent nights in Orléans and Toulouse en route to Carcassonne and then Barcelona. Three days were enough to convince him that the rough proletarian city was not for him. They sailed to Majorca, having booked in advance at Palma's Hotel Royal, moving from there shortly afterward to the Principe Alfonso.

Writing to Rhys Davies, he explained why he didn't think he would be staying long, even though the hotel was nice and "in the morning when it is lovely and sunny and blue and fresh, I am reconciled again, for a time." Yes, he liked the sea and the sunshine "and the pink convolvulus flowers all on the rocks." And there were some pleasant people about, residents. It was Spain itself he could not bear, and the Spanish wine, "my God, it is foul, cat-piss is champagne compared, this is the sulphureous urination of some aged horse . . . and my malaria came back, and my teeth chattered like castanets—and that's the only truly Spanish thing I've done."

He went on putting pressure on Secker not to publish a bourgeois "inoffensive" *Pansies*. While he was in Bandol two copies of the manuscripts of *Pansies* had gone missing, and his correspondence with his publisher was being intercepted. The home secretary was closing in and Secker had good reason to be nervous. Lawrence was safe from arrest on a charge of obscenity while he stayed out of England, but his publisher was not. If any words seemed offensive, said the exasperated author, just put a dash. Or let him know if the content was alarming. Secker was by now in a funk about most of the book, especially things like "What Does She Want?"

> What does she want, volcanic Venus, as she goes fuming round?
> What does she want?
> She says she wants a lover, but don't you believe her.
> She's seething like a volcano, and volcanos don't want lovers.
> Besides, she's had twenty lovers, only to find she didn't really want them.
>
> So why should I, or you, be the twenty-first?
> How are we going to appease her, maiden and mother, now a volcano of rage?
>
> I tell you, the penis won't do it.
> She bites him in the neck and passes on.

He changed his mind about the island when his health seemed to improve. Any place where he felt better became at once agreeable to him, though he had no intention of taking a house there. Frieda, now "moaning for a house," kept harping vociferously in favor of Italy, either in the Florence or Lake Garcia regions, and Lawrence agreed that if they *had* to settle he wanted a whole house this time, not the top story of someone's villa, and all in all he thought Italy was best, and France second. *"Triumphat Frieda!"*

One balmy day in early May they motored to Valdemosa, "where Chopin was so happy and George Sand hated it." Looking out from the monastery, he wrote to the Huxleys in prose that took on the resonance of his writing about Monte Cassino as he gazed into the dim mystery of the plain below "and the great loose roses of the monastery gardens so brilliant and spreading themselves out— then inside, the cloisters so white and silent." They picnicked on the mountainous north coast high over the sea. The vista bewitched him, the bluest sea he ever saw—"not hard like peacocks and jewels, but soft like blue feathers of the tit . . . and no people—olives and a few goats—and the big blueness shimmering so far off?" They went on to Soller, where the orange blossom was strong in the air and "one felt like a bee." Always alert to the spirit of place, he found in an old Moorish garden where they stopped, among big bright roses, the ground yellow from the blossom of jasmine, that there lived "a queer stillness where the Moors had been, like ghosts—like a pause in life." He ended with his old diatribe against humanity: "The world is lovely if one avoids man—so why not avoid him! Why not! Why not!"

Frieda, whose opposition to Spain even extended to not learning a word of Spanish, finally turned on Majorca with a vengeance. Lawrence confided to Davies that a man had pinched Frieda's bottom on a tram—"I wasn't there—don't tell her I told you—so she despises every letter in the word Mallorca and is rampant to sail to Italy—to Marseilles anyhow—where her squeamish rear has never been nipped."

By the time they came to leave it was June 18. They traveled together to Marseilles and then separated, so that Frieda could go to London to oversee the exhibition of his pictures while he made his way to Cannes and a villa the Huxleys had rented along the coast. The opening of the show had still not been finalized by "that wretch Dorothy Warren," who was proving dilatory. The Mandrake Press edition of his paintings was meant to coincide with the show's opening, whenever that was. Frieda, who had sprained her ankle bathing at Majorca, nevertheless was elated by the prospect of her new role as business manager. She limped off to see Edward Titus in Paris on her husband's behalf before going on to London. Lawrence, dubious but resigned, did not feel up to a journey to England, and he would be risking arrest if he did so, according to his agents who had been visited by detectives.

AN EXCITED FRIEDA arrived at the Warren Gallery in Mayfair to find that the private view had been and gone and the show was in full swing. Dorothy Warren's gallery had mounted Henry Moore's first one-man show in 1928. She and Phillip Trotter were an odd couple to be promoting Lawrence's work, though they did specialize in showing paintings and sculpture by artists from the working classes. When their lawyer represented the Trotters in court in due course he referred to "Mr. Lawrence, who began as a miner in England."

The Warren Gallery exhibition was nearing the end of its successful three weeks' run, attracting thirteen thousand visitors, when two detective inspectors from Scotland Yard appeared and asked the owners to close the show. The Trotters held their ground and refused. Back came the detectives an hour later with reinforcements in order to carry away thirteen of the twenty-five pictures. During the course of this farce they came across the Nonesuch edition of William Blake's *Pencil Drawings* and were about to confiscate this item too before someone pointed out that Blake was beyond the reach of prosecution.

The police action and Lawrence's notoriety attracted the public in increasing numbers. While lawyers got to work to defend the owners and Lawrence and the premises stayed open, gaps on the walls were filled by early copies of paintings by Lawrence which Ada Clarke sent down from Nottingham. Frieda, relishing the commotion and in particular the feeling of being "no end of an important person," spoke later of having a terrific time. The fight was on to retrieve the confiscated pictures and have them brought out of England. Frieda, caught up in the fiasco, sent a telegram to Lawrence to say that she had been delayed in London, but without mentioning the police raid.

In Huxley's villa her husband was suffering in the heat and from feverish attacks that made his cough worse, his breath more shallow and rapid, and he was devoid of energy. Orioli had come to keep him company, but now he hated the place for adding to his distress. Maria Huxley drove him to catch the train to Pisa and somehow he got himself to Florence, to be looked after in Orioli's flat and to hear for the first time about the seizure of his pictures. His health continued to deteriorate until a frightened Orioli sent Frieda a telegram to say that her husband was dangerously ill. She left immediately and was in Florence late on July 11. As often happened, her presence was enough for him to rally at once. It was as if in such crises he received a transfusion of energy from her. Orioli had brought in a bowl of peaches. He asked his friend, "What will Frieda say when she arrives?" Lawrence indicated the peaches. "She'll say, 'What lovely peaches,' and eat the lot."

Aldous Huxley, upset by the sight of Lawrence's woeful decline, had urged immediate medical help. But if he thought that by getting Lawrence into a sanatorium he would have saved him he was being wildly optimistic. The process had gone too far.

As soon as he was able to travel, Frieda carried him off to Baden-Baden. There was her mother's seventy-eighth birthday to celebrate, and then Frieda's fiftieth, when he dreaded "the effect on Frieda of four large boxes of chocolates." This time his visit to the Black Forest threw him into a black mood, as did the pine trees without leaves and a mother-in-law he now saw as greedily gulping down life, with her selfish need to have one of her family always in attendance.

At the end of August the Lawrences moved briefly to Rottach in Bavaria. Frieda, still in pain with her ankle, went to see a local farmer who set bones. The man manipulated the bone back into the socket and Frieda was cured in no more than a minute. Lawrence fumed at the money he had paid out to specialists in London and Baden-Baden. "Doctors should all be put at once in prison," he wrote to his sister Emily. "It makes one mad."

Frieda, convinced now that Lawrence was soon going to die, though she never spoke of it, would be frightened by her husband's stillness as he lay in his bedroom. He was glad to be out of Baden, writing to Davies his feeling that "the Germans, underneath, *aren't* nice. And these huge German women sitting round one like mountains that would never even know if they sat on one . . . they simply give me the horrors. I want to go somewhere where the women are a bit *smaller*: and where their hats don't sit so menacingly on their heads." And perhaps he was now admitting the truth to himself about dying, if to no one else. His *Last Poems* are a preparation for death that he believed we all needed to make. One of the most famous of these was prompted by a vase of blue flowers by his bed at Rottach:

Not every man has gentians in his house,
in soft September, at slow, sad Michaelmas.

Bavarian gentians, big and dark, only dark,
darkening the day time, torch-like with the smoking blueness of
    Pluto's gloom,
ribbed and torch like, with their blaze of darkness spread blue
down flattening into points, flattened under the sweep of white day
torch-flower of the blue-smoking darkness, Pluto's dark blue daze,
black lamps from the halls of Dis, burning dark blue,
giving off darkness, blue darkness, as Demeter's pale lamps give off
    light,
lead me then, lead the way.

Reach me a gentian, give me a torch!
let me guide myself with the blue, forked torch of this flower
down the darker and darker stairs, where blue is darkened on
    blueness
even where Persephone goes, just now, from the frosted September
to the sightless realm where darkness is awake upon the dark
and Persephone herself is but a voice
or a darkness invisible enfolded in the deeper dark
of the arms Plutonic, and pierced with the passion of dense gloom,
among the splendor of torches of darkness, shedding darkness on
the lost bride and her groom.

His rage had not left him, but he had little strength for it. Often he wrote touching, gentle letters. To the Brewsters' daughter Harwood he wrote fondly as Uncle David. She was seventeen, about to begin studying to be a doctor. He pretended to be "very much healed up," but his "asthma" plagued him, and his everlasting cough annoyed everyone or made them nervous. "And I suppose cough I shall—though perhaps one day I shall leave it behind, I suppose." She should hurry up and be a doctor and cure him, "for you've only got half an Uncle David instead of a whole one."

IT WAS AUTUMN, he kept reminding himself. "The Ship of Death," his great autumnal poem, is thunderous with the fall of apples on the grim, frost-hardened earth, death on the air "like a smell of ashes." He conjures up for his solace the homely scenes of the afterlife by those Etruscans he loved so much, their little ships

> with oars and food
> and little dishes, and all accoutrements
> fitting and ready for the departing soul . . .
>
> A flush of rose, and the whole thing starts again.

He speculated again and again on the possible causes of his sickness, ruling out the diagnoses of doctors. In one of his pansies, "Healing," he concludes that

> I am ill because of wounds to the soul . . .
> and the wounds to the soul take a long, long time, only time can
>   help
> and patience, and a certain difficult repentance
> Long, difficult repentance, realization of life's mistake and the
>   freeing oneself
> from the endless repetition of the mistake
> which mankind at large has chosen to sanctify.

To Witter Bynner he is more specific. "I do believe the root of all my sickness is a sort of rage. I realize now, Europe gets me into an inward rage, that keeps my bronchials hellish inflamed. . . . I can't digest my inward spleen in Europe—that's what ails me."

Too ill to go searching for a new place when they left Bavaria, he returned to Bandol because of its familiarity and its pleasant associations, since he had been relatively well there the previous year. It was a good place in his mind, as the ranch in New Mexico still was. To please Frieda he took on the tenancy of an ugly little house of concrete, Beau Soleil, not far from the Hotel Beau Rivage, looking from the photograph more like a suburban bungalow with dormer windows. Built in a vulgar imitation of a Roman villa, it at least had central heating and a marble bathroom. And he liked the name and its splendid views over the Mediterranean, putting up with its Parisienne love-nest decor of purple walls and gold-framed mirrors, its lack of an open fire. He slept by himself, as he had done for years, waiting sleeplessly for the cyclamen dawn, his curtains pulled back. His worst bout of coughing came in the early hours. Frieda was banned from entering until he had recovered. "Come when the sun rises," he told her.

His *Last Poems* kept flowering, even in the dark:

> The breath of life is in the sharp winds of change
> mingled with the breath of destruction.
> But if you want to breathe deep, sumptuous life
> breathe all alone, in silence, in the dark,
> and see nothing.

Yet while he was still able to look out on his beloved Mediterranean world he was never utterly alone.

In November he was well enough to take little walks in the brilliant weather, enjoying three blue days, the yellow sun sinking down into the sea at four o'clock, the wind strong but kindly. They had a *femme de ménage* coming and going, Madame Douillet, who bounced about angrily when they baked their own bread, burning Frieda's apple cake in her agitation. "But I sat in the kitchen like a lion and watched my bread bake safely."

He had said to Bynner that he was really an amiable person if given the chance, even though catty, as Bynner told him. "But cats are really very easy animals. I feel a rather bedraggled one at present—wish a few people would stroke my fur the right way and make me purr."

One day he was astonished to see a cat saunter through the doorway to his room where he lay in bed. He called excitedly to Frieda. When she came in the cat had vanished, but Lawrence insisted that it was yellow and white, big and handsome, and had come walking in as if it owned the place. She shook her head in disbelief. "Look under the bed," he insisted. "They like to go under things, they're explorers." He wondered who its owner might be. Frieda was down on her knees, wanting to see this splendid animal for herself: and there it was. A discussion began, with Lawrence not willing to take responsibility for a stray. What would happen if they went off somewhere? When it jumped up on the bed he shooed it away. She would have to show it the door, he said. She refused. Micky could stay or go, just as he preferred. How did she know its name? Frieda said laughing that it looked like a Micky, so Micky it was.

A little later they were given two goldfish in a bowl, a present from Madame Douillet's old mother "pour amuser Monsieur." She should have told her they had a cat, said Lawrence, and they had better be placed on the table in the corner of his room by the plants, out of the cat's reach. Frieda carried them up at once, followed by Micky. The cat was warned not to stare "with your fixed stare. Those fish," Frieda warned, "are not for your breakfast."

"Pour amuser Monsieur le chat," remarked Lawrence.

Frieda exclaimed with her usual exuberance that the fish looked radiant as they swam to and fro. So did the plants, so did Mickey. "Radiant!"

"All except me," Lawrence mourned.

Naively she gushed on, saying that indeed everything seemed to flourish except Lawrence, plants and cat and goldfish. "Oh, why can't you be like them?"

He answered sadly that he wished he could. The defeated note in his voice, so uncharacteristic, made her cry. "Stop it," he said sharply. Then he asked in a gentle voice, "Why, why did we quarrel so much? Can you tell me?"

She answered, "Because we are violent creatures. We couldn't help ourselves."

He said after a pause, "In all our years together I could always trust your instinct to know the right thing for me. . . . Now you don't seem to know any more, do you?"

She shook her head, for once at a loss. "Never mind," he said.

The unstoppable stream of poetry kept flowing: lovely meditations imbued with the sweetness of his imagination, the language simple as only his could be:

> The sea will never die, neither will it grow old
> nor cease to be blue, nor in the dawn
> cease to lift up its hills
> and let the slim black ship of Dionysos come sailing in
> with grape-vines up the mast, and dolphins leaping . . .

And there were pansies jumping up, seeding and blooming, some banal, some spiteful, or mere sparks, as if to prove that a broken spark or bit of blossom in him lived on: some of them mere handfuls of words that were miraculously deft and right:

> A lizard ran out on a rock and looked up, listening
> no doubt to the sounding of the spheres.
> And what a dandy fellow! the right toss of a chin for you
> and swirl of a tail!

> If men were men as much as lizards are lizards
> they'd be worth looking at.

In another he swiped yet again at the mosquitolike persistence of the ubiquitous Murry, almost from habit:

> A man wrote to me: We missed it, you and I.
> We were meant to mean a great deal to one another;
> but we missed it.
> And I could only reply:
> A miss is as good as a mile
> mister!

The loyal Brewsters, wanting to be near him, had come from Capri to rent a villa close by for six months. Workmen moved in to the Chateau Brun and whitewashed the inside, and Earl and Achsah "are supposed to be painting the doors and windows, also white. The whole interior is to be snow white, like a pure, pure lily. . . ." Like a tomb, Lawrence added sardonically. He wrote to Emily King, the sister he addressed as Pamela, to say on November 30 that yes, they would love a Christmas pudding, a small cake, and a bit of mincemeat, and half a pound of tea. Harwood Brewster would bring them from England when she came to her parents for Christmas. He gave Pamela Harwood's address, and asked her to give Ada a message. Would she send Frieda "2 large meridian undervests and 2 knickers." The Brewsters would be having Christmas dinner with them, so they would have to pretend the mincemeat and pudding were made with nut fat. They were vegetarians, and "would faint at the thought of suet."

As he neared the end of the year he completed an essay, "A Propos of Lady Chatterley's Lover," and his last book, *Apocalypse*. In the first, in what he called his postscript or afterthought to the novel, he set out his defense by replying in effect to the question: If sex in the head is our modern disease, how can true sex be restored to us through the medium of the conscious mind? Answering his critics, and especially the one inside himself, he called now for a "realization of sex."

Today the fully conscious realization of sex is even more important than the act itself. After centuries of obfuscation, the mind demands to know and know fully. . . . The mind has to catch up, in sex: indeed, in all the physical acts. . . . Balance up the consciousness of the act, and the act itself. Get the two in harmony. And it is obvious, there is no balance and no harmony now. The body is at the best the tool of the mind, at the worst, the toy.

HIS LITTLE BOOK *Apocalypse* came about as a result of his correspondence with Edward Carter, whose mystical theories interested him. On October 29 he wrote saying that he had carefully read Carter's book on St. John the Divine, *The Visionary Way*. He had provisionally agreed to write an introduction, and invited Carter down to Bandol to discuss the matter further. He had met him once six years before, and found him changed, depressingly so. In the end he expanded his introduction and it became his own book, *Apocalypse*. He had confessed to Carter that he had come "to hate St. John the Divine and his bloody Revelations," but saw that one could launch oneself off from them: they were "a very useful start for other excursions." He much preferred to write about the pre-Christian heavens, "the great pagan religions of the Aegean, and Egypt and Babylon."

It was the discarded Chaldeans who fascinated him, not John of Patmos. In his effort to recover the old pagan world with its splendor, long before John's day, a yearning nostalgia takes hold of him. The language of his prose has a majesty that transfixes us, not least because we know this is his valediction. "Don't let us imagine we see the sun as the old civilizations saw it," he writes. "We have lost the cosmos, by coming out of responsive connection with it, and that is our chief tragedy. . . . We may see what we call the sun, but we have lost Helios for ever, and the great orb of the Chaldeans still more. . . . And we have lost the moon, the cool, bright, ever-varying moon. It is she who would caress our nerves, smooth them with the silky hand of her glowing. . . . For the moon is the mistress and mother of our watery bodies, the pale body of our nervous consciousness and our moist flesh."

How hard he strives to lift us, to give us back our lost wonder. "We and the cosmos are one. The cosmos is a vast living body, of which we are still part. The sun is a great heart whose tremors run through our smallest veins. The moon is a great gleaming nerve-center from which we quiver forever." What begins as a work of exposition ends as a hymn to abounding life.

He weakened daily. The gentle Earl Brewster called to massage him with olive oil. Scarcely able to walk, he was taken on brief motor trips. Frieda grieved that he was stooped and so thin, when he had once been so straight and quick. He wrote now out of sheer defiance:

> And if, in the changing phases of a man's life
> I fall in sickness and misery
> my wrists seem broken and my heart seems dead
> and strength is gone, and my life
> is only the leavings of a life . . .
>
> then I must know that still
> I am in the hands of the unknown God,
> he is breaking me down to his new oblivion
> to send me forth on a new morning, a new man.

"Never in all that illness," said Frieda, "did he let the days sink to a dreary or dull or sordid level. Those last months had the glamour of a rosy sunset." Lawrence would have mocked her sentimentality: her very words sent a German "into a swoon of love," whereas in truth she secretly hated it all. "My God, why are people *never* straightforward!"

Visitors came and went. In the New Year he was worse, losing weight drastically, pretending as always in his letters that he was about to turn the corner, "warily." On Christmas Eve he struggled to his feet to make lemon tarts. Now his bed was his almost permanent sickbed. Their friends the di Chiaras had come from Capri and on January 1 wanted to give him lunch in the village.

In London the rumor circulated that he was dying. Koteliansky and Gertler, hearing that Dr. Andrew Morland of the Mundersley Sanatorium, who happened to be Gertler's physician, was traveling to the south of France, asked him to visit Lawrence. Frieda wanted it, and Lawrence was too weak to oppose her. Pinned to his bed, he dreamed impossible dreams, of starting a school somewhere with Frieda, perhaps New Mexico, and wondered if his real vocation all along was to be a teacher. His malice flickered out like a lizard's tongue in a letter to the Huxleys on January 6, 1930: "I hear Wells and Maugham and Co. were rolling their incomes round Nice for Xmas, rich as pigs, Hugh Walpole sunning himself in the glow of their lucre. . . ." Brett Young, his income "an easy four thousand a year, has got a 'hall' in the Lake District, in which he can become a little more damp than he already is, to be a last lake poet, instead of a mere puddle poet." He hated them all, these "mere incomes on two legs." A letter from Brett reminded him of London and how "they all so eagerly *expect* me to die—Murry and the London lot. How they want to bury me!"

His final surrender came in his words to Ada on February 3: "I have decided to go to the sanatorium." He was down to eighty-four pounds, a walking skeleton, except that he could no longer walk. Dr. Morland had called and advised a higher altitude, recommending a sanatorium above Vence, not far away. Friends drove him to Ad Astra, three thousand feet above Cannes. Telling his sisters that he had been forced to give in and come here but would rather they did not visit him, he said that "when one feels so weak and down, one doesn't want to see anybody, and that's the truth."

It was a banal experience, the large chaletlike building just like a hotel with doctors. The regulations seemed to make no sense: he was taken off milk and had to walk down two flights of stairs for his meals. He told Frieda she would bury him there and she said no, the place was too ugly. She was nearby at the Hotel Nouvel in Vence with her daughter Barbara. Everyone jabbered in French, children cried, and he was spared by his deafness from hearing the worst cries of distress. "It is very stupid to be ill," he said, reprimanding himself bitterly.

From his balcony he looked down on the garden, where the mimosa was out "in clouds, like Australia," and the almond blossom that he had loved in Sicily. He asked Frieda to try to find a life of Columbus for him to read, since he could read only history. That could be an exploration in itself, she laughed, but she did find one, and he read fitfully. His letters dwindled to a few lines of adverse comment on his worsening condition and the sanatorium he would never accept. He wrote a short review of *Art Nonsense and Other Essays* by the Catholic artist Eric Gill. Uncompromising as ever, he began, "Mr. Gill is not a born writer: he is crude and crass. . . . like a tiresome uneducated workman arguing in a pub." But he endorsed the truth of Gill's opinion that a man was free when his activity pleased God. The teacher in Lawrence explained that this meant "being livingly absorbed in an activity which makes one in touch with—with the heart of things: call it God."

Missing the one person who had always revived him, he asked Frieda to stay with him. A bed was moved into his room, and he joked feebly with his stepdaughter, "It isn't often I want your mother, but I do want her tonight to stay." The experiment was not a success. In a reaction against her he said, "Your sleeping here does me no good." She went away in tears, but when she returned he said wistfully, "Don't mind me. You know I want nothing but you, but sometimes something is stronger than me." Withdrawing again another time he told Barbara, "Your mother does not care for me any more: the death in me repels her."

A month in the sanatorium was all he could bear. The Huxleys came from London, helping Frieda to find a villa in Vence. The last move of his life was accomplished on Saturday, March 1. Never before had he allowed Frieda to help him put on his shoes. He was taken in a taxi to the Villa Robermond, where the exertion brought on a collapse. Again he wanted her to be where he could see her, so she slept on a couch in his room.

The next morning he was asked if he would like a little breakfast. He said it didn't feed him: nothing did. "Not even you." She burst into tears and left him. A little later he said, "I only want you. It's the devil in my body speaking."

She told him that Aldous and Maria Huxley were below. Did he want to see them?

He said he liked them, but it was not love. "They're not my sort." When Maria Huxley sat with him his face was contorted with pain. He had the illusion he was split in two. He asked her to hold his hands. He said again, "I'm two people. I can see myself." When in fear she asked where, he cried out, "Look at *him* there in the bed!"

Later that day he asked for morphine. Huxley hurried away to fetch the Corsican doctor who was attending him. Lawrence called to Frieda, as if to someone far away, "Hold me, hold me, I don't know where I am. . . . If I could only sweat it would be better."

At ten that night on March 2 he died, aged forty-four. He weighed eighty-five pounds. It was a Sunday. Frieda wrote that, "The minutes went by. Maria Huxley was in the room with me. I held his left ankle from time to time, it felt so full of life. . . . All my days I shall hold his ankle in my hand. . . ."

Later she told Rhys Davies, "His death was so simple and somehow great, his courage in facing death and fighting inch by inch and then at the end asking for morphia. He looked so proud, so beyond all these silly ugly dogs barking, so unconquered when he was dead—I know you grieve too." When she came to write her memoir, *Not I, But the Wind*, she called Lawrence "the last green leaf on the English tree."

Postscript

FRIEDA WAS the least literary of all the women in Lawrence's life, something she would have pugnaciously denied. Because of this she was able to write more freely than anyone, about what it was like to be in his presence, in both the good and bad times. In her letters and remembrances she wrote as she talked, in a flow that gushed forth—impetuous, candid, simple, sometimes stupid, and often humorous. Only she would have said of her husband's funeral in Vence on March 4, 1930, "We buried him simply, like a bird."

Probably as a consequence of his outspoken wife's influence, Lawrence came to see himself as a spokesman for women, as Elaine Feinstein points out, announcing to Sallie Hopkin in December 1912 that as a writer he intended to "do my work for women, better than the suffrage." Frieda was no intellectual, and that could have been part of her attraction, but she brought into the relationship, along with undigested theories, a cultural dowry that enriched him. In marrying her he also married Munich, named by Martin Green as "one of the two great nodes of the anti-Bismarck movement." By the time she and Lawrence met she had begun to think of herself as a force of nature, a muse whose destiny was to nurture and mold a genius. Ernest Weekley, who had once taught Lawrence, invited the young Nottinghamshire author of *The White Peacock* to lunch a year after he had published this first novel. The *English Review* had enthused over "a new writer, one most certainly to be reckoned with." Frieda took one look at the lonely, unsure Lawrence and thought how like a previous lover, Otto Gross, he was—"only nicer." Lawrence for his part had never met such a forthright woman.

After his death his widow flailed about wildly, trying to enlist the help of friends and protectors, and was soon in financial chaos. Lawrence had kept her wilder impulses in check, and now he was gone. Her daughter Barbara was ill, and with her lover Angelo Ravagli in the wings she struggled with problems created by the fact that her husband had not left a will.

Why someone so careful had not done so remains a mystery, but he had died intestate, and of the four thousand pounds he had left she was entitled to a payment of only a thousand pounds, his furniture and personal effects, and no automatic right to his manuscripts and paintings. Extraordinary as this now seems, letters of administration had been granted to his elder brother George, who, like Ada and Emily, made no secret of his hostility to Frieda, seeing her as immoral. Over the years he had become a lay preacher in Nottingham and had had no contact with his brother after a quarrel about Frieda. Edward Nehls in his *Composite Biography* records him as saying, "Oh, Bert was a grand little lad—he was always delicate. . . . We all petted and spoiled him from the time he was born—my mother poured her very soul into him."

The fight was on to keep the administration of the estate in the hands of the family. Frieda's solicitors went to court to retrieve the letters held by George. The probate court hearing took place in London on November 3, 1932. Frieda was now the Enemy, an unscrupulous woman the Lawrence family saw as capable of anything. Her appearance in court, looking eccentric, was obviously a ruse. George's son William described her as "dressed up like a Guy Fawkes effigy—thick woolen stockings, heavy old boots, thick woolen skirt, smoking Woodbines" in order to plead poverty.

It was Murry of all people who gave Frieda some hope. He and

Lawrence, he recalled, had both made wills in Buckinghamshire at the start of the war, bequeathing everything to their wives. Could the missing will be among papers left behind in New Mexico? Urgent telegrams went off to Brett, who searched high and low and could discover nothing. But Murry was willing to testify in court that he had seen such a will, and this in the end won over the judge. If the court had known that this independent witness had been Frieda's lover for a short spell, only two months after Lawrence's death, the outcome might have been different. In answer to one of her many distress calls he had gone to Vence and then, as she put it, "the worst happened!" Later she confided to her Taos ex-rival, who had married her Indian and was now Mabel Luhan, "There really is something *perverse* in him!"

She was delighted to be vindicated by the words of the judgment. The Lawrences, declared Lord Merrivale, were a committed couple, and as citizens of the world could have mislaid documents on their travels. It was reasonable to suppose that Lawrence intended his whole estate to go to his widow. Of the four thousand pounds awarded to Frieda, she offered five hundred each to George, Ada, and Emily, a generous gesture that won the court's approval. Ada would have nothing to do with this settlement from her hated sister-in-law.

Frieda was now able to buy Ravagli out of the army and carry him off to New Mexico with her. He left a wife and three children behind in Italy, and Frieda, on good terms with Signora Ravagli, compensated her in 1933 with a financial settlement. Angelo Ravagli was no angel but was fundamentally honest and straightforward, and she found lasting happiness with him. He worked hard and was a practical man, building a log ranch farther down the mountain from the Kiowa cabins. She wrote in 1931 that he was "so human and nice with me and real, no high falute, but such a genuine warmth for me—I shall be all right. . . . We have been fond of each other for years and that an old bird like me is still capable of real passion and can inspire it too seems a miracle."

Ravagli stayed in touch with his family, visiting them in Italy from time to time. He and Frieda were not married until October 31, 1950, and only then to avoid the possibility of Angelo's deportation from the United States. To satisfy the Taos County Court, a certificate had been produced giving Ina-Serafina Ravagli's consent to the dissolution of her marriage. Angelo was free to apply for an American divorce, though the divorce and remarriage would not be legal in Italy.

Georgia O'Keeffe paints a vivid picture of Frieda in these later years, "standing in a doorway there, with her hair all frizzy, wearing a cheap red calico dress that looked as if she'd wiped the frying pan with it," filling the house with her big voice. Now that she was legally Ravagli's wife, she felt able to travel to England in June 1952. She met Murry, happily married with his fourth wife, and was able to see her five grandchildren. Back in New Mexico she suffered a stroke outside Taos on August 18, 1956, dying three days later, on her seventy-seventh birthday. Ravagli returned to Italy and lived again with his Italian wife and family.

Lawrence's letters, now all published in the seven-volume Cambridge Press edition—though there will probably be others—have resurrected him yet again, and more freshly than ever. His poetry, he wrote once, "needs the penumbra of its own time and place and circumstance to make it full and whole," and this is true of all his work. The spontaneity and humor alone in these letters are enough to inspire any biographer, whether describing a break with Murry— "he's licked all the gum off me, I'm no longer adhesive"—or at his happiest at Irschenhausen in 1913, "the living spit of Paul Dombey grown up," when the rain hammers down nonstop—"positively stands up on end. Sometimes one sees the deer jumping up and down to get the wet out of their jackets, and the squirrels simply hang out by their tails, like washing. I take one morning run around the house in my bathing suit in lieu of a shower bath." Let us leave him running, unquenchably alive to the end, writing letters when he feels happy or spiteful, "like having a good sneeze."

Acknowledgments

A BIOGRAPHER of Lawrence is fortunate in having such a vast quantity of letters at his disposal, and from a writer whose epistolary achievement has always been seen as remarkable. Lawrence communicated from his real self and rarely gave up on any correspondent. The exemplary seven-volume Cambridge edition of the letters, now complete, has been called a major new literary work in itself, and I am indebted to James Boulton and his fellow scholars for delivering up this immense treasure trove. Also invaluable has been the *Selected Letters*, containing 330 letters compiled and edited by James Boulton. Chronological and descriptive introductions are featured in each section, and a biographical list of correspondents, so that one is caught up at once in the drama of Lawrence's life as he travels the world and battles with his soul.

But why so many letters? Once embarked on his often hand-to-mouth career, he found them a means of acting decisively at a distance, essential for someone constantly on the move who needed to keep his literary and business affairs under control. There was, too, his hunger for intimacy, which never abated, as he sought to combat isolation and exile, and to maintain contact with the family who thought they knew him. Nothing isolates more than genius; nothing is lonelier.

Another boon for biographers has been the publication by Cambridge of an enormous life in three parts, the task being shared by three scholars, John Worthen (1991), Mark Kinkead-Weeks (1996), and David Ellis (1998), and this meticulous reconstruction of Lawrence's story must surely now be the definitive biography.

Two recent books that have shed light for me are Brenda Maddox's expansive and worldly *D. H. Lawrence*, entitled *The Married Man* in its London edition, and Elaine Feinstein's *Lawrence's Women*, both of them with slants of their own.

Ivan Dee, my editor-publisher in Chicago, has kept faith with my work as always, and my friends Stanley Middleton, John Lucas, Jim Morgan, and Richard Young have heartened me with their interest and encouragement. My agent and friend Elizabeth Fairbairn has tracked down Dorothy Brett's *Lawrence and Brett*, a rare book which has eluded me, and I have depended on her yet again for her scrupulous checking of the typescript, and for guiding me through the final stages of production.

To Anne, with me through many difficult months, goes my devoted love.

Selected Bibliography

Peter Ackroyd. *Introduction to Dickens*. London, 1991.

Richard Aldington. *Portrait of a Genius, But.* . . . London, 1951.

———. *Pinorman: Personal Recollections of Norman Douglas, Pino Orioli, and Charles Prentice*. London, 1954.

———. *Life for Life's Sake*. London, 1968.

A. Alvarez. *Life After Marriage*. London, 1982.

Armin Arnold. *Lawrence and America*. London, 1958.

Lady Cynthia Asquith. *Remember and Be Glad*. London, 1952.

———. *Diaries: 1915–1918*. London, 1968.

Nicola Beauman. *Lady Cynthia Asquith*. London, 1987.

Sybille Bedford. *Aldous Huxley: A Biography*. New York, 1985.

Harold Bloom, ed. *D. H. Lawrence: Modern Critical Views*. New York, 1986.

James T. Boulton, ed. *Lawrence in Love: Letters from D. H. Lawrence to Louie Burrows*. Nottingham, 1968.

James T. Boulton, *et al.*, eds. *The Letters of D. H. Lawrence* (7 volumes). Cambridge, England, 1979–2001.

———. *The Selected Letters of D. H. Lawrence*. Cambridge, England, 1997.

Dorothy Brett. *Lawrence and Brett*. Philadelphia, 1933.

Earl and Achsah Brewster. *D. H. Lawrence: Reminiscences and Correspondence*. London, 1934.

Anthony Burgess. *Flame into Being: The Life and Work of D. H. Lawrence*. London, 1985.

Witter Bynner. *Journey with Genius*. New York, 1951.

Catherine Carswell. *The Savage Pilgrimage*. London, 1934.

David Cavitch. *D. H. Lawrence and the New World*. Oxford, 1979.

Jessie Chambers. *D. H. Lawrence: A Personal Record*. Cambridge, England, 1980.

Helen Corke. *Lawrence and Apocalypse*. London, 1933.

Rhys Davies. *Print of a Hare's Foot: An Autobiographical Beginning*. London, 1969.

Emile Delavenay. *D. H. Lawrence: The Man and His Work*. London, 1972.

Hilda Doolittle (H.D.). *Bid Me to Live*. New York, 1960.

Geoff Dyer. *Anglo-English Attitudes*. London, 1999.

David Ellis. *D. H. Lawrence: Dying Game, 1922–1930*. Cambridge, England, 1998.

Elaine Feinstein. *Lawrence's Women*. London, 1993.

Joseph Foster. *Lawrence in Taos*. New Mexico, 1972.

Eugene Goodhart. *The Utopian Vision of D. H. Lawrence*. Chicago, 1963.

Martin Green. *The Von Richtofen Sisters*. London, 1974.

Emily Hahn. *Lorenzo: D. H. Lawrence and the Women Who Loved Him*. Philadelphia and New York, 1975.

———. *Mabel: A Biography of Mabel Dodge Luhan*. Boston, 1977.

C. A. Hankin, ed. *The Letters of John Middleton Murry to Katherine Mansfield*. London, 1983.

Christopher Heywood, ed. *D. H. Lawrence: New Studies*. New York, 1987.

David Holbrook. *The Quest for Love*. London, 1964.

Graham Hough. *The Dark Sun: A Study of D. H. Lawrence*. London, 1956.

H. Montgomery Hyde. *The Lady Chatterley's Lover Trial*. London, 1990.

Mark Kinkead-Weeks. *D. H. Lawrence: Triumph to Exile, 1912–1922*. Cambridge, England, 1996.

Frieda Lawrence. *Not I, But the Wind*. London, 1983.

Robert Lucas. *Frieda Lawrence*. London, 1973.

Brenda Maddox. *D. H. Lawrence: The Story of a Marriage*. New York and London, 1994.

Norman Mailer. *The Prisoner of Sex*. London, 1971.

Edward McDonald, ed. *Phoenix: The Posthumous Papers of D. H. Lawrence*. London, 1936.

Knud Merrild. *A Poet and Two Painters: A Memoir of D. H. Lawrence*. New York, 1939.

Harry T. Moore. *The Priest of Love: A Life of D. H. Lawrence*. London, 1974.

Cohn Murry. *One Hand Clapping*. London, 1975.

John Middleton Murry. *Son of Woman: The Story of D. H. Lawrence*. London, 1931.

————. *Reminiscences of D. H. Lawrence*. London, 1933.

Katherine Middleton Murry. *Beloved Quixote: The Unknown Life of John Middleton Murry*. London, 1986.

Edward Nehls, ed. *D. H. Lawrence: A Composite Biography* (3 volumes). Madison, Wisc., 1957–1959.

Warren Roberts and Harry T. Moore, eds. *Phoenix II: Uncollected, Unpublished and Other Prose Works by D. H. Lawrence*. London, 1968.

Keith Sagar. *The Life of D. H. Lawrence: An Illustrated Biography*. London, 1980.

Martin Secker. *Letters from a Publisher: Martin Secker to D. H. Lawrence and Others*. London, 1970.

Miranda Seymour. *Ottoline Morrell: Life on the Grand Scale*. London, 1992.

Stephen Spender. *D. H. Lawrence: Prophet, Poet, Novelist*. London, 1973.

Mark Spilka. *The Love Ethic of D. H. Lawrence*. London, 1958.

Bruce Steele. "*Kangaroo: Fiction and Fact*." Meridian, 1991.

William York Tindall. *The Later D. H. Lawrence*. New York, 1952.

Claire Tomalin. *Katherine Mansfield: A Secret Life*. London, 1987.

John Worthen. *D. H. Lawrence and the Idea of the Novel*. London, 1979.

————. *D. H. Lawrence: The Early Years, 1885–1912*. Cambridge, England, 1991.

Index

Italy (1920–1921), 25–51; and the
Brewsters, 42–43, 48–49; Fontana
Vecchia, 25–26, 42, 43, 48–49; German
trip, 42, 43–44, 46–48; and reactions to
Women in Love, 48, 49–50; Sardinia,
26–41
Italy (1925–1926), 182–189; Ada's stay in,
184–185; Brett and, 185, 186–187;
Frieda's daughters in, 183, 184, 187,
189; Lawrence's solo trip to Capri,
185–187; quarrels of Lawrence and
Frieda, 184; Ravagli in, 182, 183, 184,
185, 187
Italy (1926–1928), 188–213; acquaintances
and visits, 193–195, 200–201, 234, 239;
Brewster and Lawrence's trip to Rome,
217–229; and the Etruscans, 190–191,
216–217, 218–229, 233; fascism, 189,
190; Florence/Tuscany, 188–213;
happiness in, 191; Huxley's visits, 201,
234, 239; Lawrence's illness, 233–234,
237–238, 243; Lawrence's reviews,
232–233, 235–236; Lawrence's writing
in, 192–193, 201–203, 206–213, 214,
216, 229, 231; return to England,
196–199; trip to Austria from, 236–238;
and Tuscan landscape, 192–193

Jaffe, Edgar, 237
Jaffe, Else, 191, 233, 237, 238, 247. *See
also* Richthofen, Else von.
Jaffe, Friedal, 174, 176
James Tait Black Prize, 54
Jenkins, Anna, 57, 61
Jews, 50–51
"Jimmy and the Desperate Woman," 135,
136–138
John Bull, 49, 253
John Thomas and Lady Jane, 203, 208–213,
214, 222, 241, 245. *See also Lady
Chatterley's Lover.*
Johnson, Willard "Spud": Bynner and, 80,
106, 107, 108–109, 127, 147;
Lawrence's trip to Mexico with, 106,
108–112, 114–115; magazine of, 142
Journey with Genius (Bynner), 108
Joyce, James, 70, 102
Juta, Jan, 21, 23

Kangaroo: aborigines reference, 62;
autobiographical information, 64, 65,
66–67, 71–72; "Bits" chapter, 69; class

in, 66; Ellis on, 68, 70, 71, 72; Joyce
and, 70; and Lawrence's love for place,
72; and Lawrence's rage, 70–71, 72;
Lawrence's self-treatment in, 66, 67,
68–69, 79, 88; "lord-and-master" beliefs
in, 69, 106; Maddox on, 6; marital
relationship and friendship between
men, 70; Murry on, 67, 68, 69, 88;
"The Nightmare" chapter, 68, 70–71;
on novel form, 69; and *The Plumed
Serpent*, 171; *Sea and Sardinia*
resemblance, 66; Stevenson allusions,
71; style of, 4, 70; women as Furies in,
88; writing of, 64, 65–67, 69, 71–72
"Kangaroo" (poem), 74–75
Kant, Immanuel, 102
King, Emily, 156, 278. *See also* Lawrence,
Emily.
King, Margaret, 190
Kiowa Ranch: the Hawks and, 160,
182–183; 1924 stay, 148, 150–152,
153–154, 160; 1925 stay, 172–174,
175–176, 178
Koteliansky, Samuel: and Frieda, 4, 133,
134, 187; Gertler's letters to, 133, 181;
invitation to New Mexico, 142;
Jewishness of, 51; and Lawrence's
illness, 281; and the Lawrences in
England, 135; and Lawrence's review of
Rozanov, 232; Mansfield's letter to, 103
Koteliansky, Samuel, Lawrence's letters
to: regarding Brett, 147; regarding
Gertie Cooper, 197; regarding financial
generosity, 85; regarding Frieda, 4, 121;
regarding Germany, 44; regarding
illness, 243, 248; regarding *Kangaroo*,
70; regarding living in America, 42;
regarding stay at Les Diablerets, 244;
regarding suits against *Women in Love*,
50

Lady Chatterley's Lover, 240–242; Arlen's
influence on, 240–241; booksellers and,
193, 247, 248–249, 263, 265;
distribution of, 248–249, 255; *The First
Lady Chatterley*, 203; Frieda's
collaboration in, 202, 209; *John Thomas
and Lady Jane*, 203, 208–213, 214, 222,
241, 245; Maddox on, 202; misogyny
charge, 242; modern world and, x,
206–207, 208–209, 213, 241, 259–260,
262, 278–279; money for, 247–248, 255;

A NOTE ON THE AUTHOR

Philip Callow was born in Birmingham, England, and studied engineering and the teaching of English before he turned to writing. He has since published fourteen novels, several collections of short stories and poems, a volume of autobiography, and six biographies—*Louis: A Life of Robert Louis Stevenson; Chekhov: The Hidden Ground; Lost Earth: A Life of Cézanne; From Noon to Starry Night: A Life of Walt Whitman; Vincent Van Gogh: A Life*; and *Son and Lover: The Young D. H. Lawrence*—all of which have received critical acclaim. He lives and writes in the Cotswolds, England.